The Golden Age of
the Quantity Theory

THE GOLDEN AGE
OF THE QUANTITY
THEORY

David Laidler

Princeton University Press
Princeton, New Jersey

© 1991 by David Laidler

Published by Princeton University Press,
41 William Street, Princeton, New Jersey 08540

Library of Congress Cataloging-in-Publication Data

Laidler, David E. W.
  The golden age of the quantity theory : the development of
neoclassical monetary economics. 1870–1914 / by David Laidler.
    p.   cm.
  Includes bibliographical references and index.
  ISBN 0-691-04295-0
  1. Quantity theory of money.   2. Neoclassical school of economics.
I. Title.
HG226.6.L35   1991
332.4′01–dc20   91–15247
                                                                CIP

Printed in Great Britain

To Antje

'as things are, gold and silver have no natural value . . . their value is artificial, because the demand for them as currency is itself artificial.' Alfred Marshall, 1887

'As the years go on it seems to become even clearer that there ought to be an international currency; and that the – in itself foolish – superstition that gold is the "natural" representative of value has done excellent service.' Alfred Marshall, 1923

Contents

Preface

I have written this book as much for monetary economists as for historians. The history of economic thought is a fascinating subject in its own right, but it is also a vital component of the discipline of economics. If many university departments neglect to teach it nowadays, then so much the worse for them; and, sadly, so much the worse for their students.

To begin with, it is simply not the case that everything known to previous generations and still worth knowing, is to be found in modern textbooks. Anyone who believes such nonsense is invited to consider how the textbooks of the 1950s and 1960s treated the quantity theory of money. If this book is easier reading to an economist trained recently than it would have been to someone graduating in, say, 1960, that is because much of what we regard as the progress made by monetary economics during the last three decades has involved the rediscovery of ideas that verged on the commonplace a century ago, but which had become lost in the intervening years. The modern monetary economist still has a few things to learn from the literature surveyed here: exponents of the 'backing' theory of money's purchasing power could do worse than spend an hour or so reading Laughlin (1903), Fisher (1911) or Wicksell (1915) on this topic; advocates of free banking must still deal with the issues raised by the economies of scale which banks can exploit by centralising their reserves, and which were discussed by Edgeworth (1888) and Wicksell (1898); students of currency substitution will find that their models have much in common with those used by Walras (1886, 1889) and Fisher (1894, 1911) to analyse bimetallism; and so on.

But there is more to the task of the historian of economic thought than the provision of reading lists based on the older literature, valuable though such a service might be. We have long known that the conduct of economic policy requires the policy-maker to have a theory of how the economy works. More recently, the creators of rational expectations analysis have reminded us that private agents too hold such theories, which condition their behaviour. Furthermore, policy-makers are subject to control by private agents through political processes, and economic ideas affect the way in which such 'public choices' are exercised. Economic ideas profoundly affect the way in which economies function, and if economics is to help us explain empirical evidence, such effects must be recognised and incorporated into our analysis. But economic ideas do not remain the same over time. One decade's 'true' model of the economy has been known, justifiably or not, to turn into an object of ridicule in the next.

Philosophers of science stress that creative conjecture is a large part of the process whereby knowledge advances. Thus the interaction of economic ideas with the economy is not a static phenomenon, nor is it unidirectional. The economy's current behaviour has a great deal to do with which creative conjectures fail, and which evolve into well established doctrines, which in their turn affect the economy's future behaviour. The processes to which I am referring here may or may not be susceptible to the techniques of formal modelling at which economic theorists are so adept. To say that they have not yet been modelled is not to deny that, in future, some creative conjecture about how the trick could be managed might turn out to be fruitful. Failing such a breakthrough though, the only way we have of learning about these processes, which are at the very heart of our discipline's subject matter, is to study particular instances of them at work. Even if a theoretical breakthrough does come along, and models are constructed, those same particular instances will provide the data against which they are tested. 'The history of economic thought' is simply the label which we attach to the study of the data in question. That is why it should be of interest to every economist.

There is no need to labour the foregoing argument. Suffice it to say that this book does not purport to be a general and comprehensive history of monetary economics between 1870 and 1914. Rather it highlights certain aspects of that history, and in particular the uneasy relationship that existed between, on the one hand, the evolving Gold Exchange Standard, which was partly the result of

historical accident and partly a response to the economic orthodoxy of an earlier period, and on the other, the neoclassical
quantity theory of money which replaced that earlier orthodoxy. It
is intended as a study of a particular instance of the dynamic
interaction of economic ideas and economic history discussed
above, as well as being a survey of a body of literature still
interesting in its own right as economic analysis.

Acknowledgements

I have received much help from others in writing this book. Horst Raff and George Stadler checked certain translated passages against German language originals for accuracy; Tony Bernardo gave advice about bimetallism, on which topic he completed an honours paper of his own in 1988-9 and, with Jian-Guo Cao and Quan Wen, checked quotations for accuracy; Jane McAndrew provided expert bibliographic help; and Yvonne Adams and her colleagues saw the typescript through more drafts than anyone cares to remember. My colleagues Ann Carlos, Joel Fried, Knick Harley, Peter Howitt and Michael Parkin read and commented on various sections of the book as they were prepared, as also did Arie Arnon, Haim Barkai, Michael Bordo, Milton Friedman, David Glasner, Charles Goodhart, Samuel Hollander, Susan Howson, Lars Jonung, Donald Moggridge, Johan Myhrman, Don Patinkin, Franco Spinelli and Lawrence White.

I am grateful to the Social Science and Humanities Research Council of Canada for indispensable financial support, and to the University of Western Ontario for an appointment as Faculty of Social Science Research Professor during the academic year 1988-9 when first drafts of Chapters 3-6 were prepared.

An early version of Chapter 2 was published in *Oxford Economic Papers*, March 1988, under the title 'British monetary orthodoxy in the 1870s'. I am indebted to the editors of the journal, and to Oxford University Press for permission to incorporate this material here. Also, sections of Chapter 5 were presented under the title 'Was Wicksell a quantity theorist?' at the Jerusalem Economic Seminar held in May 1990 in honour of Don Patinkin. I am grateful to the organisers of that seminar, Haim Barkai and Nissan Liviatan, for their permission to include those sections in this book.

1 • An overview

To the monetary economist, the period 1870–1914 was a golden age, in more than one sense. Most obviously and literally, in those years the Gold Standard developed from something close to an exclusively British institution into an international monetary system which even today is held up as a model of stability. But this was also the period in which the quantity theory of money, conceived of as a theory of the general price level, reached the peak of its development. In the years before World War I, both well-known formulations of that theory – the transactions approach mainly associated with Irving Fisher, and the stock supply and demand for money approach of Alfred Marshall and his pupils – were brought to full fruition by their exponents. This fact, and the then ruling idea that it was the principal business of monetary economics to explain the behaviour of the general price level, combined to give the quantity theory a more central position in monetary economics than it has enjoyed at any other time, whether before or since.

During the period in question the quantity theory was deployed, as it had been in earlier years, to deal with policy issues, prominent among which were, in the case of the controversy about bimetallism, those involving the choice of monetary standard. However the analytic precision which the quantity theory acquired after 1870 owed more to a concern on the part of its exponents to eliminate a certain logical incompleteness in the body of knowledge which they had inherited from classical economics, than it did to any immediate desire on their part to contribute to contemporary policy debates. In the years before World War I, the literature of monetary economics became much less a series of *ad hoc* responses to questions posed by current events than it had been before, and began consistently to display that internal dynamic which is the basic characteristic of a mature branch of economic science. In this sense too, then, the phrase 'golden age' seems an appropriate characterisation of the period.

There is nevertheless an element of irony implicit in this book's title. The spread of the Gold Standard between 1870 and 1914 had much to do with the growing international influence of what Frank Fetter (1965) called 'British monetary orthodoxy'. This orthodoxy had developed over the preceding century, and the quantity theory too was part and parcel of it. But the refinement of the quantity theory after 1870 did not strengthen the intellectual foundations of the Gold Standard. On the contrary, it was an important element in bringing about its eventual destruction. I hasten to add that I am aware that World War I happened, and that the monetary upheavals associated with it and its aftermath were undoubtedly the immediate causes of the Gold Standard's final collapse in the 1930s. However, the notion of a managed money, available to be deployed in the cause of macroeconomic stability and capable of producing a better economic environment than one tied to gold, was not an intellectual response to the monetary instability of the post-war period. The idea appeared in a variety of guises in the pre-war literature as a corollary of the quantity theory there expounded.

Whether the idea of managed money would have triumphed over tradition and practice to destroy the Gold Standard had World War I not happened is hard to say. My own instinct is to doubt it: exponents of the quantity theory were, on the whole, more satisfied with the monetary status quo on the eve of the war than they had been twenty years earlier. Though they did not give up arguing the theoretical superiority of other ways of organising matters, they did recognise that the Gold Standard, or to be more precise the Gold Exchange Standard, seemed to be working, and working rather well at that. At the same time, I find it even less likely that notions of managed money would have attracted so much support so quickly in the 1920s and 1930s, had their intellectual foundations not been so firmly developed in the preceding forty years or so.

This book does not pretend to offer a comprehensive account of what is to be found in the literature of monetary economics between 1870 and 1914. It concentrates on the development of the quantity theory of money, and discusses alternative approaches to the extent that they seem to throw light on that development, making no attempt to weight the latter by the relative frequency with which they were discussed in contemporary literature. Two major themes are developed in the following pages, as I have already hinted: namely, that the evolution of monetary economics owed more to its own internal dynamics than to outside events, and that the logic of the quantity theory subverted the intellectual authority of the Gold Standard. These themes are explicit in many of the details of the exposition that follows. More importantly, though less obviously, they are implicit in the order in which topics are taken up in the following chapters. In particular, the nature of the quantity theory as it evolved after 1870 is dealt with before its application to policy questions is discussed in any detail.

There is some justification for my chosen order of exposition: Marshall's (1871) manuscript on 'Money', unpublished (until 1975), which contains an essentially complete account of the Cambridge version of the quantity theory, was indeed a product of the early 1870s, and hence antedates its author's involvement in the bimetallic controversy of the 1880s and 1890s; but this defence cannot be pushed too far. Irving Fisher's work, not to mention that of Knut Wicksell, did not even begin to see print until the debate in question was more or less over, and both of them were well aware of, and commented extensively on, the issues that had been raised during its course. My main reason for treating topics in the order that I do stems, however, not from chronological but from theoretical considerations. The chronology of the development of monetary economics during this period, as indeed during any other, is capriciously untidy. The logical relationships which exist among theoretical ideas that were developed then, and between those ideas and the policy problems to which they were relevant, have an altogether clearer shape. My perception of that shape has, as I have already remarked, determined the design of my narrative, which I shall now outline.

The main purpose of Chapter 2 is to give an account of the 'monetary orthodoxy' of the early 1870s, an account which stresses the following three weaknesses in its structure. First, that orthodoxy distinguished between the short and long run when it discussed price level determination under commodity convertibility, espousing the quantity theory for the short run and the classical cost of production theory of value for the long run; but, because it treated mining as a rising marginal cost activity, while simultaneously lacking the theoretical tools to analyse precisely the influence upon that marginal cost of the monetary demand for the precious metals, its treatment of these matters was logically incomplete, or at least unclear.[1] Second, that orthodoxy treated the cycle as being mainly a phenomenon of short-run price level fluctuations, but did not satisfactorily explain the speculative behaviour which drove them; nor did it integrate output and employment fluctuations into the corpus of facts with which cycle theory was expected to deal. Finally, classical economists often had difficulty distinguishing systematically between money and credit, and hence in integrating their analysis of banking with their theory of the price level.

These three flaws in classical monetary economics are precisely those which the neoclassical quantity theorists, notably, but not exclusively, Fisher, Marshall and Wicksell, attempted to repair. As I show in Chapters 3 and 5, they carefully analysed the influence of the monetary demand for the precious metals on their value. In the process they demoted the metals' cost of production from the status of a major, and in some treatments unique, determinant of money's 'natural' value to that of a secondary and remote influence on its quantity. They simultaneously promoted the quantity theory to the status of general theory of the price level, valid in both the short and long run. As to the cycle, Chapter 4 shows that the idea of expected inflation and its corollary the nominal–real interest rate distinction, and the notion of money wage stickiness, taken together led most quantity theorists (though not, as is shown in Chapter 5, Wicksell) to give pride of place to price level fluctuations in its analysis. Though not all of them regarded monetary shocks as being the major impulse leading to cyclical fluctuations, all of them emphasised the interaction of money and prices in explaining how the consequences of initial shocks were propagated and amplified. Wicksell's unique role in the development of the quantity theory is described in Chapter 5, where it is shown to have involved tackling the third of the above-mentioned problems implicit in classical monetary economics. Wicksell integrated an already well articulated classical account of the role of interest rates in the transmission mechanism with contemporary capital theory, and went on to expand the analysis of credit market effects in that mechanism. In doing so, he laid the groundwork for the later abandonment of the quantity theory by his disciples.

Chapter 6 describes how the theoretical developments just out-lined affected thinking about policy. Specifically it is argued: that the destruction of the idea that a commodity money has some natural value independent of its monetary use removed an important theoretical support from the Gold Standard, whose victory over bimetallism, therefore, occurred despite, rather than because of, developments in monetary theory; and that the quantity theorists' insistence on price fluctuations as a key factor driving the cycle naturally led them to look for monetary arrangements that would either eliminate such fluctuations or render them harmless. Marshall, early in his career, wanted to replace the Gold Standard with a form of bimetallism and advocated indexed contracts; Fisher argued for indexing money itself; and as early as 1898 Wicksell was urging the abandonment of any kind of metallic money and its replacement by an international paper standard. None of those proposals attracted support from contemporary policy-makers. Their effect was less direct and more subtle, but in the longer run no less important. They helped to change the political status of the Gold Standard from that of an unquestioned constraint on choices about monetary arrangements to that of one object of choice among several. That change of status was, I believe, crucial once the monetary instability associated with World War I put the choice of monetary arrangements back on the political agenda.

Now the foregoing is a summary of this book's major thrust, but many other subsidiary, yet important, topics are taken up along the way: the relationship between Fisher's version of the quantity theory and the Cambridge formulation; Ralph Hawtrey's use of Marshallian ideas to construct a thoroughgoing monetary theory of the cycle; Wicksell's failure to integrate inflation expectations into the heart of his cumulative process analysis; Francis Y. Edgeworth's important contribution to banking theory to name but a few. Nor should this very broad brush summary lead anyone to believe that, by the outbreak of World War I, the edifice of neoclassical monetary economics, built around the quantity theory, was any more complete than the classical orthodoxy, from which it developed, had been in the early 1870s. It contained gaps and inconsistencies of its own, and the development of monetary economics continued after World War I in response to those gaps and inconsistencies just as it had earlier. The scientific maturity which marked monetary economics during the period 1870–1914, persisted into the post-war period. The final chapter of this book, therefore, briefly discusses the deficiencies of neoclassical monetary theory as it stood in 1914, and how subsequent attempts to cope with them were to evolve.

Note

1. I do not mean to suggest here that classical monetary theorists always neglected demand side effects. Thus one important factor motivating David Ricardo's (1816) *Proposal for an Economical and Secure Currency*, which would have replaced gold coin with paper convertible into bullion, was his fear of the deflationary consequences of re-introducing gold coinage into Britain in the wake of the preceding inflation. On this, see Samuel Hollander (1979), Chapter 8.

2 • The orthodoxy of the 1870s

Introduction

The early 1870s were rather quiet years in monetary economics. The great policy debates that dominated the development of the subject in the first half of the century had no real parallel in its third quarter, and by 1870 the effects of the gold discoveries in California and Australia of 1849–51 had been absorbed by the international economy, and analysed by economists; while the 'Great Depression' of prices, and the debates about bimetallism that were to accompany it had not yet begun. Moreover, though Marshall's unpublished manuscript on 'Money' was probably written in 1871, and shows quite clearly that by this early date he had a firm grasp of all of the essential ingredients of what was later to be called 'Cambridge Monetary Theory', these ideas did not begin to enter the published literature until the late 1880s. What Frank W. Fetter (1965) termed 'British monetary orthodoxy', a comprehensive body of doctrine about theory and policy which encapsulated the major achievements of classical economics in the monetary area, was then at the height of its influence.

This chapter surveys the principal ideas of that orthodoxy, and draws in particular on the writings of John Stuart Mill, William Stanley Jevons and Walter Bagehot. Mill's *Principles* was first published in 1848 and the seventh edition of 1871 was the last to appear during its author's lifetime. Furthermore, under the influence of John Cairnes, Mill had made important revisions to its treatment of monetary issues in the sixth edition of 1865, and the authority of this great work was still at its height in the 1870s. Jevons, along with Cairnes, had carried out important empirical work on monetary issues in the 1860s, and his little book *Money and the Mechanism of Exchange* (1875) rapidly became a widely read primer on the subject. Though not everything it contains, (notably its proposals for indexation) belong to classical orthodoxy, it nevertheless provides a textbook account for the general reader of that orthodoxy's theoretical aspects as they stood in the 1870s. As to Bagehot, his celebrated *Lombard Street* appeared in 1873, and is the *locus classicus* of the theory of central banking which formed an integral part of the orthodoxy of the 1870s.

The classical theory of the price level

Nowadays monetary economics places overwhelming emphasis on money's capacity to act as a store of value but this was not the case in the 1870s. Individual choice was not then conventionally regarded as the proper starting point for any kind of economic analysis, let alone monetary theory, and even such a self-consciously revolutionary exponent of marginal utility theory as Jevons never thought to extend it to monetary economics. For him, as for all of his contemporaries, monetary theory was about *The Mechanism of Exchange*, and money's fundamental and distinguishing role in the economy was recognised to be that of a means of exchange. Classical monetary economics recognised that money has to be durable (and in this sense a store of value) in order to fulfil this primary function, but the idea that money might be held as an asset independently of its role in the process of exchange (an idea absolutely central to much modern monetary theory) was, with one significant exception to be discussed later in this chapter, quite alien to it.[1] Thus in discussing the functions of money in his *Principles* (1871) Mill did note that, 'The thing which people would select to keep by them for making purchases, must be one which, besides being divisible and generally desired, does not deteriorate by keeping' (page 503), but to say that durability is a desirable quality of the means of exchange is not the same thing as attributing to money a store of value function in its own right. Jevons' (1875) comment that 'It is worthy of enquiry whether money does not also serve a fourth distinct purpose – that of embodying value in a convenient form for conveyance to distant places' (page 15) comes a little closer to modern views, but still stops far short of them. Even this step was one too far for the American economist Francis A. Walker (1878, pages 11–13), who explicitly argued that anything held as a store of value had *ipso facto* ceased to function as money.

The monetary economists of the 1870s were well aware that money's unit of account function did not need to be performed by the means of exchange itself. Schemes for 'tabular standards' – indexed contracts using something other than money as their unit of account – had been current during the Napoleonic Wars, and Jevons in particular, who distinguished between the 'unit of account' and 'standard of deferred payment' functions of money was an ardent exponent of them in the 1870s. Jevons' views on this issue were exceptional however, and indeed attracted scornful criticism from Bagehot (1875). The institutional fact of contracts denominated in terms of the means of exchange was usually taken as a datum by classical analysis.

Even though the proposition that, 'the introduction of money does not interfere with the operation of any of the laws of value' (Mill, 1871, page 507) was central to classical economics, and even though the real economy was usually analysed without direct reference to monetary mechanisms, computational costs arising from the absence of a common unit of account, not to mention the inconveniences of barter, were regarded as an essentially impossible barrier to trade. A smoothly functioning system of monetary exchange was therefore recognised to be a *sine qua non* for economic development and the efficient operation of the real economy; and the ultimate purpose of monetary theory was, in keeping with the utilitarian ethos of classical economics, the solution of a policy problem, namely how to design monetary institutions so as to promote the efficient operation of the real economy.[2] Price level instability disrupted money's efficient performance as a unit of account, and, because it was associated with financial crises and panics, it also undermined money's effectiveness as a means of exchange. Understanding the interaction of money and the price level was thus the central scientific problem for classical monetary economics.

The nature of the interaction between money and prices had long been understood to depend upon the nature of monetary institutions. The eighteenth and nineteenth centuries had seen many experiments with inconvertible paper monies, and exponents of classical monetary economics knew well enough that, under such arrangements, variations in the quantity of money did indeed cause variations in the price level. Even though, according to Jevons (1875), 'There is plenty of evidence to prove that an inconvertible paper money, if carefully limited in quantity, can retain its full value' (page 235), inconvertible paper money was nevertheless regarded as an 'abnormal phenomenon' (Jevons, 1875, page 191) associated in particular (though not exclusively) with wartime finance. Thus Jevons cites the British currency after 1797, and the 'present notes of the Bank of France' as examples of 'undisguised *paper money*' (page 234), and he also notes that:

> It is a common resource for insurrectionary or belligerent govern-
> ments in want of funds to issue documents promising to pay cash [i.e.
> commodity money] after their successful establishment . . . there are
> few instances in which such bills have been eventually paid (page
> 233).[3]

For Jevons and for the classical economists generally, the norm was a commodity-based monetary system, with the liabilities of banks being convertible at a legally stipulated rate into gold or silver (or both). Under such an arrangement, the value of money was ultimately the value of the precious metals, and was to be explained as a special case of the general theory of relative prices. Subject to certain qualifications involving terms of trade effects (see pages 28-9), the value of money, to put it in Mill's (1871) words 'is determined . . . temporarily by demand and supply, permanently and on the average by cost of production' (page 507). The relevant cost of production was marginal cost, because the Classics viewed mining as a diminishing returns activity (see, e.g. Mill, 1871, page 519).

To modern eyes, there are obvious difficulties here. Interactions among the size of the existing stock of specie, the proportion of that stock devoted to monetary uses, and hence its current rate of flow of output, are all relevant to the determination of its marginal production cost which is not, therefore, an exogenous variable. A Marshallian supply and demand apparatus modified to incorporate the stock flow distinction is indispensable to the analysis of these interactions. Though the supply and demand apparatus was available in the 1870s, it had not, in any published form, acquired the powerful simplicity that Marshall was to give it. Moreover the significance of the stock flow distinction was not widely understood. Marshall's unpublished manuscript on 'Money' of 1871 shows that he had, even at this early date, both grasped and solved the problems to which I am here alluding, but they were not squarely addressed in any published, or even readily available unpublished, source until much later. Rather, it was simply asserted that in the long run 'the ultimate regulator' – the phrase is Mill's (1871, page 517) – of the price level was the marginal production cost of the precious metals. The vagueness of classical economics about the means by which this regulator operated, and hence about the ultimate significance of technological factors in determining the value of a commodity-based money was, as we shall see, to play an important role in the debates about bimetallism, and its resolution by Marshall and Fisher would in due course be one of the major achievements of neoclassical monetary economics.

Of course, classical economics had long recognised that the above-mentioned cost of production, and therefore the equilibrium general price level, could be changed by the discovery of new and more cheaply worked sources of supply of gold and silver. The effects on the price level of the discovery of new sources of the precious metals in New Spain had been a factor giving strong impetus to the development of the quantity theory in the seventeenth century, and their theoretical analysis had taken a recognisably classical form as early as the 1730s with the work of Richard Cantillon (1734), whose treatment of the quantity theory in many important respects anticipates that of David Hume (1752). By the 1870s such effects had once more attracted considerable attention as the result of the gold discoveries in California and Australia of 1849–51. Both Cairnes (1873) and Jevons (1884) devoted much time and effort in the 1860s to analysing the consequences of these discoveries. For them, the problem was first to show that the new discoveries had indeed caused an increase in the general price level, and secondly to trace out the mechanisms whereby this change was brought about.

From the 1820s onward, there had been no real disagreement among monetary economists that the long-run equilibrium price level under specie convertibility was determined by the cost of producing the precious metals. There had, though, been disagreement about short-run issues. What we might call the quantity theory position (as epitomised, for example, by Nassau Senior (1840)) was that, in the case of a commodity-based monetary system, changes in the quantity of money could play an active though short-run role in moving the price level away from equilibrium when they were engineered by a banking system, and that such changes were the key factor moving the price level towards its new equilibrium in the wake of gold discoveries. This view underpinned the policy recommendations of the Currency School, embodied in the Bank Charter Act of 1844, though this group applied it only to a very narrow concept of money consisting of coin and bank notes. There had also existed an anti-quantity theory position, however, particularly associated with the Banking School who opposed the Bank Charter Act as likely to be ineffective. Though this group's broader view of what constituted money was not inherently antithetical to the quantity theory, their argument that under a commodity-based monetary system the quantity of money was a purely passive variable (which adjusted to a price level determined, even in the short run, by relative costs of production) certainly was.

The gold discoveries in California and Victoria provided empirical evidence not only about long-run equilibrium relationships, but also about the short-run interaction of money and the price level. They led, beyond a doubt, to a sudden fall in the cost of producing gold. They were followed in Gold Standard countries by a steady increase in the prices of at least primary commodities, an increase which appeared to be proximately caused by the growing quantity of gold money coming into circulation as a result of mining activities. The price level in a country such as Britain, could, it appeared as a result of this experience, deviate from its long-run equilibrium time path for a considerable period of time. The factor which kept it away from this equilibrium was an initially 'too low' quantity of money; and the forces which moved it towards this equilibrium were an increased rate of gold production, an initial disturbance of relative price levels between gold-producing areas and the rest of the world, and subsequent balance of payments surpluses and money supply growth in the latter, not least Britain itself.

This causative sequence, which had been postulated by Cantillon as early as 1734, was thoroughly documented by Cairnes and Jevons, particularly the former, as having occurred in the 1850s.[4] Thus the same theory of the nature of the relationship between money and prices which commanded virtually universal agreement in the case of inconvertible paper money – namely, that money caused prices and not *vice versa* – had by the 1870s become accepted as holding in the case of convertible money as well, at least in the short run. As Cairnes put it, in a passage quoted by Bordo (1975):

> The value of a circulating medium, convertible on demand into gold, of course, depends in the long run on the cost of obtaining gold; but its value at any given time and the fluctuation in its value, are determined by the quantity which happens to be in circulation, compared with the functions which it has to perform, and its efficiency in performing them: (pages 339–40).

Mill (1871) also made this point, and explicitly concluded that 'it would . . . be an error both scientifically and practically, to discard the proposition which asserts a connection between the value of money and its quantity' (page 522) when discussing the determination of the price level under convertible currency.

From the late eighteenth century onwards institutional development in general, and the growth of banking in particular, created difficulties for exponents of the quantity theory. These were partly analytic and partly semantic, but this borderline was not always clearly delineated during nineteenth-century debates. There was much confusion about what ought and ought not to be considered as 'money', and about what such a choice implied for the validity of the quantity theory. Here it is helpful to recall once more the classical economists' insistence on the central importance of money's role as a means of exchange. Coin and, as their use spread, bank notes (convertible or not) clearly performed this function, and hence were usually characterised as 'money' or 'currency', though the latter term was sometimes reserved for coin alone. However, as a simple matter of fact, bank deposits (and/or cheques drawn upon them) not to mention bills of exchange of various sorts, also circulated, particularly in the wholesale trade, becoming increasingly important from the late eighteenth century onwards. Though a modern economist would have no great difficulty incorporating at least some of these instruments in a 'broad' concept of 'money', the classical economists chose to distinguish between the 'circulating medium' and 'money', usually (though not always) using the former phrase to describe the broader aggregate.

The semantics of classical monetary economics differ from ours in a way well calculated to confuse the unwary reader, but substantive problems too were created for the quantity theory by the growth of banking. During the debates of the 1830s and 1840s, the Currency School insisted that variations in the quantity of 'money', defined as bank notes and coin, and 'money' alone, were crucial to the behaviour of prices. They argued that an institutional framework which ensured that the quantity of this aggregate behaved appropriately would be sufficient to guarantee price stability. It might be tempting to defend this position by referring to the role of 'money' thus narrowly defined as the base of an inverted credit pyramid, and by arguing that the Currency School understood this and were early supporters of treating 'high powered money' as a strategic variable. However, it would be difficult to carry such a defence very far.

With the exception of those ruling with respect to the note issue after 1844, reserve ratios in nineteenth-century Britain were at the discretion of individual institutions, and were subject to much variability. Moreover, the mechanism of the simple bank credit multiplier was not fully or widely understood. A more accurate interpretation of the Currency School position on this matter is given by Mill (1871, page 552), namely, that its members were misled by a purely semantic distinction between 'money' and other components of the 'circulating medium' into making a theoretical one; and that in arguing that 'bank notes and no other forms of credit influence prices' (page 552) they were simply wrong. Jevons expressed similar views in 1862 (reprinted 1884, page 7). By the 1870s then, this particular aspect of Currency School doctrine was widely agreed to be erroneous. The Banking School view, that variations in other components of the circulating medium were also relevant, had become an uncontroversial part of classical monetary economics.

The exponents of this view did not express it in the way that twentieth-century quantity theorists would: they did not systematically broaden their usage of the word 'money' to encompass a wider range of instruments. Rather they wrote about the limited validity of simple versions of the quantity theory in the presence of a sophisticated financial system, and emphasised that variations in 'credit' as well as 'money' could and did affect prices. Thus Mill (1871), having stated that 'the amount of goods and of transactions being the same, the value of money is inversely as its quantity multiplied by what is called the rapidity of circulation' (pages 513–14), went on to warn his readers that,

> When credit comes into play as a means of purchasing, distinct from money in hand, we shall hereafter find that the connection between prices and the amount of the circulating medium is much less direct and intimate, and that such connection as does exist no longer admits of so simple a mode of expression.

Sometimes the classical economists argued, as in this just-quoted passage, that the existence of credit, and variations in its quantity, would affect the relationship between prices and the quantity of money (or of the circulating medium), and stressed that credit *per se*, as opposed to the type of instruments to which it gave rise was the key factor influencing prices. At other times they attributed effects on prices (and hence implicitly different velocities) to different credit instruments. Thus Mill (1871) says:

> I apprehend that bank notes, bills, or cheques, as such, do not act on prices at all. What does act on prices is Credit, in whatever shape given, and whether it gives rise to any transferable instruments capable of passing into circulation or not (pages 538–9).

Only a few pages later (pages 545–6) he tells his readers that 'It appears . . . that bank notes are a more powerful instrument for raising prices than bills, and bills than book credits' and a little later still (page 551) he points out that,

> there is a fourth form of credit transactions, by cheques on bankers, and transfers in a banker's books, which is exactly parallel in every respect to bank notes, giving equal facilities to an extension of credit, and capable of acting on prices quite as powerfully.

The manner in which ideas about the extent to which the simple quantity theory had to be modified to deal with a sophisticated financial system were expressed was thus sometimes confusing; but by the 1870s the confusion in question stemmed from the fact that different authors (and indeed sometimes the same author) used different modes of reasoning to reach similar conclusions.[5] It did not stem from any inconsistency or error in the conclusions themselves, as it did in the Currency School literature of the 1830s and 1840s.

The 'rapidity of circulation' concept incorporated in classical monetary economics was a transactions (as opposed to income) velocity idea. Discussions of its determinants, particularly in a secular context, went in terms of the technical institutional characteristics of the trading system in general, and the financial system in particular, rather than referring to factors conditioning individual portfolio choices.[6] Because the nature of communications, and the structure of the banking system do not change suddenly, it is normal to associate the transactions velocity approach to the quantity theory with the view that velocity is rather stable over time and that large variations in the price level require large variations in the quantity of money if they are to occur. Classical quantity theorists, however, did not argue that velocity was an empirically stable parameter in this sense. They were as much concerned with the cyclical interaction of money and prices as with secular relations, and in this context they stressed not the role of a given institutional structure in stabilising velocity in the long run, but rather the short-run scope for prices to vary independently of the quantity of money which that structure provided. This emphasis was central to their analysis of the credit cycle, so-called, as we shall see below. It will be convenient, however, to discuss their views on what we would now call the transmission mechanism before we take up the cycle.

The transmission mechanism

Classical monetary economists frequently argued that the general level of prices was determined by supply and demand, but in doing so they were not referring, as would a modern economist, to the interaction of a stock supply of nominal money with a stock demand for real balances. They were referring, to put it in terms of Fisher's equation of exchange (which is discussed in Chapter 3), to the interaction of a flow of money expenditure (MV) and a flow of goods offered for sale – T rather than Y – and arguing that prices (P) had to move in order to reconcile these two largely independently determined flows. Mill puts the matter in the following way:

As the whole of the goods in the market compose the demand for money, so the whole of the money constitutes the demand for goods. The money and the goods are seeking each other for the purpose of being exchanged. They are reciprocally supply and demand to one another (1871, pages 509–10).

To think about price level determination in this way had a number of consequences for classical monetary economics.[7]

To begin with, and as we have already seen, exponents of the classical quantity theory were much more willing than their modern successors to entertain the possibility that changes in velocity might be autonomous sources of price level variations in their own right. Although from the early eighteenth century onwards, just about everyone who wrote about the quantity theory argued that a change in the quantity of money would lead to a proportionate change in prices, the argument was usually accompanied by the explicit qualification that this prediction depended upon the assumption of a constant velocity of circulation, and the warning that this assumption did not usually hold in the real world. Mill was far from alone in defining the quantity of money relevant to the quantity theory as notes and coin *in active circulation*, excluding 'hoards' of such assets from the relevant aggregate. We have also seen how keenly aware were he and his contemporaries of the presence of other assets in the circulating medium, and the role of 'credit' in determining prices. Indeed, the occasional semantic inconsistency among Mill's discussions of the role of money and credit in determining the price level, noted above, also probably stems from this emphasis on flows of expenditure. Credit, after all, permits goods to be exchanged without money simultaneously passing from buyer to seller.

A further, closely related, consequence of this classical view of the interaction of money and prices was the belief of virtually all of its exponents that an injection of money into the economy would have significantly different real consequences depending upon whose hands it passed through first when it came into circulation. This point was made by Hume (1752) and as Fridrich von Hayek (1932) showed, it was also clearly present in the work of Cantillon (1734), Henry Thornton (1802) and Thomas R. Malthus (1811) among others; but Cairnes and Mill added details to the story, in particular concerning the influence of monetary expansion and contraction on the rate of interest, details which were to be of great importance for the later evolution of monetary economics.[8]

It was an article of faith in classical economics that, in the long run, interest was a real economic variable:

> the natural rate . . . about which the market rate oscillates . . . partly depends upon the amount of accumulation going on in the hands of persons who cannot themselves attend to the employment of their savings, and partly on the comparative taste existing in the community for the active pursuits of industry, or for the leisure, ease, and independence of an annuity (Mill, 1871, page 648).

Cairnes and Mill, like many of their classical predecessors, sought to explain not just the natural interest rate, but also the above-mentioned oscillations. They noted that Britain, not being a gold producer, received its share of newly mined gold through the balance of payments. They further noted that such gold inflows increased the banking system's reserves and generated domestic money as an accompaniment to an expansion of bank credit. They argued that, because 'the rate of interest will . . . equalize the demand for loans with the supply of them' (Mill, 1871, page 647) this flow of new money into credit markets would serve to raise the prices of credit instruments and lower the rate of interest even if nothing happened to the economy's underlying saving rate. 'The same operation . . . which adds to the currency also adds to the loans: the whole increase of currency in the first instance swells the loan market . . . it tends to lower interest' (Mill, 1871, page 656).

By the 1870s, classical economics had thus evolved a full-fledged loanable funds, as opposed to 'productivity and thrift', theory of interest, but the analysis did not stop there. Cairnes and Mill understood that the flow supply of bank credit would run ahead of voluntary saving for as long as new money was entering circulation through the banking system. This newly created money placed in the hands of investors by the banks would, they believed, at least in the all-important first round, enable them to bid resources away from consumers, thereby generating 'forced savings'. Hence capital accumulation at an increased rate would accompany monetary expansion.[9]

It is easy to read into classical analysis of these matters more than is actually there. As Kohn (1985) has pointed out, it seems to prefigure certain insights of the literature on 'money and growth' of the 1960s and 1970s; but as he has also noted, the classical economists were not in fact here discussing long-run super-neutralities and non-neutralities. The idea of a *continuous and fully anticipated inflation*, which is central to this modern literature, was quite alien to their analysis, which dealt with non-neutralities arising during periods (albeit perhaps quite long periods measured in years rather than months) of *transition from one equilibrium price level to another*. Moreover, it would not be quite correct to argue that Mill was ignorant of the effects of anticipated inflation on nominal interest rates. Thus a passage, quoted in part earlier, about the effects of monetary expansion on the rate of interest, also tells us that 'Considered as an addition to loans [an operation which adds to the currency] tends to lower interest more than *in its character of depreciation it tends to raise it*' (Mill, 1871, page 656; my italics).[10] However, neither Mill nor any other economist of the 1870s incorporated such insights as they had about this matter into the heart of their analysis. The effects of anticipated inflation on the demand for assets are, however, a *sine qua non* of the modern analysis in question.

If we must be careful not to attribute to Cairnes, Mill or any other classical economist even an embryo theory about the long-run super-neutrality (or non-neutrality) of money, we must also avoid the more modest suggestion that they envisaged a theory of the business cycle in which forced saving plays a key role during the upswing. They did not relate their analysis of this phenomenon to the 'credit cycle'. By the 1870s classical economists had most of the ingredients necessary for the creation of a theory of the cycle which stressed fluctuations in fixed capital formation as its key 'real' feature. However, as we shall see in Chapter 5, even in the hands of Wicksell (1898), who greatly extended and refined the Cairnes–Mill insights into the effects of money creation on the interest rate, these remained a component of an analysis of secular price level changes. It was only later, and outside the period covered by this book, with Ludwig von Mises and Hayek in Austria and Dennis Robertson and Lionel Robbins in England, that forced saving came to be placed in an explicitly cyclical context.[11] Furthermore, though the effects of credit creation on the price of storable commodities certainly played a key role in classical analysis of the cycle, which *could* have been expanded into a systematic theory stressing fluctuations in the quantities as well as prices of inventories, it was not. This development had to await the work of Hawtrey, which will be discussed in Chapter 4.[12]

The classical theory of the cycle

The financial crisis of 1825 was the first peacetime example of a series of such events that recurred at ten to eleven-year intervals for the rest of the century. These crises were associated with fluctuations in the levels both of prices and of real economic activity. Though their occurrence was clearly perceived and much commented on from the outset, their regularity only revealed itself gradually to contemporary observers. Indeed it is the principal contribution of Clément Juglar (1860) that he documented and systematically analysed the decennial nature of the cycle. The fact that real as well as financial fluctuations were integral to the cycle was even more slowly discerned. Thus, during the nineteenth century, a theory of financial crisis in due course evolved into a theory of the credit cycle, and eventually into a theory of the business cycle. The evolution here was not, however, quite as orderly as this summary might suggest. Mill, from his earliest writings onwards, showed an awareness that the cycle involved fluctuations in real variables (see Hollander, 1986, pages 501–2), while Jevons and his associates in the Manchester Statistical Society were also well aware of the existence of a real cycle by the 1860s.[13]

Marx (whose connections through his friend Friedrich Engels with Manchester are surely significant in this context) went much further than did any representative of classical orthodoxy. As is well known, he claimed that fluctuations in real economic activity were a regular and inherent feature of capitalist growth. His jibe that, 'The superficiality of political economy shows itself in the fact that it looks upon the expansion and contraction of credit, which is a mere symptom of the periodic changes of the industrial cycle, as their cause,' (1867, page 633) is surely more justified than many similar attacks which he launched on classical economics: notwithstanding the qualifications noted above, its exponents did place much more emphasis upon the financial aspects of the cycle than upon its real characteristics even as late as the 1870s. Classical monetary theory dealt with a 'credit cycle', rather than a 'business cycle', and stressed price fluctuations as its dominant endogenous characteristic. Output fluctuations, though discussed, were not systematically integrated into orthodox analysis until Alfred and Mary Marshall did so in 1879, a development to be discussed in Chapter 4.

Classical economists paid particular attention to the 'crisis' phase of the cycle or, as we would now put it, the upper turning point. This 'crisis' was treated as a phenomenon mainly of the financial system, and its prelude seemed to involve the banking system expanding its note issue, and indeed credit generally, thereby contributing to speculative activity in financial and commodity markets. Its actual occurrence was attributed to a drain of specie from the banking system, both abroad as a result of an adverse trade balance (an *external drain* as it was often called) and at home (an *internal drain*). As Bagehot put it: 'periods of internal panic and external demand for bullion commonly occur together. The foreign drain empties the Bank till, and that emptiness, and the resulting rise in the rate of discount, tend to frighten the market' (1873, page 27).

In the crisis itself, market participants sought to rid themselves of speculative inventories of commodities and financial assets whose convertibility into specie seemed to be at risk. Such a crisis could degenerate into a panic which threatened the convertibility of banking system liabilities into Bank of England liabilities, and Bank of England liabilities into specie; but further credit contraction undertaken to counter this threat not only exacerbated it, but also led to much commercial distress, and many outright business failures.

The Currency School–Banking School debate, which culminated in the 1844 Bank Charter Act, has been in large measure about the causes of this sequence of events. Before 1844 the Bank of England was not subject to any fixed specie reserve ratio against its note issue, and Country (i.e. outside London) and Scottish banks were free to issue notes in quantities limited only by the public's willingness to keep them to circulation. According to the Currency School, whatever gave the cycle's upswing its initial impetus, the subsequent issue of notes permitted by these arrangements exacerbated the boom, drove up domestic prices, and precipitated a drain of specie abroad. Such a state of affairs could persist long enough to create a financial crisis because the requirement that bank notes be convertible into specie was not, in and of itself, sufficient to guarantee that their quantity would begin to shrink in harmony with the country's specie stock when the first consequences of 'overissue' manifested themselves. The Banking School, on the other hand, treated the quantity of money (however defined) as a passive variable even in the short run. They attributed the onset of specie outflows to such exogenous events as bad harvests, and the subsequent panic to inadequate specie reserves.

A cure for crises was implicit in the Currency School's analysis, namely to prevent the preceding boom. This was to be accomplished by depriving the Country banks (and the Scottish banks) of their discretionary note issuing rights, and by requiring the Bank of England to hold 100 per cent specie reserves against its notes over a fixed maximum fiduciary issue. In this way, any incipient tendency of the note issue to rise excessively would automatically and immediately be checked as specie began to leave the country and notes were withdrawn from circulation. Any boom, accompanied and/or caused by 'excessive money creation' on the part of the banks, would always be nipped in the bud, while the convertibility of paper money would be guaranteed. Crises, like those of 1825 and 1836 would thus be forestalled and rendered things of the past.

It has already been remarked that the Currency School's notion that only money as they defined it could affect prices had been thoroughly discredited by 1870. It was empirical evidence as much as any theoretical arguments that had done so. The Bank Charter Act of 1844 went a good way towards embodying the Currency School's proposals for control of the note issue. Their suggestions for regulating the Bank of England issue were implemented, while the Country bank note issue was frozen. A separate Act of 1845 put the Scottish note issue on a 100 per cent marginal reserve requirement. Moreover, the 1844 Act also established a separate unregulated banking department at the Bank of England to run its deposit business. Nevertheless, even though these measures ensured that the note issue varied in lock step with the country's specie reserves, financial crises, which as we have seen were recognised by the middle of the century to be features of a regular cycle rather than simply random events, occurred in 1847, 1857 and 1866.

These crises had all the important characteristics of their predecessors save one, namely that the convertibility of Bank of England *notes* into specie was no longer in question. However, on each occasion, the convertibility of the Bank of England's *deposit liabilities* (which themselves played the role of the reserve base of the rest of the banking system) into notes (and hence into specie) *was* at risk. The Bank, not to mention the rest of the financial system, was saved from collapse in each case only by the suspension of the 100 per cent marginal reserve requirement against its note issue. This experience ensured that, by the 1870s, the Currency School's analysis of financial crises was widely understood to be inadequate.

However, the extreme Banking School view that the financial system played an essentially passive role in their generation had also been given up. Instead, the expansion and contraction of bank credit (as well as trade credit), which generated price fluctuations independently of the behaviour of the quantity of 'money' had been identified as a crucial mechanism in propagating the cycle.[14] Mill's account of the credit cycle, which, when the first edition of *Principles* appeared in 1848, embodied important elements of a moderate Banking School (and hence minority) view of the phenomenon, had by the 1870s become quite representative of mainstream classical opinion.

> Some accident which excites expectation of rising prices . . . sets speculation at work in several leading departments at once. The prices rise, and the holders realize, or appear to have the power of realizing, great gains. . . . At periods of this kind a great extension of credit takes place. Not only do all whom the contagion reaches employ their credit much more freely than usual; but they really have more credit, because they seem to be making unusual gains, and because a generally reckless and adventurous feeling prevails, which disposes people to give as well as take credit more largely than at other times, and give it to persons not entitled to it. . . . When . . . the reaction comes and prices begin to fall, though at first perhaps only through the desire of holders to realize, speculative purchases cease: but were this all, prices would only fall to the level from which they rose, or to that which is justified by the state of consumption and of the supply. They fall, however, much lower, for as, when prices were rising and everybody apparently making a fortune, it was easy to obtain almost any amount of credit, so now, when everybody seems to be losing, and many fail entirely, it is with difficulty that firms of known solidity can obtain even the credit to which they are accustomed. . . . There is superadded, in extreme cases, a panic as unreasoning as the previous over-confidence; . . . Thus general prices, during a commercial revulsion, fall as much below the usual level as during the previous period of speculation they have risen above it: the fall, as well as the rise, originating not in anything affecting money, but in the state of credit (1871, pages 542–3).

The fact that Mill makes much of the role of speculation, particularly in commodity markets, in giving an impetus to credit expansion during the boom is typical of classical accounts of the cycle; and, as Sir John Hicks (1983) has argued, the notion that under a specie standard prices have a 'normal' level may be used to construct a model of the lower turning point that hinges upon the perception of gains to be made by buying at prices below this normal level. However, and again typical of classical accounts of the cycle, Mill does not systematically analyse the lower turning point. On the other hand, the absence from the preceding quotation of any systematic analysis of the role of balance of payments mechanisms generating what we would now call the upper turning point of the cycle reflects the influence of the Banking School on a book that was first written in the 1840s.

Elsewhere in the *Principles* Mill refers to the possibility of an external drain of specie exacerbating the severity of the crisis (see Hollander, 1986, page 571), while Bagehot (see page 21) and Jevons, both identified an adverse trade balance, financed by a drain of specie abroad, as a crucial factor at work in precipitating financial crisis; as indeed had the Currency School in the debates of the 1830s and 1840s. Jevons' words are typical of the orthodox position on this issue as it has evolved by the mid-1870s:

> the rise of prices thus produced turns the foreign exchanges against the country, and creates a balance of indebtedness which must be paid in gold. The basis of the whole fabric of credit slips away, and produces that sudden collapse known as a commercial crisis (1875, pages 315-16).

One other aspect of Mill's treatment of the cycle also sets it apart from that of Jevons and Bagehot, and is of considerable theoretical interest. It involves an insight which, as Hollander (1979, pages 491-5) has pointed out, occurs in the writings of Jean-Baptiste Say, and which, as Gary Becker and William Baumol (1952) note, also appears with some frequency from the 1880s onwards, but which does not appear in the writings of Mill's contemporaries. The insight in question concerns the notion of a 'general glut' of commodities; and the cycle, specifically its upper turning point, is the context in which he discusses it, first in his 1829 (but not published until 1844) essay 'On the influence of consumption upon production', but (contrary to many assertions to the contrary) also in his *Principles*.

Like all orthodox classical economists, Mill denied Malthus' assertion that the process of growth in a capitalist economy could break down as a result of oversaving. In long-run analysis he firmly adhered to the view that 'supply creates its own demand' and denied that a general oversupply of everything to be traded was possible.[15] However, and crucially different from any economist who viewed money *solely and always* as a means of exchange, Mill recognised in this context the logical possibility of agents wishing to acquire cash balances in order to hold them, rather than to spend them on goods. Furthermore, he argued that while agents sought to accumulate cash, there would indeed be a general oversupply of commodities *other than money*. Now agents would only wish to accumulate money *per se* if they wished to hold it as an asset, and such a possibility could, according to Mill, arise as a short-lived phenomenon during a financial crisis.

> Persons in general, at that particular time, from a sudden expectation of being called upon to meet sudden demands, [like] better to possess money than any other commodity. Money, consequently, [is] in request, and all other commodities [are] in comparative disrepute. (1844, page 72)

Such behaviour would mean that, a temporary, *but nevertheless general* oversupply of commodities would accompany a financial crisis. In Mill's own words, as they appear in *Principles*,

> I have already described the state of the markets for commodities which accompanies . . . a commercial crisis. At such times there is really an excess of all commodities above the money demand: in other words, there is an undersupply of money (1871, page 574)

However, he also warned his readers,

> It is a great error to suppose . . . that a commercial crisis is the effect of a general excess of production. It is simply the consequence of an excess of speculative purchases . . . its immediate cause is a contraction of credit, and the remedy is, not a diminution of supply, but the restoration of confidence (1871, page 574).

The only 'general glut' that Mill countenanced was thus a short-term one in organised commodity markets. The idea that a general excess demand for money might be related to an excess supply of current output, let alone of labour, was quite alien to him.

Even so, the presence of this admittedly narrowly focused analysis of Mill's in his *magnum opus*, as well as in a youthful essay, does mean that later analysis of the role of monetary factors in the business cycle such as, for example, that of Marshall and Marshall (1879) or Marshall (1887), which clearly build on Mill's insights, have roots in classical economics.[16] It also implies that the notion of a demand for a stock of money to hold was not entirely absent from classical theory; although the fact that Mill viewed such a demand as a temporary phenomenon, arising only at times of financial crisis, does mean that the notion was peripheral to his version of the quantity theory of money. As we shall see below, a generalisation of this idea became, in the hands of Mill's successors, the basis of conventional neoclassical analysis of what we usually call 'cash balance mechanics'.

Money and the balance of payments

Nowadays monetary theory typically starts with the assumption of a closed economy, but it will already be apparent that English classical economists took an open economy for granted: a theory of the balance of payments was an integral part of their monetary economics, and had been since the days of Cantillon and Hume, whose price–specie flow mechanism, so-called, formed the starting point for virtually all subsequent work on this matter. According to Hume (1752) the mechanism in question operated to ensure that, under a commodity currency shared with the rest of the world, or a significant part of it, the domestic supply of money and price level would be endogenously and simultaneously determined. 'Too large' a domestic supply of the precious metals in circulation would temporarily cause 'too high' a domestic price level, in the well defined sense that a balance of trade deficit and a gold outflow would occur. The money supply would therefore automatically contract until domestic prices had fallen sufficiently to restore and then maintain balance of trade equilibrium. Long before the 1870s, this Humean analysis had been extended to accommodate paper money and a banking system, not to mention the influence of autonomous capital movements on the balance of payments; its implications for the behaviour of the exchange rate of an inconvertible paper money had also been thoroughly explored.

The first extension of classical monetary analysis to accommodate paper money was the work of Adam Smith, and his insights were refined and consolidated during the Bullionist Controversy, notably by Thornton and Ricardo, into a form which Mill was still expounding in the seventh (1871) edition of his *Principles*. Starting from an equilibrium situation, paper money issued domestically (and indeed other forms of paper and book credit too) would tend to raise domestic prices and lead to a balance of payments deficit, just as would an increase in a metallic currency. Paper was not acceptable abroad but specie was, and would therefore replace specie in domestic circulation without affecting the long-run equilibrium domestic price level, except to the extent that the addition of paper in one country to a world-wide circulation raised world-wide prices; but according to Mill (1871) 'This effect . . . would be too trifling to require notice except for the illustration of a principle' (page 642).

Provided that convertibility, and confidence in convertibility, were maintained, the replacement of specie with paper was, according to the Classics, beneficial because it economised on real resources in the provision of a circulating medium.[17] In Mill's words,

> The substitution . . . of paper for the precious metals, should always be carried as far as is consistent with safety; no greater amount of metallic currency being retained than is necessary to maintain, both in fact and in public belief, the convertibility of the paper (1871, page 643).

The extent to which price level fluctuations, as opposed to not very well articulated direct real balance effects, were stressed in the mechanisms at work as paper drove gold abroad varied from writer to writer. Smith, with his notion of a fixed 'channel of circulation' that tended to 'overflow' when more money was poured into it, certainly ignored price level effects, and may, without doing too much violence to his text, be interpreted as relying on a real balance effect to generate a trade imbalance.[18] In this he was later followed by Banking School writers. Ricardo, on the other hand, and the Currency School after him, focused on price level variations as an essential link in the mechanism. Cairnes and Jevons, as we have seen, had identified price level effects as critical in their empirical studies of the consequences of the mid-nineteenth-century gold discoveries. As to Mill, he found room for both price level and direct real balance effects in his analysis, but stressed the former.

The mechanisms which we have discussed so far involve trade flows only, and indeed, trade balance questions dominate the classical literature on balance of payments issues. Mill's 'equation of international demand' stated that: 'The produce of a country exchanges for the produce of other countries, at such values as are required in order that the whole of her exports may exactly pay for the whole of her imports' (1871, page 604), and thus identified trade balance equilibrium with balance of payments equilibrium. Classical economists knew about capital movements, of course, but they tended to associate them with once and for all payments of subsidies to allies, or of reparations to victorious enemies, or with the temporary financing of trade imbalances associated with bad harvests. Classical economics normally treated capital flows as complicating factors of temporary duration.

Autonomous capital movements had attracted serious attention in the context of Britain's payments of subsidies to her continental allies during the French Wars. Smith's earlier correct but incomplete insight that such transfers ultimately involved a movement of goods rather than of specie, was the starting point of what was to become the orthodox classical theory of the transfer mechanism. This mechanism involved, as a first step, international movements of money which had incipient effects on price levels and the exchanges, as well as real balance and income effects on the supply and demand for goods in the countries involved. These effects in turn provided incentives for goods to begin to move internationally to complete the transfer. As with the analysis of paper money and the balance of payments, different writers stressed different aspects of this general framework; and here too, Mill building particularly and explicitly upon Thornton's work, provided his readers with a comprehensive account of the transfer mechanism which paid due attention to all of the above-mentioned elements.

Though much of Mill's writing on international monetary matters, like that of such contemporaries as George J. Goschen (1861), summarised inherited wisdom, he did add insights of his own to this area, notably in working out the effects, on the balance of payments, money, and prices, of increases in labour productivity and of shifts in the pattern of world demand for various goods. He recognised the essential similarity of these two cases arguing that, in either instance, a tendency towards a balance of payments surplus in the country benefiting from either change would lead to equilibrating increases in domestic money and prices. According to Mill it was an error to suppose that,

> the value of money, in countries where it is an imported commodity, must be entirely regulated by its value in the countries which produce it. . . . On the contrary, any circumstance which disturbs the equation of international demand with respect to a particular country, not only may, but must, affect the value of money in that country. . . . The opening of a new branch of export trade from England . . . and all other events of similar tendency, would make the imports of England (bullion and other things taken together) no longer an equivalent for the exports; and [other] countries . . . would be obliged to offer their commodities, and bullion among the rest, on cheaper terms, in order to re-establish the equation of demand: and thus England would obtain money cheaper, and would acquire a generally higher range of prices (1871, pages 621).

Finally, it should be noted that Mill understood and clearly stated that, under inconvertible money, exchange rate movements would replace specie flows and domestic price level adjustments as equilibrating mechanisms. He pointed out that,

> a depreciation of the [inconvertible] currency does not affect the foreign trade of the country. . . . But though the trade is not affected, the exchanges are. . . . In such cases, instead of saying that the exchange is unfavourable, it would be a more correct representation to say that the par was altered (1871, pages 644-5).

Bimetallism

Well into the nineteenth century, silver was a more widely used monetary metal than gold. Britain, whose adherence to a *de facto* Gold Standard since the early eighteenth century had finally been sanctioned by an Act of Parliament in 1816, was something of an exceptional case. Indeed many obscurities in the nineteenth-century British monetary literature, particularly that of the Bullionist Controversy, stem from the fact that, at times of monetary disturbance, not just the sterling price of gold, but the gold price of silver were fluctuating. Contributors to policy debates had to deal with these complications.[19] Such matters were much less important in the thirty years after 1820, but they arose again with a vengeance in the 1850s when the gold discoveries in California and Australia threatened to disturb the relative price of gold and silver. Then France, *de jure* bimetallic but whose coinage in the first half of the century was predominantly of silver, shifted rapidly to the use of a gold coinage as a long-standing relative overvaluation of silver at her mints was transformed into an overvaluation of gold. This interaction of institutions with events generated, from the 1850s onwards, a good deal of discussion of the mechanics of bimetallism, discussion which, after a pause in the late 1860s and early 1870s, was in due course to culminate in major debates during the 1880s and 1890s.

Now bimetallism was not a brand new topic of discussion in the 1850s and 1860s. Britain's movement to a Gold Standard in the eighteenth century was the accidental outcome of an attempt to place her currency on a bimetallic basis at an inappropriate, fixed, relative mint price for the metals. The United States prior to the Civil War also was on a *de jure* bimetallic standard, but there too an overvaluation of gold had led to a *de facto* gold standard. Moreover, Gresham's Law, the proposition that under bimetallism a metal overvalued at the mint – 'bad' money – would drive an undervalued one – 'good' money – from circulation, had been understood since the sixteenth century. Nevertheless, the 1850s and 1860s saw much refinement of this old insight, not least at the hands of the French economist and politician Michel Chevalier (1859) who used it to explain the 'parachute effect' which had prevented a rapid inflation ensuing from the gold discoveries of the period. He saw that the value of gold was prevented from falling continuously as its quantity increased by the fact that, instead of swelling the money supplies of existing gold-using countries, newly mined gold first replaced silver in circulation in bimetallic nations, notably France, where the relative mint prices of gold and silver were fixed.

Chevalier failed to note, in Jevons' (1863, reprinted 1884) words, that 'The French currency may and does prevent gold from falling much below its old *relative value to silver*, but it cannot prevent both gold and silver falling in value' (page 60; Jevons' italics). This point had previously been made by Cairnes in an essay dealing with Chevalier's ideas (1860, reprinted 1873), and he, like Jevons, was able to document a general rise in prices, whether measured in silver or gold, in the wake of the gold discoveries. Even so, as a matter of fact, in the 1850s and 1860s there were strong forces at work against specie inflation in general; Chevalier had predicted a rapid inflation once silver had been driven out of the French monetary system, but he was wrong here too, because, as Cairnes and Jevons both pointed out, the silver displaced by gold in Europe was absorbed by Silver Standard countries such as India and China without a large fall in its value. The amount of silver displaced from Europe was rather small relative to already existing stocks in the East, and, as Cairnes (1860, reprinted 1873, pages 92–6) noted, the absence of a well developed banking system there precluded the possibility of a multiple expansion of bank credit on a silver reserve base taking place. Thus, though during the 1850s, France moved from being close to a *de facto* Silver Standard towards a *de facto* Gold Standard, she was nevertheless able to maintain the relative price of silver and gold at her mints at 15½ to 1 and in so doing also to keep the world market price of the metals close to that range too. As a side effect (but a very important one), she therefore succeeded in maintaining an essentially fixed exchange rate between the gold pound sterling and the silver Indian rupee.

The stabilising effect that the existence of bimetallic arrangements no doubt had on the gold price level in the 1850s was to be much cited during the 1880s and 1890s by those supporting their reinstatement. The American bimetallist S. Dana Horton's (1887) views are typical: 'Gold performed its functions in England in the satisfactory manner so often referred to with praise, by favour of the maintenance of Silver and Gold in other countries' (page 52). As we shall see in more detail in Chapter 6, during this later debate supporters of bimetallism argued that such a system would provide a more stable price level than a monometallic one based on either silver or gold alone because, it was argued, the 'parachute' would begin to work whenever the value of either metal was disturbed by the discovery of new sources of supply or by a change in its productivity in non-monetary uses. This position did, of course, rest upon an empirical assumption, as Jevons (1881, reprinted 1884), drawing upon his analysis of the 1860s pointed out.[20]

it is indispensable to remember the fact . . . that the values of gold and silver are ultimately governed, like those of all other commodities, by the cost of production. Unless clear reasons, then, can be shown why silver should be more constant in its circumstances of production than gold, there is no ground for thinking that a bimetallic gold and silver money will afford a more steady standard of value than gold alone (page 318).

Implicit in this passage, and explicit in his treatment of the issue in *Money and the Mechanism of Exchange*, (as Léon Walras (1889; see 1954 edition, pages 359–60) pointed out), is Jevons' view that bimetallism in practice would be alternating monometallism. He took it that, with given sources of the metals and given technology, their relative cost of production would also be given, and except in exceptional circumstances would differ from their relative mint price. The cheaper metal would then dominate the monetary system. Any technical change or discovery of new mines that reversed the relationship between relative production costs and mint price would set Gresham's Law to work, replacing one metal with the other.

If, as Jevons believed, gold production was likely to be relatively undisturbed by new discoveries and technical changes, and silver production was prone to such disturbances, a bimetallic system would be less stable than gold monometallism. That is why Jevons, an ardent exponent of an international money, was equally ardent in his insistence that such a money should be based on gold, thus embracing a position that Horton (1887) was later to disparage as 'transcendental single-metallism'.[21] This is not the place to discuss subsequent debates about bimetallism in detail. We shall return to them briefly in Chapter 3 and in more detail in Chapter 6 below. The important point to note at this stage of the narrative is that, though as we shall now see, a commitment to gold monometallism was an important component of British orthodoxy in the 1870s, it was also implicit in the theoretical element of that orthodoxy that questions about the viability of bimetallism were essentially empirical in nature.

The theory of monetary policy

The explicit inflationism which had characterised the monetary proposals of the Birmingham School in the earlier part of the nineteenth century, and which would soon flare up again among some American supporters of bimetallism, was at a low ebb in the 1870s as was the not unrelated view that monetary measures could be taken actively to promote a high and rising level of real economic activity. Classical orthodoxy was deeply concerned about price level instability, both secular and cyclical. The classical economists were good utilitarians, and therefore believed that social and economic problems should be tackled by designing the institutional framework so that the pursuit of individual self-interest would promote the social good. Hence they sought their solutions to monetary problems primarily in the design of monetary institutions within which market mechanisms could function, rather than in the creation of principles to govern discretionary behaviour on the part of some policy authority. Nevertheless, by the 1870s, their confidence in an institutional solution to the problem of price stability was greater in a secular context than a cyclical one. The Bank Charter Act 1844 had been intended to deal with both problems in such terms, but by the 1870s, it was widely accepted that suitable discretionary conduct on the part of the Bank of England, within the institutional framework created by that Act, was required to deal with problems engendered by cyclical fluctuations.

For any quantity theorist, a necessary condition for control over the general price level is control over the money supply, and Jevons' views on this matter were completely representative of British classical opinion in general. In 1875 he listed no fewer than fourteen methods whereby a paper currency, by the 1870s an accepted institution, could be regulated. He conceded that, in principle, inconvertible paper could be manipulated so as to maintain price level stability, and that such a system had indeed delivered more or less desirable price level behaviour in a number of historical instances. He was far from recommending such an arrangement, though, because he feared that unpredictable fluctuations in velocity would make the business of managing inconvertible paper difficult; although he did note that such technical problems could be overcome by managing an inconvertible currency so as to stabilise the exchange rate, or the market price of the precious metals.

However, 'The great temptation which it offers to overissue and consequent depreciation' (1875, page 229) was the primary basis of Jevons' objection to inconvertible paper. Mill opposed it in similar terms. 'All variations in the value of the circulating medium are mischievous: they disturb existing contracts and expectations, and the liability to such changes renders every pecuniary engagement of long date entirely precarious.' (1871, page 558) The power which inconvertibility gave to the issuers of money to 'add to it indefinitely, lowering its value and raising prices . . . is . . . in whomsoever vested, . . . an intolerable evil', particularly so when vested in governments, who 'always have a direct interest in lowering the value of the currency, because it is the medium in which their own debts are computed' (1871, page 558).

In order to prevent such abuses, then, commodity convertibility was, for classical monetary economics, a *sine qua non* of a sound monetary system. By the 1870s, subsequent debates about bimetallism notwithstanding, it is fair to say that, particularly in Britain, the commodity of choice was gold. This despite the fact that the experiences of the 1850s and 1860s had rendered untenable the easy identification of a constant price of paper money in terms of gold, with a constant purchasing power of such money over goods in general; and despite the fact that, if forced to choose, it was the latter kind of constancy that the classical economists favoured. Without systematically arguing the reasons for their position, they particularly feared a falling value of money. Redistribution of wealth away from frugal creditors was apparently regarded as particularly reprehensible, and although Jevons (1863, reprinted 1884, page 96), for example, was willing to agree that a lightening of the burden of debt in the economy might be conducive to economic growth, that was not sufficient reason for him to soften his opposition to inflation.

As we have noted earlier, there was considerable doubt about how serious the wealth redistributions brought about in the 1850s and 1860s by fluctuations in the purchasing power of gold had in fact been, and about how pressing a policy problem such redistributions might present in the future.[22] Jevons showed much more concern about this matter than did most of his contemporaries, making proposals (to be discussed in more detail in Chapter 6) that government regularly compute and publish price level measures, a 'tabular standard', to which private parties could voluntarily index contracts. Indeed Bagehot (1875), and later Robert Giffen (1892b), poured scorn on such proposals. On the whole, despite the experience of the 1850s and 1860s, and particularly in Britain, maintenance of gold convertibility was regarded as an adequate institutional defence of long-run stability in the purchasing power of money. The worries about secularly *falling* prices and associated proposals for adopting bimetallic arrangements which were to come to the fore in the later 1870s and 1880s were not evident in the literature of the early 1870s.

Even Jevons' doubts about gold convertibility only extended to its *sufficiency* as a guarantee of a sound monetary system. Its *necessity* (or at least great desirability) was as strongly accepted by him as by anyone, and he expressed considerable satisfaction about the 'unmistakable tendency to the adoption of gold as the measure of value, and the sole principal medium of exchange' among the 'principal nations' (1875, page 144) that was then under way. Indeed, Jevons devoted a good deal of energy towards helping this process along. He actively supported proposals, which originated from a conference held in Paris in 1867, for establishing a common European gold currency based upon the French 25 franc piece, proposals which he defended with reference to the promotion of efficiency in international transactions, and linked to a scheme for decimalising the British currency.[23] The failure of Bagehot (1875) to appreciate the arrangement, notwithstanding Jevons' support for a 'tabular standard', should be seen in the context of these other proposals, and as reflecting a desire to make a gold-based monetary system more efficient, certainly not a wish to replace it.

The classical economists of the 1870s, concerned as they were with promoting price level stability, defended the 1844 Bank Charter Act, and were just as opposed to 'free banking' in the sense of an unregulated competitive note issue, as had been the Act's architects. However, they took an altogether narrower and more modest view of its importance than had their predecessors.[24] Bagehot's (1873) judgement that the Act was 'only a subordinate matter in the Money Market . . . the phenomena connected with it . . . magnified into greater relative importance than they at all deserve' (pages 1–2), would have deeply disappointed its creators, whose aim had been nothing less than to eliminate financial crises by putting a stop to the fluctuation of the 'money supply' (that is bank notes) originating in bank lending, without at the same time violating *laissez-faire* principles in the organisation of credit markets.

We have already seen that the Currency School had attributed altogether too great an importance to the note issue *per se* in the monetary system; but they also envisaged no unique role for the Banking Department of the Bank of England in the financial system. The separation of the Issue Department from the Banking Department of the Bank, brought about by the 1844 Act, was intended to confer upon the latter the status of just another, albeit large, deposit bank with no special responsibilities beyond those to its shareholders. The 100 per cent marginal specie reserve requirement against notes, on the other hand, left no room to the Issue Department for discretionary activity at all and removing as it did any real possibility that a financial crisis would make notes inconvertible, was intended to render it unnecessary that the Bank play a 'lender of last resort' role in the monetary system.

The Banking School had accepted none of this. They had insisted that the dichotomy between bank notes and deposits upon which the Act rested was a false one, and had argued that the need to maintain the convertibility of bank liabilities in general, and not just of the note issue, imposed what amounted to 'lender of last resort' obligations upon the Bank of England. They had lost the debate in 1844, and the Bank of England had eagerly embraced its new status. As one of its directors, Mr T. Hankey (quoted with disapproval by Bagehot, 1873, page 84), put it:

> The more the conduct of the affairs of the Bank is made to assimilate to the conduct of every other well-managed Bank in the United Kingdom, the better for the Bank, and the better for the community at large.

However, the 1850s and 1860s saw the slow but sure re-establishment of the predominance of the Banking School view that the Bank of England had a special position in the monetary system; and the publication of Bagehot's *Lombard Street* in 1873 completed the edifice of classical monetary economics with a theory of central banking. This theory had roots which can be traced to the work of Thornton (1802), but it had largely been re-created in the wake of the temporary victory of Currency School doctrines in 1844 by adherents of the Banking School, notably James Wilson, Bagehot's father-in-law and predecessor as editor of *The Economist*.[25]

The key empirical insight of this theory of central banking was that the specie stock of the Bank of England, or to be more precise, that proportion of it held against the notes in the possession of the Banking Department, was in fact the ultimate reserve of the entire British financial system. Country (i.e. outside of London) banks held reserves against their deposits mainly in the form of the highly liquid deposit liabilities not only of London banks but also of bill brokers located in London. London banks held reserves of their own on deposit with the Banking Department of the Bank of England and also with the bill brokers who in their turn held, albeit very slender, reserves of Bank of England liabilities. The Banking Department of the bank, in its turn, held Bank of England notes as its reserve. Though gold coin was of course held as till cash at all layers of the system, only relatively small reserves of specie, the only *internationally* acceptable money, were held anywhere outside of the Issue Department of the bank. Furthermore, during crises, commercial bankers were inclined to defend or even increase any stocks of specie which they had on hand. Those stocks were not readily available to support the viability of the financial system as a whole at such times.

Bagehot did not regard this system as 'natural', in the sense that it was the inevitable outcome of free market forces. No more than any other classical monetary economist did he understand that there existed economies of scale in the holding of a centralised reserve. As we shall see in Chapter 6, recognition of this all-important point was to come with Edgeworth's 'Mathematical theory of banking' (1888), though certain passages of Jevons (1875), notably on pages 297–305, suggest that he had some insight into the issues involved. In Bagehot's view market forces alone would have produced a competitive free banking system, with each institution holding its own specie reserves. He attributed the crucial role of the Bank of England to historical circumstances and traditional practices which had their origins in monopoly privileges granted to that institution in earlier times, and not to any tendencies inherent in the very nature of banking. Nevertheless, the author of the *English Constitution* was a great respecter of tradition, and had no wish whatsoever to change the status of the Bank: 'I do not suggest that we should return to a natural or many-reserve system of banking. I should only incur useless ridicule if I did suggest it' (1873 page 34). On the contrary, Bagehot wanted the Bank to recognise its special position at the base of the economy's credit pyramid and to accept the obligations imposed upon it by this position. In particular he urged its directors to conduct their business with the aim of preserving the safety and viability of the financial system as a whole. As he put it, accurately if dramatically,

> all our credit system depends on the Bank of England for its security. On the wisdom of the directors of that one Joint Stock Company, it depends whether *England shall be solvent or insolvent* (1873) (page 17; Bagehot's italics).

To maintain the nation's solvency, the Banking Department was advised to hold an adequate reserve against its liabilities, the presumption here being that such a reserve would be larger than that dictated by simple commercial considerations. The quantification of this recommendation was not attempted, however.[26] Rather Bagehot's view was that:

> At every moment there is a certain minimum which I will call the 'apprehension minimum' below which the reserve cannot fall without great risk of diffused fear; and by this I do not mean absolute panic, but only a vague fright and timorousness which spreads itself instantly, and as if by magic, over the public mind. . . . There is no 'royal road' to the amount of the 'apprehension minimum': no abstract argument, and no mathematical computation will teach it to us. . . . Credit is an opinion generated by circumstances and varying with those circumstances (1873 pages 156–7).

Moreover, though a self-interested bank would normally reduce its loans at times when creditors were converting their deposits into notes and specie, the Bank of England was advised to lend freely at such times to all solvent borrowers.

> A panic, in a word, is a species of neuralgia, and according to the rules of science you must not starve it. The holders of the cash reserve must be ready not only to keep it for their own liabilities, but to advance it most freely for the liabilities of others (Bagehot, 1873 page 25).

Because an internal drain of specie was liable to coincide with an external drain, the need 'to treat two opposite maladies at once' dictated that a 'rapid rise in the rate of interest' by which he meant the Bank of England's discount rate, should accompany the 'large and ready loans' (page 27) needed to cope with the former. This rise in the Bank Rate would generate short-term capital inflows and ensure that the external drain associated with an adverse trade balance would be offset, hence preserving the specie reserves necessary to prevent the internal drain degenerating into a panic.

According to Bagehot, it was the Bank's duty to manage its affairs so as to mitigate, to the best of its ability, the credit cycle, and in particular to prevent its upper turning point being marked by financial panic. It was to be persuaded to act appropriately, however, not legislated into doing so. The classical economists were clear that the regulation of the *currency* was the responsibility of government, and provided an important exception to *laissez-faire* principles. Jevons spoke for all of them when he asserted that 'there is nothing less fit to be left to the action of competition than money' (1875, page 65). However, they did not extend this exception to deposit banking or to credit markets. David Glasner (1985; 1989 Chapter 9) has argued that they viewed the financial system much as they viewed any competitive industry, and that regulation of the activities of individual banks was not for them an appropriate activity for government. If we except the note issue from this claim, and the context of the above quotation from Jevons suggests that the word 'money' should be read in the sense of 'currency' in this case, Glasner is surely correct. If individual banks made bad loans, or otherwise over-extended themselves, competitive forces would cause them to fail, and it was no business of government to prevent that. However, panics could lead to the failure of solvent firms, and the fragility of the financial system was a matter of general concern. The Banking Department of the Bank of England, being a privately owned firm, was not to be regulated, but its directors were expected to recognise their public responsibilities and act accordingly. As Jevons (1875), in a passage another part of which explicitly refers to Bagehot, put it,

> The present state of things in England is not to be cured by any legislation. The only measure which can restore stability to the London market, or prevent it from becoming more and more sensitive, is to secure by some means the existence of more satisfactory cash reserves, either in actual coin, or in the Bank of England notes, representing deposits of coin in the Bank vaults (page 322).

The English classical theory of central banking was not, then, a theory of discretionary counter-cyclical policy. To the extent that the cycle was a product of competition in credit markets, it was not to be interfered with. Discretionary intervention in markets by the central bank was only required in order to prevent the upper turning point of the cycle leading to a dislocation of the monetary system, and because the central bank was a privately owned profit-making institution, such limited intervention had to be strictly voluntary. Such a limited view of monetary policy will hardly appear convincing to an economist of the 1990s and indeed, neoclassical views on what monetary policy could accomplish, which we shall discuss in Chapter 6, were often much more ambitious. But in the 1870s the system had begun at last to function better than it had in the past. That, for Bagehot, as for most of his contemporaries, was more than sufficient reason for not tampering with it.

Concluding comments

It was asserted at the outset of this chapter that classical monetary economics of the 1870s was a coherent body of theoretical and policy-related analysis. More than enough has surely now been said to justify this claim. It is useful at this point to draw attention to the factors, not present or not fully developed in classical monetary economics, which were later to become of central importance to the sub-discipline, particularly those that played a role in its development during the next forty years.

From the point of view of pure economic analysis, one striking absentee from the classical economics of the 1870s is the notion that monetary theory requires that attention be paid to individual choice in establishing its results. Marshall's (1871) manuscript shows that he had completely adopted this position even at this early date, but that manuscript was never part of the published record, and the ideas it contained did not begin to enter the public arena until the 1880s by which time the ideas of the so-called Marginal Revolution were becoming central to economics in general. Before the 1880s, the analysis of individual choice and its social consequences was by no means absent from economic theory, and indeed as Hollander has argued with great persuasiveness and persistence, a concern with allocative questions was a good deal more pervasive in classical economics than much of the standard secondary literature would lead one to believe. Even so, the analysis of individual choice *per se* did not lie at the heart of the discipline.[27]

However, the absence of a well worked-out choice theoretic basis for economics in general is only part of the explanation for its absence from monetary theory in the 1870s. For classical economists, and in this context the term even includes that pioneer of marginal analysis Jevons, money was primarily a social phenomenon which existed to facilitate the workings of market mechanisms. It was only in the 1880s that marginalists such as Walras (e.g. 1886) and Marshall (e.g. 1887) tried in published work to apply a general choice theoretic approach to the special case of money and began to bridge the gap between the analysis of money as a social institution on the one hand and an object of individual choice on the other.[28] Furthermore, it was only when this analysis had been worked out that the uneasy tension existing in classical monetary theory between cost of production and quantity theory explanations of the price level was resolved.

Classical monetary economics' treatment of the cycle too was incomplete by later standards. Nowadays the cycle is the 'business cycle'; its salient characteristics are persistent fluctuations in real variables such as output, investment, employment, and so on. For the Classics it was the 'credit cycle' and principally involved fluctuations in the volume of bank lending, the money supply, interest rates and prices in commodity markets. As much as anything, perhaps, this emphasis in classical economics reflected the fact that fluctuations in well-organised financial markets were readily observable and hence attracted attention, whereas the more pervasive economy-wide fluctuations which we nowadays stress were less easily discerned by observers in the 1870s. However, this gap also reflects slowness on the part of economists to put two and two together.

Jevons and his Manchester Statistical Society associates *did* know that the cycle had an important real dimension; transitional effects of monetary changes on real variables through forced savings mechanisms *were* understood by Cairnes and Mill. Every classical economist who had read Hume knew that the rising prices which accompanied the upswing of the cycle might involve a temporary increase in output; Mill certainly did, and he *also* knew that, at the downturn of the cycle, a general excess demand for cash would involve a general glut of commodities. Most key components of a monetary theory of real economic fluctuations *were* available by the 1870s, but their interconnectedness was not appreciated. Jevons associated the cycle with fluctuations in agricultural output induced by sunspot activity; neither Mill nor anyone else investigated the possibility that a glut of currently existing commodities might have implications for the production of new goods; and Mill and Cairnes treated forced saving as a phenomenon of the transition between different equilibrium values of the price level, and divorced its analysis from that of the cycle. All of these interconnections, and more, would in due course be recognised and developed, but they had not been in the 1870s.

On the policy front too, classical analysis was very different from that which would eventually follow. In the 1870s, specie convertibility, and in Britain in particular gold convertibility, was regarded as a *sine qua non* of sound monetary management. By 1923 Keynes, whose authority on such matters later approached that of Mill in an earlier time, was arguing that the Gold Standard was outmoded, and eventually (for good or ill is not the issue here) helped to persuade the majority of his professional colleagues and successors of the justice of this position. As to short-run policy directed at the cycle, its proper design came to look very different from that advocated by Bagehot, as economists' perceptions of the nature of the cycle, and the desirability of stabilising it, evolved over time. Moreover, though the classical theory of central bank policy behaviour was fully articulated by Bagehot, neither he nor anyone else provided a theoretical basis for the existence of a central bank other than the accident of history. For him the 'natural system – that which would have sprung up if Government had let Banking alone – [was] that of many banks of equal, or not altogether unequal, size' (1873 page 32), as exemplified by 'the American banking system . . . of many reserves . . .' (1873, page 161). The underlying economies of scale in reserve holding which were leading the American system to concentrate its reserves in New York, and which were therefore one of the factors that would lead to the creation of the Federal Reserve System, and which, in the international sphere would lead to the evolution of the Gold Exchange Standard, were not recognised.

In short, though coherent and well established as an orthodoxy by the 1870s, English classical monetary economics was a very different body of doctrine from any that is nowadays popular, superficial and often semantic resemblances notwithstanding. Subsequent chapters of this study will show how, even before World War I, the foundations of modern analysis were laid by those whom it is convenient to label 'Neoclassicals', notably, but by no means solely, Irving Fisher, Alfred Marshall, Arthur C. Pigou and Knut Wicksell.

Notes

1. The exception referred to in the text is Mill's analysis of the possibility of a 'general glut of commodities' discussed on page 25.
2. Jevons begins *Money and the Mechanism of Exchange* (1875) with a vivid account of the difficulties attendant on the absence of money, in describing the case of the unfortunate Mademoiselle Zélie, a singer, who, having given a concert in the Society Islands received

   > In exchange for an air from Norma and a few other songs . . . 3 pigs, 23 turkeys, 44 chickens, 5000 coconuts, besides considerable quantities of bananas, lemons, and oranges, this being her agreed fee of a third part of the receipts (page 1).

   The notion that the inconveniences of barter were so great that the economy could not function in the absence of a monetary system had been a central feature of classical economics from the beginning.
3. He cites the example of the Confederate States of America. See Jevons (1875, pages 232–7).
4. For an account of Cairnes' work on tracing through the sequence of events whereby Australian gold discoveries raised prices throughout the world, see Michael Bordo (1975). Cairnes' own account is to be found in 'Essays towards a solution of the gold question' (1860, reprinted 1873).
5. If it is borne in mind that to Mill, the 'supply of money' referred to a rate of flow of money expenditures, the essentially semantic nature of the inconsistency evident in the passages quoted in the text is more easily appreciated. On this, see pages 16–17.
6. Thus, among the factors affecting the 'rapidity of circulation', Jevons listed 'Railways and rapid steamboats . . . telegraphs . . . and the acceleration of the mails', (1875, page 337). Jevons did note in the same passage that the propensity of people to hoard coin would also affect velocity, but linked variations here to the type of banking institutions in place, and to the 'thrifty' or 'improvident' nature of the population. Hence there is no trace of an embryo theory of the speculative demand for money in his work. Mill dealt with the problems raised by hoarding for the quantity theory by excluding the quantity of hoarded coin and notes from the money supply: 'The supply of money, in short, is all the money in *circulation* at the time' (Mill, 1871, page 509; Mill's italics).
7. I have already commented above on the lack of clarity in classical

economics about the stock-flow distinction. In putting Mill's supply-and-demand for money notions into more up-to-date terminology, I have taken the liberty of introducing anachronistic clarity about this point. The passages from pages 513–14 of Mill (1871), quoted on pages 14–15 suggest that, in doing so, I am not doing any great violence to Mill's views, for he does there explicitly introduce the idea of velocity into his discussion of the mechanism linking money, transactions and prices. However, Hugo Hegeland (1951, pages 68–9) does, quite correctly, draw attention to Mill's uncertain grasp of the fact that the notion of velocity has a time dimension to it.

8. Hollander (1986, pages 540–1) discusses the influence of Cairnes on Mill on this issue, and also the extent to which Mill arrived at the relevant results on his own account. Meir Kohn (1985) has recently revived the questions dealt with by Mill.

9. Such effects as these would not, according to classical economics, accompany just any type of money creation. On the contrary, issues of inconvertible government paper money were, for them, associated with the deficit finance of government consumption, and Mill, for one, argued quite explicitly that, in this case, the economy's interest rate would be raised by the government bidding away for its own use resources that would otherwise have been saved and therefore invested by the private sector. On this, see Mill (1871, page 656) and Hollander (1986).

10. This is not the only place that Mill refers to what was later to become known as the 'Fisher effect'. Note that Thornton had drawn attention to the effects of anticipated inflation on the nominal interest rate in a parliamentary speech of 1811. However his *Paper Credit* (1802) referred to no such matter nor does the *Bullion Report of 1810* (Edwin Cannan, 1919) of which he was a part author. The above-mentioned speech was delivered in defence of that report, however. It is reprinted in the edition of *Paper Credit* edited by von Hayek in 1939.

11. And in the case of the Austrians, it was Wicksell's (1898) elaboration, of the factors driving the market interest rate away from its natural rate during the celebrated cumulative process, which formed the link between Mill's work and theirs. Wicksell's analysis of these matters, like that of his classical predecessors, was in the context of secular price level changes and not the cycle, see Chapter 5, page 143ff.

12. See Chapter 4, page 104ff. See also Patrick Deutscher (1990).

13. On the matter of the cycle, of course, Jevons was by no means an orthodox classical economist. Not only does his 1863 work on the 'Value of gold' contain a striking discussion of the role of fixed investment fluctuations in the cycle, which he did not follow up in his later work, but he was also later to be the great populariser, though not originator, of the 'sunspot theory'. This was by no means as ridiculous an idea as it is sometimes made out to be, though Jevons' enthusiasm for it was, perhaps, excessive. (On all this see David Laidler (1982, pages 340–5) and Sandra Peart (1990).) Though Jevons did on various occasions pay attention to real variables in the cycle, among them fixed

investment, agricultural output and the volume of textile exports, prices and financial variables nevertheless loomed very large in his analysis. In this his work contrasts sharply with that of Karl Marx (1867) for whom fluctuations in output and employment were of the very essence of the cycle. Marx barely discussed price fluctuations and financial factors.

14. The preceding few pages draw heavily, and obviously, on the work of Jacob Viner (1937) and Fetter (1965). For a modern account of the controversy, which shows considerable sympathy with the Banking School, see Arie Arnon's forthcoming study of Thomas Tooke. For accounts of the Bullionist controversy and the Currency School–Banking School debate by this writer, see Laidler (1987a) and (1973) respectively.

15. Malthus' denial of Say's Law is to be understood as applying to the stability of the economy's long-run growth path, and not to any short-run processes. Thus, John Maynard Keynes' (1936) claim to the contrary, notwithstanding his analysis of this issue, did not foreshadow *The General Theory*. It is in the context of Malthus' views, and others like him, that Mill's defence of Say's Law in the classical system must be read. On this, see Bernard Corry (1962).

16. See Marshall (1887; reprinted 1925, pages 184–92). Many standard interpretations of Mill's views on Say's Law do not acknowledge the presence even of this limited analysis of a 'general glut' in his *Principles*, presumably because it occurs in his discussion of monetary issues, and is not referred to in that section of the book dealing with capital accumulation where the celebrated assertion that 'demand for commodities is not demand for labour' occurs. For a discussion of this issue, see Hollander (1986).

17. In Smith's analysis, which confined itself to considering the replacement of metallic money with bank notes, specie would flow abroad in exchange for wage goods. These could be added to the stock of circulating capital, and so generate an increase in the domestic labour force and output level. Smith's analysis is the starting point of Ricardo's (1816) *Proposal for an Economical and Secure Currency* which was to consist of paper convertible on demand into gold ingots held by the Bank of England. In discussing this matter, Mill (1871, page 642) cited Smith's comparison of 'the substitution of paper in the room of the precious metals, to the construction of a highway through the air' with approval, and a little inaccuracy, since Smith referred to a wagonway, a primitive form of railroad, not a highway.

18. On this matter, see Laidler (1981). The reader's attention is drawn to the fact that I refer to the real balance effects in classical economics as 'not very well articulated'. To analyse them properly a clear notion of a demand for money is needed, and, classical economics, with the exception of the analysis of 'gluts' referred to above, (page 25ff.) did not use such a device. Becker and Baumol (1952) provide an excellent guide to the role of the real balance effect in classical theory. Before the 1880s, they find few satisfactory accounts of it, Mill's above-

mentioned analysis being the principal exception. On the transfer mechanism, see Mill (1871, pages 637–8). For a comprehensive account of the evolution of the classical analysis of the transfer problem, see Fetter (1968).

19. Thus, the Bullionist Controversy saw much debate about the state of the British exchange rate on Amsterdam and Hamburg, where a silver standard was in place. It should also be noted that the 1844 Bank Charter Act permitted the Bank of England to hold up to one quarter of its specie reserves in silver, a measure intended to facilitate transactions with silver standard countries, notably India.

20. Fisher (1911) unfairly attributed to Jevons a belief in the necessarily stabilising effects of bimetallism on the price level (see Laidler, 1982, page 346). In a recent paper, Arthur Rolnick and Warren Weber (1986) have suggested that Gresham's Law is invalid. The empirical evidence with which they support this extraordinary suggestion is drawn from times at which the mint prices of the two metals were not fixed, as they themselves admit (page 192). However, they then go on to argue (page 193) that no mint with finite resources could effectively hold its price for two metals away from the market price indefinitely, failing to note that precisely this prediction of Gresham's Law played a major role in nineteenth-century and early twentieth-century discussions of bimetallism. Since they fail to cite Mill, Jevons or even Fisher on these issues, it is perhaps not surprising that they seem unaware of this fact.

21. Only in his commitment to gold monometallism was Jevons orthodox. His support of an international decimal money based on the French 25 franc gold piece, like his promotion of indexation, lay well beyond the bounds of contemporary conventional wisdom.

22. Much of the difficulty here stems from the fact, already noted, that although Cairnes and Jevons were able to document systematic commodity price increases in the wake of the gold discoveries, productivity changes apparently did much to prevent these increases coming through in what we would nowadays call a 'consumer price index'. Cairnes and Jevons, true to their classical heritage, seemed to regard the purchasing power of gold over primary commodities as the correct measure of its 'value', presumably because the labour input needed to produce them had not changed significantly during the period they studied. Even Jevons did not entertain the idea that the purchasing power of money over utility might be a relevant measure of its value. On this issue, see Laidler (1982).

23. On this issue, see Jevons (1868, reprinted 1884). This study mainly dealt with the feasibility of replacing the sovereign with the slightly ligher 25 franc piece. The scheme in question attracted some attention, but very little political support in Britain. The sections of *Money and the Mechanism of Exchange* dealing with 'International money' contain Jevons' retrospective account of it. The scheme, not to mention the Paris Conference where it was first developed, are also discussed by Horton (1887) and Walker (1897).

24. Though the suppression of a competitive note issue, along with the

maintenance of competition in deposit banking made sense in terms of Currency School doctrine, which attached undue significance to notes *per se*, it is hard to defend those writers such as Jevons who supported the Bank of England's note issue monopoly while simultaneously recognising the importance of competitively provided deposits in the circulating medium. As Lawrence White (1984) has argued, the example of Scottish banking, of which Jevons was, of course well aware, shows that competition among note-issuing banks could be an effective means of ensuring their soundness just as it was among deposit banks.

25. The story summarised here is, of course, told in considerable detail in Fetter (1965). Laidler (1973) deals with Banking School views on the importance of maintaining the convertibility of banking system liabilities in general, as opposed to bank notes in particular, and also with their views on the Bank of England's lender of last resort role. See also Arnon forthcoming.

26. In this Bagehot differed from earlier Banking School writers. Thus, Tooke (1844) proposed that the Bank of England should usually hold a reserve of 10 million pounds and never let it fall below 5 million pounds (see Laidler, 1973 and Arnon, forthcoming).

27. There is no better evidence in favour of this, surely, than that the theory of value in general, and the concept of utility in particular, do not appear in John Stuart Mill's *Principles* until Book 3. The standard text of a discipline which put individual choice at the centre of things could hardly have delayed introducing the concepts fundamental to such an approach until nearly half of the way through its length, nor would it have found it possible to discuss production and distribution, before it got around to discussing utility and value. This is not to say that value, considered as a market, as opposed to individual phenomenon, does not play a role in the classical theory of distribution. It obviously does.

28. By this I mean that they developed the idea of a demand for money relationship based on the idea of individual choice. Don Patinkin (1965, Notes D and E) discusses this aspect of the early development of the marginal utility approach to monetary theory. Carl Menger's (1893) analysis of money as a social institution was, like everything else in his work, based on an individualist methodology, and in this sense did have a choice theoretic foundation.

3 • The neoclassical theory of the price level: the Cambridge School and Fisher

Introduction

We have seen that in the early 1870s, there existed in Britain, a theory of monetary policy which complemented orthodox classical monetary theory. This theory of policy had two components. First it taught that the Gold Standard was the best foundation for the monetary system. Second, it suggested that apart from maintaining that standard, the appropriate authorities, the Bank of England as far as Britain was concerned, should limit their interventions in the system to those calculated to preserve its viability at times of financial crisis. Such interventions would normally involve the Bank lending freely at a penalty rate of interest at times when the banking system was both simultaneously confronted with an internal (domestic) and external (foreign) drain of reserves, and would serve both to restore the confidence needed to correct the former, and generate the short-term international capital flow required to reverse the latter.

This theory of monetary policy came to dominate British practice before World War I, and it also had considerable international influence during this period. In particular, monometallic gold convertibility, which in 1870 had been an almost uniquely British institution, became the basis of the international monetary system by the turn of the century. Thus the United States, nominally bimetallic, but *de facto* on a Gold Standard before the Civil War, restored convertibility of the dollar into gold alone in its wake; Germany replaced silver with gold after the Franco–Prussian War, France and the rest of the Latin Union closed their mints to silver in the early 1870s thereby adopting monometallic gold currencies; the Scandinavian Monetary Union moved to a Gold Standard in the

1870s; Russia adopted gold in the 1890s; India shifted from silver to a Gold Exchange Standard between 1893 and 1914; many colonial economies in Asia and Latin America, and some other economies in Europe, also adopted this framework; and so on. As to the principles of central banking as set out by Bagehot, these too had an international influence, not least in the United States where the foundation of the Federal Reserve System in 1913 was intended to provide sufficient elasticity in the supply of currency to enable financial crises to be averted. The system was also initially expected to cater to the perceived regional diversity of that economy, by providing geographically dispersed lenders of last resort for its monetary system.[1]

As the above-mentioned developments took place, classical monetary theory was also evolving. In particular the quantity theory of money was brought to a high degree of refinement, and the monetary analysis of cycles also made great progress. It is easy to jump to the conclusion that these theoretical developments went hand in hand with those on the policy front, and provided the theoretical underpinnings for the smooth spread of the international gold standard. As I noted in Chapter 1, and shall now begin to show in more detail, however, such a conclusion would be extremely wide of the mark. To begin with, the spread of the Gold Standard was by no means uncontroversial. It is well known that the 1873–96 period was one of falling prices in terms of gold, and saw a continuous and vigorous political debate in the United States about the virtues of gold monometallism relative to those of bimetallism; but there was a parallel debate in Europe too, not least in Britain whose commercial relations with India made the fall of the (silver) rupee in the mid-1870s and 1880s, if not quite as sensational as Oscar Wilde suggested, then at least a matter of considerable contention.[2]

The quantity theory and the bimetallic controversy

In the above-mentioned debates, far from being associated with policy orthodoxy, what we now think of as mainstream neoclassical monetary economics, and particularly the quantity theory, was usually associated with the case for bimetallism and was treated with much hostility by the advocates of 'sound money'. We shall discuss the debate about bimetallism in more detail in Chapter 6. In this and the next two chapters we shall concentrate upon theoretical developments, because these must be described before the tensions between neoclassical monetary theory and classical policy orthodoxy can be fully understood. We begin, in this chapter, with an account of the development of the quantity theory, at the hands of the Cambridge School and Irving Fisher. Two interlinked elements gave impetus to this work. The first stemmed from tensions implicit in the logical structure of classical monetary theory, and the second from the above-mentioned debates about bimetallism.

We have seen that the classical theory of the price level consisted of a sometimes uneasy blend of the cost of production theory of value and the quantity theory of money. The first of these had it that, with a commodity-based system, the purchasing power of money was set by the marginal cost of producing the money commodity; and the second had it determined by the interaction of the 'supply of money', conceived of as a flow of money expenditures, (MV in later terminology) with the 'demand for money', conceived of as the flow of goods and services offered for sale (T in that same later terminology). In Mill's work, as in Senior's (1840), the cost of production theory provided an explanation of money's long-run equilibrium, or 'natural', value, leaving the quantity theory as the preferred but essentially complementary explanation of short-run behaviour. In the debates of the 1830s and 1840s, however, the two theories had sometimes been treated as alternatives, rather than complements, and as we shall see in Chapter 6, so it was again in the controversy over bimetallism, and that controversy focused economists' attention on the unsatisfactory nature of the classical theory of the price level.

Marshall had in fact worked out the basic analysis of what was to be called the 'Cambridge cash balance approach' as early as 1871 (and therefore before the bimetallic controversy began) in an unpublished and purely academic exercise, but he first publicly deployed his analysis in an 1887 *Contemporary Review* article entitled 'Remedies for fluctuations in general prices' which dealt explicitly with bimetallism.[3] He later submitted this piece as evidence to the 1888–9 Gold and Silver Commission, a committee set up by the British government to deal with, and make recommendations about, bimetallic proposals; while his oral evidence to this commission (reprinted in *Official Papers of Alfred Marshall*, Marshall, 1926) was for years a standard reference on his monetary thought. Marshall's paper appeared one year after Walras (1886) had published the first algebraic formulation of the quantity theory as a cash balance equation, and Walras' exposition was also in the context of a discussion of issues raised by the bimetallic controversy. As to Fisher, his first journal article on monetary matters dealt with the 'Mechanics of bimetallism' (*Economic Journal* 1894) and his famous monograph, 'Appreciation and interest' (1896), also dealt with issues raised by this debate. Moreover, the primary purpose of Fisher's comprehensive treatise *The Purchasing Power of Money* (1911) was to reinstate the quantity theory as a scientifically respectable doctrine in the wake of the American bimetallist controversy. As Fisher noted in his preface:

> since the 'quantity theory' has become the subject of political dispute it has lost prestige and has even come to be regarded by many as an exploded fallacy. The attempts by promoters of unsound money to make an improper use of the quantity theory – as in the first [1896] Bryan campaign – led many sound money men to the utter repudiation of the quantity theory. The consequence has been that, especially in America, the quantity theory needs to be reintroduced into general knowledge. (page viii)

Though the bimetallic controversy provided part of the background to the evolution of the quantity theory, however, that evolution mainly involved the resolution of *theoretical* tensions in the classical version of that doctrine. It can therefore be analysed and understood independently of contemporary policy debates.

In this chapter, I shall show that the Cambridge School and Fisher alike, though the details of their analysis differed, both developed the quantity theory which they inherited from their classical predecessors into a general theory of the price level; that they were in substantial agreement in downgrading the role of the cost of production of the precious metals to that of one, rather remote and indirect, influence on the quantity of money, where in classical economics it had usually been treated as the main determinant of money's purchasing power in the long run; and that both paid attention to institutional factors, notably bank behaviour, as well as the role of individual choice in determining money's value. Moreover, a constant theme of my exposition will be that, the influence of contemporary debates about bimetallism on them notwithstanding, the work of the Cambridge School and Fisher alike should be seen as strongly motivated by a desire to develop monetary theory *per se*, rather than merely by a wish to contribute to those debates. I shall begin with an account of the work of the Cambridge School, and then turn to Fisher.

The fundamentals of the Cambridge approach: Marshall's 1871 note on 'Money'

Keynes reviewed Fisher's *Purchasing Power of Money* in the 1911 *Economic Journal*. The basic message of his review was that much of what Fisher had to say had been anticipated, indeed superseded, by developments in monetary theory which had already taken place in England (by which Keynes meant at Cambridge). The tradition to which Keynes referred was, he agreed, largely an oral one, because in 1911 the only published accounts of what we would now call the Cambridge version of the quantity theory of money existed in transcripts of Marshall's evidence to the Gold and Silver Commission of 1888-9 and to the Indian Currency Committee of 1899.[4] These publications were not entirely unknown, and indeed Wicksell (1898) referred quite extensively to the first of them. However, the extent of the theoretical innovation underlying them must have been hard indeed to discern for anyone otherwise unaware of it. Marshall was, at the best of times, prone to hide his theoretical apparatus when addressing the general public, and the main purpose of his two bodies of evidence was not to expound fundamental ideas about monetary theory to his colleagues, but to apply them, for a general audience, to policy questions concerning, respectively, the roles of gold and silver in the British monetary system and the reform of Indian monetary arrangements.

Marshall's own attempt at a systematic exposition of monetary economics in *Money, Credit and Commerce* did not appear until 1923. This was very much an old man's book and large parts of its text are drawn directly from the above-mentioned evidence. Indeed the book as a whole does little more than arrange in a more orderly way the ideas set out in that evidence. Anyone seeking a comprehensive account of Cambridge monetary theory in a single source would do better to turn to Pigou (1912), or better still to the same author's (1917) *Quarterly Journal of Economics* essay on 'The value of money', than to Marshall's book; but in either case it is important to bear in mind that the analysis expounded is of much earlier origin. The unpublished manuscript on 'Money' to which reference has been made earlier, and to which Keynes referred extensively in his obituary of Marshall (Keynes, 1925) probably dates from 1871, and along with some accompanying, albeit fragmentary, mathematical notes, contains all the essential theoretical ideas to be found in later Cambridge writings.

Thus Keynes' (1911) claim that important theoretical advances had been made at Cambridge was undoubtedly true. Moreover, those advances were made *before* the policy issues to which Marshall first applied them arose. They clearly represented not a response to the bimetallic controversy but to problems inherent in the classical monetary theory which Marshall had inherited from Mill. We have seen that, in Mill's view, the quantity and cost of production theories of the value of money were complementary to one another, but we have also seen that his attribution of rising marginal production costs to mining, along with his lack of clarity about the stock-flow distinction, left the details of that complementarity unclear. Marshall's original work of 1871 on money both clarified and completed Mill's analysis, and in particular put cost of production considerations in their proper place (cf. Marshall (1871), volume 2, pages 277–8).[5]

Marshall's (1871) analysis is cast in terms of an abstract model of a simple corn-producing economy which used as its currency, the 'shells of a certain extinct fish'. He began by assuming the quantity of shells constant, and argued that 'If . . . there be a million such shells, and the income of the country be sixty million bushels of corn' then, if the average individual wishes to hold purchasing power equal to one tenth of income in the form of money, 'a shell will be worth . . . six bushels'. Postulating a 'change in habits' leading to desired money holdings falling to a twentieth of income, he went on to show that 'the value of each shell will diminish . . . until each shell is worth only three bushels' (Marshall, 1871, Volume 1, page 168). Hence, Marshall developed the stock demand for nominal money function as a rectangular hyperbola, a form which he explicitly gave it in a diagram in his mathematical notes.

Marshall successively generalised this exogenous money stock special case, first to a situation in which the stock of shells may be increased by dredging, second to one in which they have alternative uses 'for ornament and for other purposes' (Marshall, 1871,

Volume 1, page 172) and finally to the case in which 'other things beside shells are used as money, paper or whatnot' (Marshall, 1871, Volume 1, page 173), in the process bringing his model successively closer to the complex commodity-based monetary system of the nineteenth-century world. In the first case Marshall noted that a downward shift in the economy's demand for money might leave the value of shells 'permanently below their cost of production' but that an upward shift would make it 'profitable to dredge in deeper and deeper water' (Marshall, 1871, Volume 1, page 172); in the second he remarked that the influence of the demand for shells as a commodity would break (except in a very special case) the proportionality relationship between the quantity of shells and their value; and in the third he pointed out that:

> The effect of these contrivances [paper money and whatnot] is to cause other modes of exchange to be substituted for those into which money enters. . . . They cause the amount of commodities over which persons choose to keep a command in the form of money to diminish: they thus diminish the value of shells or (as we may now say) of gold and silver: thereby setting free more of them to be used as commodities and at the same time diminishing the labour spent in working the mines to obtain the means of doing what can in many cases be better done by the avoidance of than by the use of gold and silver (Marshall, 1871, Volume 1, page 173)

It will be noted that, throughout this exposition, the emphasis is on factors affecting the demand for commodity money, rather than its supply, and that to the extent that variations in the supply of money are discussed, alternative uses for the commodity receive as much attention as new production. Cost of production is thus treated as one rather unimportant factor among many affecting the value of money, operating through its influence on changes in the quantity of money. Only in the special case of a stationary economy in which the purchasing power of money is just equal to the cost ruling on the margin of production in the most fruitful mine, and hence when output is zero, does Marshall's analysis permit the price level to be thought of as determined by the marginal cost of production of the money commodity, a result which Marshall explicitly derived in his mathematical notes with the aid of both a differential equation and a discrete time diagrammatic approximation to the model yielding that equation.

Institutional influences on the price level

Marshall's 1871 note was not to be published until 1975, but the analysis it contains was nevertheless influential. He lectured regularly on monetary economics at Cambridge from the 1870s onwards, and according to Keynes (1925), the 1871 analysis still formed the basis of his lectures as late as 1906. Its influence on Pigou's (1912, 1917) expositions of Cambridge monetary theory is unmistakable, and it clearly underlies Marshall's own (1887) 'Remedies for fluctuations in general prices', not to mention his oral evidence to the 1888-9 Gold and Silver Commission and to the 1899 Indian Currency Committee. Indeed, the 1887 paper contains perhaps the clearest of all of Marshall's statements of the implications of his theory for the status of the cost of production theory of money's value:

> as things are, gold and silver have no natural value. They are so durable that the year's supply is never more than a small part of the total stock, and therefore their values do not conform closely to their costs of production. And, insofar as their values are regulated by the relations between the demands for them and the existing stocks of them, their value is artificial, because the demand for them as currency is itself artificial. (*Memorials of Alfred Marshall*, page 200)

In this quotation, as elsewhere in Marshall's writings, the emphasis is on the influence of demand on the value of currency, that is coin and notes backed by specie, rather than on any broader idea of a 'circulating medium' which might include bank deposits.[6] As we shall see, Marshall and the Cambridge School suffered from none of the confusion that had marked Mill's work about the role of bank liabilities in the monetary system, but they nevertheless usually put the supply and demand for currency, rather than some broader monetary aggregate, at the centre of their analysis. The institutional framework taken for granted in most of their writings, furthermore, was that of pre-World War I Britain, where there had taken place (and indeed continued to take place) a rapid growth of deposit banking. These two factors combined to ensure that the Cambridge economists paid more attention to variations in the demand for currency than its supply when they analysed the determinants of the price level, and also that they placed considerable emphasis on institutional factors in this context.

Marshall's view of the relative importance of variations in the demand and supply of currency for the determination of prices, and hence of the *empirical* validity of the quantity theory proposition that the price level moves in proportion to the quantity of money (narrowly defined) was expressed as follows in a written memorandum to the 1888–9 Gold and Silver Commission:

> While accepting the doctrine that, *'other things being equal,* prices rise or fall proportionately to every increase or diminution in the metal or metals which are used as the standard of value,' I consider that the conditioning clause, 'other things being equal,' is of overwhelming importance (Marshall, 1926, page 21; Marshall's italics).

In his oral evidence he reiterated and elaborated his view that 'changes in the other things which are taken as equal are very often, perhaps generally, more important than the changes in the volumes of the precious metals.' (Marshall, 1926, page 34) noting explicitly that 'changes in the volume of business and methods of payment' (Marshall, 1926, page 22) were crucial here. Marshall pointed out that '[t]he relation which the amount of bankers' money bears to the amount of currency has to be discussed as a part of a larger inquiry as to the influence which is exerted on prices by the methods of business' (Marshall, 1926, page 37) and he followed up this remark with an essentially correct verbal sketch of the bank credit multiplier process.

It is true that, in 1912 Pigou did indeed assert that:

> the supply of money in modern civilized states is made up of two parts, money proper in the possession of the public, and bank money, whether in the form of deposits subject to cheque or of banknotes redeemable on demand (page 426).

and treated the ratio of 'bank money' to 'money proper' as a factor affecting (increasing) the elasticity with which the total supply of money (broadly defined) could respond to a shift in the demand for money. By 1917 however, and without changing the substance of his analysis, he had reverted to Marshall's practice of concentrating upon the supply and demand for 'legal tender money' (i.e. 'money proper') as determining the price level, and hence transformed banking institutions from a factor affecting supply into one affecting demand:

First, the proportion of titles to legal tender held in the form of actual legal tender will be smaller the more people have banking accounts, and, therefore, are *able* to keep their titles to legal tender in the rival form of bank balances. . . . Secondly, the proportion of titles kept in actual legal tender will be smaller the more readily cheques are accepted in ordinary transactions. . . . Thirdly, this proportion will be smaller the longer shopkeepers allow their accounts to run before requiring payments. . . . Lastly, the proportions will be smaller, the more convenient and less costly is the machinery by which payments can be made direct from bank balances, without resort to actual legal tender by the paying public (1917, page 170; italics in original).

In short, and not to labour the point further, the most important influences on the price level as far as the Cambridge economists were concerned lay on the demand side of what we might call the market for currency, and an important sub-set of these were institutional in nature, having mainly to do with banking arrangements. Thus when Marshall told the Indian Currency Committee that:

there is something fiduciary in the value of gold and silver; that is, that part of their value depends upon the confidence with which people generally look forward to the maintenance and extension of the monetary demand for them. Of course, their value is, in the long run, controlled by cost of production; but that influence is remote, and new supplies are always small relative to the existing stock. And so fluctuations of their value *are mainly governed at any time by currency legislation*, actual and prospective (Marshall, 1926, page 269; my italics).

he was not making a point specifically about India. Rather he was reaffirming the general importance for price level behaviour of institutional factors relative to those affecting the supply of what Pigou was to call 'money proper', in this specific case the cost of producing the precious metals.

Now though I here attribute considerable importance to institutional factors in the determination of the price level, I am well aware that it is common to argue that the emphasis placed by the Cambridge economists on matters of individual choice, as opposed to institutional factors sets their work apart from other versions of the quantity theory. Certainly Marshall's (1871) critique of the classical quantity theory emphasised individual choice:

> But, when we come to the theory of money we are told that its value depends upon its amount together with the rapidity of circulation, . . . we do not find a clear statement of that balancing of advantages which in the ultimate analysis must be found to determine the magnitude of every quantity which rests upon the will of man (Marshall, 1871, page 166).

Note however, that Marshall here does not complain of an undue emphasis on institutional factors in classical monetary theory. Rather it is the concept of the 'rapidity of circulation' that concerns him. We shall see below that, though Fisher was much closer to classical monetary economics than the Cambridge School in the use he made of the latter concept, he nevertheless paid considerable attention to the influence of individual choice-making behaviour on velocity. The contrast between Cambridge and other neoclassical versions of the quantity theory, does not lie in a difference of emphasis on institutional factors versus individual choice as influences on the price level. Rather it lies in the fact that traditional quantity theorists, including Fisher, put velocity, and transactions velocity at that, at the heart of their analysis, while the Cambridge economists *abandoned this concept*. For Marshall, and even as early as 1871 'the rapidity of circulation is not the most convenient thing to be made the basis of our investigation' (Marshall, 1871, page 166); and, as we have seen, he *substituted* for it the concept of 'the amount of commodities over which people . . . keep command in a ready form' (Marshall, 1871, Volume, 1, page 171) or as we would now say, following the terminology of Keynes (1923), their demand for a stock of real balances.[7] I shall turn to a more detailed discussion of this concept and the way in which the Cambridge School developed it, but it must first be explained why it is their formulation, rather than that of Walras which merits attention.

I have already noted that, in 1886 Walras gave an explicitly algebraic treatment of the cash-balance approach to the quantity theory. His is thus the first *published* account of the approach. However his formulation in which the demand for nominal money is made to depend upon the nominal value of goods traded appears to have had no influence on his contemporaries, and remained unappreciated until Arthur Marget (1931) drew attention to it; this despite the fact that it found its way into the second (1889) and subsequent editions of his *Élements*. As Jaffé notes, in his commentary on the various editions of this work, in both eds. 2 [1889] and 3 [1894] the monetary theory was not integrated with his general equilibrium theory. Walras apparently contented himself . . . with a vague institutional explanation of the *demand for desired cash balances* . . . the problem of incorporating the equations representing the demand for cash balances into his more general system of equations proved, however, to be extremely difficult . . . it was not until 1899 that Walras first published his solution (1954, page 601; Jaffé's italics).

Thus Wicksell's analysis of the motives for holding money and of the real balance effect, which I shall discuss in Chapter 5, antedates Walras' integration of his version of the quantity theory with his analysis of the real economy. Furthermore, between his first exposition of his analysis of the demand for money in 1886 and his incorporation of it into the *Élements* in 1889, Marshall's (1887) 'Remedies for fluctuations in general prices' had appeared, and indeed Walras refers to this article in the second and subsequent editions of the *Élements* (page 339, Footnote 1). Thus Walras' claim to priority involves only the *publication* of an algebraic formulation of a stock demand function for money. Marshall's 1871 version of the same concept was more sophisticated than that of Walras, as was the analysis in which he later deployed it.

The stock demand for money

In his 1871 manuscript Marshall specified the demand for money idea that underlay his analysis as follows:

> If any man keeps accounts accurately by subtracting his payments up to any day from his receipts up to that day we know the cash he has on hand at the beginning of that day. Add up these sums for each day, divide by the number of days, and we have the amount of cash he has on hand each day on average. (Marshall, 1871, Volume 1, page 175)

Marshall clearly conceived of this 'amount of cash' as being the outcome of a wealth allocation decision. He referred explicitly to 'that portion of his *wealth* which each person retains in the form of money' (Marshall, 1871, Volume 1, page 167; my italics) and in his mathematical notes, having defined u as representing the 'general wealth of [the] community' he wrote the equation

$$\alpha = \chi(u)$$

as determining the 'amount of wealth over which community cares to keep command in ready form'. (Marshall, 1871, Volume 1, page 177).

Unfortunately the precision with which Marshall treated this issue in 1871 did not carry over to any of his later published writings.[8] He *measured* money holdings in units of current income from the outset, but after 1871 he sometimes wrote as if income was not just the unit of measurement, but also what we would now call the 'scale variable' of his demand for money relationship. Thus, in 1899 he told the Indian Currency Committee that 'the fact is that in every state of society there is some fraction of their *income* which people find it worth while to keep in the form of currency', and he ambiguously referred to people holding a 'command of *resources* in the form of currency' (Marshall, 1926, pages 267–8; my italics). Pigou too was sometimes unclear on this matter. In 1912 he treated real income as the scale variable in the function: 'the demand schedule for money, [measured] in terms of commodities, rises and falls as the volume of the national dividend of commodities rises and falls' (page 424), but by 1917 he had begun to use that same thoroughly ambiguous word 'resources' as had Marshall.

> Let R be the total resources, expressed in terms of wheat, that are enjoyed by the community (other than its bankers) whose position is being investigated; k the proportion of these resources that it chooses to keep in the form of titles to legal tender; M the number of units of legal tender, and P the value, or price, per unit of these titles in terms of wheat. Then the demand schedule just described is represented by the equation $P = kR/M$. When k and R are taken as constant, this is, of course, the equation of a rectangular hyperbola (1917, page 165).

In Pigou's subsequent discussions, the context sometimes makes it clear whether 'resources' should be read as income or wealth; but the fact remains that neither he nor any other Cambridge economist until Keynes (1930) took any care to distinguish between the two when discussing the demand for money (and of course the distinction is not conceptually clear in a period of production framework). Thus, the full potential of Marshall's analysis to become what we would now term a portfolio allocation approach to the demand for money was no more appreciated by his immediate successors than it was by its originator, and remained unrealised until the emergence of Keynesian economics.[9]

This same problem with the pre-Keynesian Cambridge theory of the demand for money may be seen from another perspective, namely that theory's treatment of the influence of opportunity cost variables on the demand for money. Marshall's equation for the demand for money set out above contains no interest rate variable, and in this it faithfully reflects his verbal discussions of this issue. Marshall recognised that income yielded either in cash or in kind by other assets was forgone when money was held, but the assets he chose to illustrate his argument were (with the one late exception in 1923 of 'a stock exchange security' (Marshall, 1923, page 39) of which he made nothing further) highly indivisible consumer and producer durables. Thus, the 1871 manuscript notes that

> if instead of keeping on hand a large stock of money he diminishes the stock which he so keeps by fifty pounds and invests this amount in an horse, he derives from it the benefit of the excess of the value of the horse's work over the cost of his keep. (Marshall, 1871, Volume 1, page 167)

The choice portrayed here is hardly made on the margin, and Marshall's subsequent examples of alternative assets to money – 'furniture', 'machinery or cattle' ((Marshall, 1926, page 268; Marshall, 1923, page 45) or 'some business plant' (Marshall, 1923, page 39) – are no better calculated to point the analysis in that direction. Nor did he treat the influence of expected inflation on money holding with any more precision. He did tell the Indian Currency Committee that:

> the level of prices which a given volume of currency will sustain, is liable to be affected by any lack of trust and confidence in the currency itself. . . . The lower is the credit of the currency, the lower will be the share of their resources which people care to keep in the form of currency . . . if the credit of a currency falls, its value falls relatively to commodities, even when there is no change in its volume. (Marshall, 1926, page 269)

but this statement falls far short of characterising a nicely calibrated marginal choice.

In contrast to his uncertain handling of the income wealth

distinction, Pigou treated the opportunity cost issue with much more precision than Marshall ever achieved.

> This proportion (k) depends upon the convenience obtained and the risk avoided through the possession of such titles [i.e. money], by the loss of real income involved through the diversion to this use of resources that might have been devoted to the production of future commodities, and by the satisfaction that might be obtained by consuming resources immediately and not investing them at all. These three uses, the production of convenience and security, the production of commodities, and direct consumption, are rival to one another (1917, page 66)

Though the relevant decisions are not quite properly formulated here, for current consumption should have been compared to the *present value* of streams of convenience and security and of commodities, the choice on which Pigou concentrated in his subsequent analysis, that between holding money and productive assets was formulated as follows, and in explicitly marginal terms.[10]

> Thus the curves that represent the desire for resources to be used in production and in money respectively both slope downward; and resources will be devoted to the two uses up to the point at which the last unit of resources devoted to each of them yields the same quantity of satisfaction. (1917, page 168)

Pigou's handling of the effects of expected inflation too was more precise than Marshall's:

> Any holding of titles to legal tender is always capable of being exchanged against some quantity of commodities. Clearly, if it is expected that the quantity of commodities for which, say, a note for one pound can be exchanged will be greater a year hence than it is now, the inducement to hold pound notes now is increased; and, conversely, if it is expected that a pound will buy fewer commodities a year hence, it is diminished. Thus any expectation that general prices are going to fall increases people's desire to hold titles to legal tender, and any expectation that they are going to rise has the contrary effect. (1917 page 169)

Even so, although Pigou formulated his analysis in explicitly algebraic as well as verbal terms, he did not write the parameter k as a smooth function of any opportunity cost variable. Once again, it was not until the development of the theory of liquidity preference in the hands of Hicks (1935) and Keynes (1930, 1936) that this next important step in the development of monetary economics took place.

Now we must be careful not to make too much of the above criticism of Cambridge monetary theory. Seen through the eyes of anyone brought up on the monetary economics of the Keynesian and Monetarist 'revolutions' its lack of precision about these issues is no doubt a glaring fault. But the Cambridge economists were, like Fisher, interested in analysing the determinants of 'The value of money', to invoke the title of Pigou's 1917 paper. For *this* purpose (and not, for example, for constructing some theory of real income determination the need for which had not yet arisen) their supply and demand approach was surely quite adequate.

The Cambridge transmission mechanism

It is something of a mystery that when Keynes drew attention to the Cambridge oral tradition in 1911 he did not select the supply and demand apparatus as its major distinguishing characteristic. Rather he stressed the superiority of Cambridge analysis of what we would now term the transmission mechanism, whereby changes in the quantity of money affect the price level. We have seen that the overwhelming emphasis in Marshall's 1871 manuscript, and in Pigou's 1917 paper, was on analysing the effects of shifts in the demand for currency on the *equilibrium* price level, and that in his evidence both to the Gold and Silver Commission and the Indian Currency Committee, Marshall paid particular attention to the influence of the development of banking on the relationship between the demand for currency and the price level. Questions about the transmission mechanism are largely irrelevant to these concerns.

In his Gold and Silver Commission evidence, however, Marshall did consider an alternative experiment, set in motion by a money supply shock. Here the context was not an abstract hypothetical economy, but rather nineteenth-century Britain, and the question he addressed was indeed by what channels would an inflow into the country of specie raise the price level. As we saw in Chapter 2, the latter question was a time-honoured one in British monetary economics, having received much attention during the Bullionist

Controversy, the Currency School–Banking School debates, and more recently during discussions of the effects of the gold discoveries of 1849–51 on the British price level. It was Keynes' contention (1911) that, in dealing with this matter, Marshall provided analysis that both differed from, and was superior to that of Fisher. More important, he argued that the analysis in question was highly innovative, a claim that he repeated in his obituary of Marshall (cf. *Memorials of Alfred Marshall*, page 30).

Fisher did in fact pay considerable attention to the role of interest rates and inflation expectations in dealing with 'transition periods', but, as we shall see later, Keynes was correct when he argued that, before the mechanisms which Fisher stressed could begin to work, an increase in the quanity of money would first have to start prices rising. He was on weaker ground with his assertion that Fisher ignored this latter issue however, because, as we shall also see, Fisher did in fact give a brief sketch of the operation of cash-balance mechanics (though not in the context of the transition period). Nevertheless, Fisher paid no attention to explaining how an inflow of specie into the reserves of the banking system would get translated into an increase in the quantity of money in circulation in the first place. Marshall, on the other hand, did indeed face up to just this question, and gave pride of place to interest rate behaviour in the answer he provided. To this extent, then, he did better than Fisher, but his analysis was nevertheless a good deal less original than Keynes persistently claimed.

I have already stressed that Marshall's monetary economics had roots in the classical tradition, in particular as it appeared in Mill's *Principles* and nowhere is this more evident than in his analysis of the interest rate. He started from the proposition, which can of course be traced all the way back to Hume (1752), that the rate of interest is fundamentally a 'real' variable. He told the Gold and Silver Commission, with regard to the discount rate, that:

> the average level is the rate of interest which can be got for the investment of capital, and this is being lowered by the rapid and steady growth of capital – I do not mean the growth of credit, I mean the growth of things, the actual excess of production over consumption (Marshall, 1926, page 49).

Marshall was equally clear that 'the supply of gold exercises no permanent influence over the rate of discount. . . . All that the influx of gold does is to make a sort of ripple on the surface of the water' (Marshall, 1926, page 41). Nevertheless, he regarded the ripple in question as a key element in the process whereby an influx of gold raised prices just as had Cairnes and Mill, as was noted in the previous chapter (see page 18). It is worth quoting Marshall at length on this point.

> the influx of a good deal of bullion into the City . . . does not increase the amount of capital, in the strictest sense of the word; it does not increase the amount of building materials, machinery, etc., but it does increase the amount of command over capital which is in the hands of those whose business it is to lend to speculative enterprise. Having this extra supply, lenders lower still more the rate which they charge for loans, and they keep on lowering it till a point is reached at which the demand will carry off the larger supply. When this has been done there is more capital in the hands of speculative investors, who come on the markets for goods as buyers, and so raise prices. Further, it must be remembered that the influx of bullion would have caused people meanwhile to expect a rise of prices, and, therefore, to be more inclined to borrow for speculative investments. Thus it might not be necessary to lower the rate of discount very much. The increased demand would meet the increased supply half-way, and, after a time, might outrun it, causing a rise in the rate of discount. But as this rise would be merely an incident in a series of changes which put more command over capital in the hands of speculative investors, it would go with an increased demand for goods and a continued rise of prices. This then is my account of the way in which this extra supply of the precious metals would bring prices up (Marshall, 1926, pages 51-2).

Now the last few sentences of this passage, with their emphasis on expectations and their hint at the cumulative nature of credit expansion, look very much like an embryonic account of the expansion phase of Fisher's 'transition period', which is discussed below, and this is no accident. Similar passages, some of which discuss in much more detail the influence of inflation expectations on interest rates and borrowing and lending occur elsewhere in Marshall's writings – in *Economics of Industry* (Marshall and Marshall, 1879), in the 1887 *Contemporary Review* article referred to earlier (*Memorials of Alfred Marshall*, Chapter 8), not to mention in all editions of the *Principles* – and Fisher quoted from the latter source both in his 'Appreciation and Interest' (1896) and, crucially, in the transition period chapter of *The Purchasing Power of Money* (1911). Though it would be wrong to deny Fisher's originality in this context, for we shall see that he went far beyond Marshall in analysing these effects, it is clear that this analysis of Marshall's provided one of his starting points.

However, there is no parallel in Fisher's analysis to the first part of the passage quoted above. It is only in Marshall's evidence to the Gold and Silver Commission that he discusses the effects of bank lending on the discount rate in getting the process of rising prices started, and Fisher seems not to have been aware of this source. If one looks for signs that this specific element in Marshall's analysis was influential, one must turn from Fisher to Wicksell, who was indeed familiar with Marshall's Gold and Silver Commission evidence; but, as we shall see in Chapter 5, Wicksell (unlike apparently Keynes) was well aware that the interest rate mechanism discussed by Marshall had also figured prominently in the work of his classical predecessors.

It is worth noting that Marshall's analytic tools, and specifically his notion of the stock demand for currency, enabled him to be far clearer than those predecessors about the way in which the process of rising prices might end with a new sustainable price level. The passage quoted above continues as follows:

> Having been raised [prices] would be sustained because the methods of business remaining stationary, if a man with an income of £1,000 keeps on the average £12 in his pocket, and if there is more currency in the country so that his share is increased from £12 to £14; then what was bought by £12 would in future be bought by £14; the higher prices are sustained by the fact that the amount of cash which a person cares to keep depends upon the habits of business in his particular rank of life, together with his individual peculiarities; if they are not changed any increase in the amount of currency which falls to his share will raise proportionally prices so far as he is concerned (Marshall, 1926, page 51).

The idea that rising prices initiated by an inflow of gold would create a demand for that gold as currency, and hence equilibrate the price level, was to play a central role in Wicksell's application of his celebrated 'cumulative process' analysis to an international commodity money case – the typical one which he analysed – and here we see that the idea in question was sketched out by Marshall in a passage with which Wicksell was familiar.

There was, in short, much that was influential in Marshall's analysis of the transmission mechanism, though the 'part played by the rate of discount' on which Keynes (1925) laid so much emphasis was probably its least original component. After all, the proposition that, if 'a new acquisition of money will fall into a few hands, and be gathered in large sums', then 'The increase of lenders above the borrowers sinks the interest and so much the faster if those who have acquired those large sums find no industry or commerce in the state, and no method of employing their money but by lending at interest' is due to Hume (1752, page 314), as is the proposition that 'after this new mass of gold and silver has been digested . . . the money may make itself felt by the increase of prices . . . and the high interest returns.' Marshall certainly gave a clear and important account of the transmission mechanism that paid careful attention to the role of the interest rate. That much is clear from the above quotations; but he hardly originated the analysis in question.[11]

The basics of Fisher's analysis: the equation of exchange and the quantity theory

Now it has already been suggested above that certain key contributions of the Cambridge School were published in response to the appearance in 1911 of Fisher's *The Purchasing Power of Money*. This is obvious in the case of Keynes' review of that book, but Pigou's (1917) *Quarterly Journal of Economics* essay on 'The value of money' also contains several references to Fisher's book and reads very much like an attempt to put Cambridge monetary theory on the record in response to it.[12] The Cambridge economists did not claim any substantive differences to exist between their work and Fisher's. Their analysis was, in their own eyes, mainly differentiated by the analytic methods they adopted, rather than by its predictions. As Pigou put it:

> I insist that, tho [*sic*] the machinery that I shall suggest in the following pages is quite different from that elaborated by Professor Irving Fisher in his admirable *Purchasing Power of Money*, and, as I think, more convenient, I am not in any sense an 'opponent' of the 'quantity theory' or a hostile critic of Professor Fisher's lucid analysis. He has painted his picture on one plan, and I paint mine on another. But the pictures that we both paint are of the same thing,

and the witness of the two, of what that thing in essentials is, substantially agrees. (1917, pages 162-3)

Given that Cambridge monetary economics represents one line of development of classical monetary theory, this conclusion is hardly surprising. Though *The Purchasing Power of Money*, which sums up close to two decades of Fisher's monetary thought, deals with much more than the determination of the general price level [containing as it does seminal contributions to index number theory, to business cycle analysis, not to mention extensive discussions of monetary policy issues] a version of the quantity theory of money, closer in many respects to the classical version of that doctrine than the Cambridge variant, provides the book's unifying framework. Indeed, we have seen that the re-instatement of that theory, which Fisher explicitly referred to as that of Ricardo and Mill (cf. 1911, pages 25-6, footnote 2), provided the book's *raison d'être*.

Fisher took as the starting point for his exposition of the quantity theory an algebraic expression known as the 'equation of exchange'. Though Fisher did not originate this formulation – he himself acknowledged Simon Newcomb (1885) and Edgeworth (1887), among other forerunners here (cf. 1911, page 25, footnote 2) – he made far more extensive use of it than had they, and the enormous advantage in clarity that his exposition of the theory of the price level has over that of, say, Mill owes much to his having organised his discussion around this expression.[13] Fisher characterised this equation as 'simply the sum of the equations involved in all individual exchanges in a year' (page 16) and stressed that it 'asserts no causal relations between [the] quantity of money and [the] price level, any more than it asserts a causal relation between any other two factors' (page 156). Hence he treated it, not as a theory, but as a 'truism' which provided a 'means of . . . demonstrating the quantity theory' (page 157).

Mill, as we have seen, had trouble extending the quantity theory to the case of an economy with a well-developed banking system. He could not make up his mind whether it was bank credit *per se* or its counterpart liabilities which affected prices. Not the least of Fisher's virtues is the clarity with which he handled this issue. He distinguished between money and circulating media, just as would have any classical economist, generally reserving the former term for what we would now call currency, and told his readers that '[c]irculating media are of two chief classes: (1) money; (2) bank deposits' (page 10). In thus classifying bank deposits as a form of what we would now term 'money', rather than, as usually did the Cambridge economists, a factor affecting the demand for 'money proper', Fisher shifted the emphasis of his subsequent analysis to the behaviour of the money supply from that of velocity. This, however, differentiates the semantics of his work from that of say Pigou, more than it differentiates its substance.

Having demonstrated that it is indeed the deposits, and not cheques drawn upon them, that circulate (1911 cf. page 35), thus avoiding another muddle prevalent in classical economics, Fisher wrote the equation of exchange as follows:[14]

$$MV + M'V' = \Sigma\, pQ = PT$$

Here M is 'money' (notes and coin), M' is chequable deposits, the Vs are their respective velocities of circulation, p is the money price of any particular good traded, Q is its quantity, so that P is the general price level, an index of the ps, and T the volume of transactions, an index of the Qs. The quantity theory could then be stated as a specific proposition about causal relationships among these variables. Fisher told his readers on the very first page of the Preface to *The Purchasing Power of Money* that:

> the purchasing power of money . . . depends exclusively on five definite factors: (1) the volume of money in circulation; (2) its velocity of circulation; (3) the volume of bank deposits subject to check; (4) its velocity; and (5) the volume of trade (page vii)

thus asserting the basic empirical prediction of his monetary theory to be that the behaviour of the general price level was an effect, but not a cause, of the behaviour of the other variables in the equation of exchange. This empirical prediction however was not itself the quantity theory.

The latter was a more specific proposition, and a 'scientific law'. Such a 'law is not a formulation of statistics or of history. It is a formulation of what holds true under given conditions' (page 320). Fisher himself stated the law in question, the quantity theory of money, as follows:

> The price level . . . normally var[ies] directly with the quantity of money (and with deposits which normally vary in unison with the

quantity of money), provided that the velocities of circulation and the volume of trade remain unchanged, and that there be a given state of development of deposit banking. This is one of the chief propositions concerning the level of prices or its reciprocal, the purchasing power of money. It constitutes the so-called quantity theory of money. The qualifying adverb 'normally' is inserted in the formulation in order to provide for the transitional periods or credit cycles. Practically, this proposition is an exact law of proportion, as exact and as fundamental in economic science as the exact law of proportion between pressure and density of gases in physics, assuming temperature to remain the same. It is, of course, true that, in practice, velocities and trade seldom remain unchanged. . . . But the *tendency* represented in the quantity theory remains true, whatever happens to the other elements involved (page 320, Fisher's italics).

We shall deal with transition periods below. For the moment though, let it be said explicitly that the foregoing statement of the quantity theory is saved from being a tautology by Fisher's argument, developed extensively in Chapter 5 of *The Purchasing Power of Money*, that though velocities and transactions volumes did vary over time, their variations were, except for transition periods, *independent of the behaviour of the quantities of money and deposits*. Hence the experiment of holding them constant while varying money was logically conceivable in a way that it would not have been had those variables systematically depended on the quantity of money.

Determinants of the elements of the equation of exchange

Fisher is often said to have stressed technology and institutions as determinants of transactions volumes and velocities, to the neglect of factors having to do directly with individual choice and his formulation of the quantity theory is sometimes termed mechanical.[15] This characterisation of his version of the quantity theory is then used as a basis for a (usually unfavourable) comparison with Cambridge analysis. As I shall now argue, the differences here are more of style than substance. Fisher summarised the determinants of transactions volumes as follows:

1. *Conditions affecting producers.*
   (a) Geographical differences in natural resources.
   (b) The division of labour.
   (c) Knowledge of the technique of production.
   (d) The accumulation of capital.
2. *Conditions affecting consumers.*
   (a) The extent and variety of human wants.
3. *Conditions connecting producers and consumers.*
   (a) Facilities for transportation.
   (b) Relative freedom of trade.
   (c) Character of monetary and banking systems.
   (d) State of business confidence (pages 74–5; Fisher's italics).

Clearly what we would now call 'tastes, technology and endow-
ments', the bases of any conventional analysis of constrained
choice, figure prominently here. As to the determinants of velocity,
these are summarised as follows:

1. *Habits of the Individual.*
   (a) As to thrift and hoarding.
   (b) As to book credit.
   (c) As to the use of checks.
2. *Systems of payments in the community.*
   (a) As to frequency of receipts and of disbursements.
   (b) As to regularity of receipts and disbursements.
   (c) As to correspondence between times and amounts of
       receipts and disbursements.
3. *General causes.*
   (a) Density of population.
   (b) Rapidity of transportation (page 79).

It is hard to square Fisher's placing the 'habits of the individual'
at the top of his list of factors affecting velocity with the view that
his version of the quantity theory is 'mechanical'. Whether or not
the 'tale' to this effect is, as Patinkin (1973, page 10) has suggested,
Cantabrigian in origin, it is certainly a tale.[16] Moreover Fisher took
and analysed a survey of the behaviour of the average money
holdings of a small sample of Yale students and their relationship to
expenditure volumes. Here, he discovered a 'law of increasing
velocity with increasing expenditure agree[ing] with the general fact
that the larger the scale of any business operation, the greater the

economy' (1911, page 381). Someone insensitive to the importance of individual behaviour for the determination of velocity would hardly have carried out what may well have been the first empirical study of the money-holding behaviour of individuals. The fact that Fisher discussed such behaviour as a factor influencing velocity, rather than some explicit demand for money concept, should not be allowed to obscure the similarity between his views and those of the Cambridge School on the importance of choices.

Critical for Fisher's formulation of the quantity theory, and with the important exception of transition period effects on 'habits as to thrift and hoarding', neither the factors which Fisher listed as determining velocity nor those affecting transactions volumes are subject to influence by variations in the quantity of money. With velocities and the volume of transactions thus tied down by factors exogenous to the equation of exchange, the transformation of that equation into the quantity theory requires consideration of the relationship between the quantity of money and the price level, and this first of all involves the effects of changes in the quantity of currency ('money' in Fisher's usual terminology) on that of bank deposits. Here he took it as a fact that 'under any given conditions of industry and civilization deposits tend to hold a fixed or normal ratio to money in circulation' (page 151). Assertions to this effect appear in a number of places in *The Purchasing Power of Money* and are hard to square with Fisher's own evidence, also presented in *The Purchasing Power of Money*, that while the quantity of money had doubled in the United States between 1896 and 1909, that of deposits had risen closer to threefold. But of course the passage of time involved here does give scope for the above-mentioned 'conditions of industry and civilization' to have evolved. Be that as it may, this step in the argument was not Fisher's primary concern.[17] He devoted far more attention to arguing another point that needed to be established to transform the equation of exchange into the quantity theory, namely that causation could not run from prices to money, and had therefore to move in the opposite direction.

The method of argument here was to show that an autonomous increase in the price level was impossible, because there was no reason to suppose that such an event would be accommodated by variations elsewhere in the equation of exchange. Thus, assuming an open economy operating under the Gold Standard, Fisher argued that if prices were to rise autonomously, they would cause the quantity of money to shrink through balance of payments effects rather than to increase, and that this would have the secondary effect of reducing the quantity of deposits too (cf. 1911, pages 169–70). Nor would velocities adapt because '[t]hese have already been adjusted to suit individual conveniences' (1911, page 171). Thus the only remaining logical possibility was that higher prices would 'diminish trade', and this he dismissed as a 'forlorn hope' (1911, page 171). In any event, he was altogether sceptical of the possibility of autonomous increases in the price level arising from conditions prevailing in the markets for specific goods. Fisher understood perfectly the importance of distinguishing between relative and money prices in this context. He argued that 'individual prices cannot be fully determined by supply and demand, money cost of production, etc., without surreptitiously introducing the price level itself' (1911, page 175) and that '[t]he reactionary effect of the price of one commodity on the prices of other commodities must never be lost sight of' (1911, page 179). Hence, he had no time for explanations of rising prices that attributed the phenomenon to the activities of 'industrial and labor combinations' (1911, page 179).[18]

Now Fisher did concede that the price level ruling elsewhere could affect that currently prevailing in the economy under study, if the latter was both open and operating as part of a larger commodity currency system. He noted that, under these circumstances:

> An individual country bears the same relation to the world that a lagoon bears to the ocean. The level of the ocean depends, of course, upon the quantity of water in it. But when we speak of the lagoon, we reverse the statement, and say that the quantity of water in it depends upon the level of the ocean (page 91).[19]

Even so, as far as factors causing a *change* in the price level in the small open economy were concerned, he was usually a more careful and thoroughgoing quantity theorist than this.

> The price level in an outside community is an influence outside the equation of exchange of [the] community [being analysed], and operates by affecting its money in circulation and not by directly affecting its price level. The price level outside of New York City, for

instance, affects the price level in New York City only *via* changes in the money in New York City. Within New York City it is the money which influences the price level, and not the price level which influences the money (page 172).

Nor was it only prices ruling in some geographically distinct economy which could, in Fisher's view, influence the current price level. Prices expected to rule in a temporally distinct economy, that is in the future, could have similar effects. In his words 'high prices at any *time* do not cause an increase in money at that time; for money, so to speak, flows *away* from that time . . . people will seek to avoid paying money at the high prices and wait till prices are lower (page 173; Fisher's italics). A modern economist would treat the hoarding of money in anticipation of its appreciation as a factor influencing velocity, but Fisher, in keeping with the normal usages of the classical quantity theory did not. For him money's means of exchange role was of the essence, and money not so functioning had by that very fact ceased to be money. When he came to apply the quantity theory to the episode of the appreciation of greenbacks in the 1870s in advance of the resumption of gold convertibility in 1879, he attributed the appreciation in question to the fact that '[s]ome of them [greenbacks] were withdrawn from circulation to be held for the rise' and, consistent with his earlier theoretical exposition, he concluded that in this case 'speculation acted as a regulator of the *quantity* of money' (page 261; my italics) and not of its *velocity*.[20]

Now I remarked earlier that Fisher had no time for the cost of production theory of the natural value of money. Nor did he have time for the views of J. Lawrence Laughlin, a leading American opponent of the quantity theory, whom Fisher quoted (page 104, footnote 1) as arguing that:

> the quantity of money used as the actual media of exchange no more determines price than the entries of deeds and conveyances in the country records determine the price of the land whose sale is stated in the papers recorded . . . price is an exchange relation between goods and the standard money commodity, whether that money commodity be used as a medium of exchange or not (Laughlin, 1903, pages 317–18).

For Fisher, on the other hand 'the value of gold bullion and the cost of production of gold affect prices by way of the quantity of money' (1911, pages 104–5, footnote 1).[21] He presented an elaborate analysis based upon a hydraulic diagram to make himself clear on this point (cf. 1911, pages 105–8). He envisaged gold as having monetary and non-monetary uses (represented as two reservoirs shaped so that the depth of liquid in them varied in proportion to its volume), and market forces (a pipe linking the reservoirs) as equalising its value (the level of the liquid) in those two uses. Given gold's value, mines whose cost of production lay below it would be at work, increasing the gold stock (adding to the amount of liquid in the system through spigots), but only to the extent that their output found its way into a monetary use would that affect the purchasing power of money (the level of the relevant reservoir). Since both reservoirs had leaks, associated with the industrial consumption of gold, etc., there existed in theory an equilibrium value of gold at which its new production would just maintain its value constant.[22] In Fisher's view 'The exact point of equilibrium may seldom or never be realized, but as in the case of a pendulum swinging back and forth *through* a position of equilibrium, there will always be a tendency to seek it' (1911, page 108; Fisher's italics). The point remained though, that gold's cost of production did not affect money's value except through its indirect, and not unique, influence on the quantity of money in circulation. In Fisher's work there thus remained hardly a trace of the concept of a 'natural' value for a commodity money. In this respect, different though his methods were, his conclusions were identical to those of the Cambridge School.

Fisher on the transmission mechanism

Now it is one thing to characterise the influence of the quantity of money on the price level as being analogous to the influence of the volume of liquid in a reservoir on its surface level. It is another altogether to describe the mechanism which links money and prices and therefore makes this analogy a useful one. Fisher discussed the transmission mechanism, dealing with both first-round effects, and their later repercussions. His description of impact effects was brief, and in fact came after his much more elaborate, and far more original, treatment of second-round effects to which he gave the label 'transition periods'. It amounted to a straightforward account of what we would nowadays call conventional cash-balance mechanics, whose historical origins lie in the Mill's analysis of the 'general glut' of commodities discussed in the previous chapter. We may let Fisher speak for himself on this matter.

> Suppose . . . that a doubling in the currency and circulation should not at once raise prices, but should halve the velocities instead . . . [p]rices being unchanged [an agent] now has double the amount of money in deposits which his convenience had taught him to keep on hand. He will then try to get rid of the surplus money and deposits by buying goods. But as somebody else must be found to take the money off his hands, its mere transfer will not diminish the amount in the community. It will simply increase somebody else's surplus. Everybody has money on his hands beyond what experience and convenience have shown to be necessary. Everybody will want to exchange this relatively useless extra money for goods, and the desire so to do must surely drive up the price of goods. No one can deny that the effect of every one's desiring to spend more money will be to raise prices . . . the only way to get rid of a plethora of money is to raise prices to correspond (1911, pages 153–4).

It should be stressed, however, that for Fisher these (by 1911), quite conventional mechanisms were not the key ones driving the price level in the wake of a disturbance.[23] Keynes was not quite correct in arguing that Fisher neglected the mechanisms that would *start* prices rising in the wake of a monetary disturbance, but Fisher certainly paid far more attention to the subsequent influence of rising prices on interest rates and profits in making price increases cumulative. As I have already noted, he had, as early as 1896, published an elaborate investigation of the influence of price level movements on interest rates. Following Marshall, Fisher here concluded that, although in principle inflation would be compensated for by an offsetting adjustment of nominal interest rates (what we now call the Fisher effect), in practice such adjustment came with only a long time lag. Hence, once some shock, often but not necessarily solely an increase in money, started prices rising at, say,

> the rate of 3 per cent a year, and the normal rate of interest – i.e. the rate which would exist were prices stationary – is 5 per cent, the actual rate, though it ought . . . to be 8.15 per cent, will not ordinarily reach that figure; but it may reach, say, 6 per cent, and later, 7 per cent (1911, page 57).

Thus begins a series of events which Fisher summarised as follows:

1. Prices rise (whatever the first cause may be; but we have chosen for illustration an increase in the amount of gold).
2. The rate of interest rises, but not sufficiently.
3. Enterprisers . . . , encouraged by large profits, expand their loans.
4. Deposit currency (M') expands relatively to money (M).
5. Prices continue to rise, that is, phenomenon No. 1 is repeated. Then No. 2 is repeated, and so on (1911, page 60).

The expansion of deposit currency in response to a price level movement does, of course violate the quantity theory as Fisher understood it, and in addition '[t]here are disturbances in the Qs (or in other words T) in V, and in V' ' (page 61). The variation in the volume of trade was not likely to be of significant magnitude, but that in the velocities of circulation might be: 'We all hasten to get rid of any commodity which, like ripe fruit, is spoiling on our hands. Money is no exception; when it is depreciating, holders will get rid of it as fast as possible' (page 63).[24]

Now the process which Fisher describes in the passages of *The Purchasing Power of Money*, from which I have just quoted, characterises, in his view, not the path taken by the price level from one stationary equilibrium value to another, but the upswing of a cycle, which reverses itself when the nominal interest rate catches up with and overshoots the inflation rate, thus precipitating a financial crisis. This is not the place to discuss the mechanics of Fisher's cycle theory in detail, but it is important to be aware of its existence in order to understand his view of the limits to the validity of the quantity theory of money as an explanation of price level behaviour.[25] He was quite clear that the feedback from prices to other elements in the equation of exchange, highlighted in his discussion of 'transition periods', violated the quantity theory, and he was equally clear that the cycle was a regular real world phenomenon. That is why, in expounding and defending the quantity theory, Fisher was usually careful to note that it did not strictly hold during such episodes. Fisher's version of the quantity theory was thus intended to provide insight into the secular behaviour of prices, insight which always had to be heavily qualified and elaborated when dealing with their year to year movements. In this respect once more, his conclusions did not differ in any important respect from those of the Cambridge School.

Statistical work

Fisher's discussion of the deflation which preceded the restoration of gold convertibility to the US currency in 1879, to which I referred earlier, is not an isolated passage in an otherwise theoretical work. Close to a quarter of the text of *The Purchasing Power of Money*, and one-third of its appendices, are devoted to assembling and deploying empirical evidence. Indeed, in the 1915 edition of his *Lectures in Political Economy*, Wicksell characterised the book as 'an interesting attempt to confirm the quantity theory statistically'.[26] Though this hardly does it justice, the book nevertheless stands as an important link between the pioneering efforts in quantitative analysis of classical economists such as Tooke, Henry Newmarch and particularly Jevons, and the later quantitative contributions of American monetary economists, not least those of Milton Friedman and Anna J. Schwartz. It provides its readers with both a systematic survey of what was known about the historical relationship between money and prices at the beginning of the twentieth century, and an account of Fisher's own work on data for the period 1896–1909 (and indeed some results for as late as 1912 were added to its second (1913) edition).

The purpose of this exercise in 'statistical verification', as Fisher termed it, was not to 'test' the quantity theory as that word would be understood by a modern econometrician. Fisher thought the quantity theory's *ceteris paribus* prediction of proportionality between money and prices to be true *a priori*, amounting as it did to a manifestation of what, in modern language, we would call the neutrality of money.[27] However, he did not expect that the 'other things' which would have to remain constant for the proposition to provide a descriptively accurate account of real world events, ever would remain constant over time in that real world. Hence the question of data refuting the theory did not arise for him, and his empirical work was directed at the (by modern standards) more modest goal of showing the usefulness of the quantity theory as an aid to understanding historical experience, and of the equation of exchange as a device for organising statistical evidence.

Fisher was at pains to point out that:

> Most . . . writers who have attempted to test the quantity theory statistically seem to have been animated by a desire not to give it a fair test, but to disprove it. They have carefully avoided taking account of any factors except money and prices (page 277)

and he agreed that 'If anyone has ever really imagined that the price level depends solely on the quantity of money, he should certainly be corrected' (page 296).[28] Even so, the overwhelming impression left by Fisher's account of the empirical evidence is that variations in the quantity of money are the principal cause of price level fluctuations. He presented evidence on the relationship between the stock of precious metals and prices in Europe from the fifteenth century onwards, in nineteenth-century Britain, and in gold and silver standard countries from the 1870s onward as what amounted to exchange rate flexibility was established between them by the collapse of bimetallism in Europe.[29] He concluded that:

> the history of prices has in substance been the history of a race between the increase in the media of exchange (M and M') and the increase in trade (T), while (we assume) the velocities of circulation were changing in a much less degree (pages 246–7).

A similar impression arises from his account of various historical episodes involving the use of inconvertible paper (including that of the greenback period discussed above, once allowance is made for what was understood by money in circulation).

Only for post-1896 US experience was Fisher able actually to present independent estimates for all the components of the equation of exchange and hence say something directly about the behaviour of velocities rather than 'assume' ('infer' might have been a better word) that they were, relatively speaking, constant. Here Fisher used the basic approach of E. W. Kemmerer (1909), but improved upon the latter's data. This approach involved creating independent estimates of the six variables that figure in the equation (M, M', V, V', T and P), using the first five to make predictions about the sixth, and then comparing these to the independent estimates of the price level's behaviour. Fisher's preferred method of comparison here was to compute the correlation coefficient between the proportional (i.e. log) first differences of the two estimates of the price level. Finding it to be 0.57 (±0.10), he concluded that this 'is a moderately high coefficient of correlation' (page 295).

Now the equation of exchange is an identity, and had the data used in the exercise just described been accurately constructed, there would have arisen no discrepancy between the actual and predicted price level. Fisher understood this, and concluded correctly that 'the remarkable agreement [cf. moderately high coefficient of correlation!] in our statistical results should be understood as a confirmation, not of the equation by the figures, but of the figures by the equation' (page 298). The above-mentioned results were thus not treated as an end in themselves, but as the starting point for adjusting the original estimates of the equation of exchange's components with a view to using it as a tool for attributing responsibility for price level behaviour among those components. The details of these adjustments need not concern us. Suffice it to state Fisher's conclusion about the behaviour of the US price level after 1896:

> We conclude, therefore, that the growth of the velocity of circulation of money [i.e. currency] was a negligible factor in raising prices; that the relative growth of deposits and their velocity were large factors; and that the growth of money was the largest (page 311).

This conclusion was, in fact, implicit in a result presented earlier by Fisher that the correlation coefficient between the first log difference of prices and money (i.e. currency) was 0.43 ± 0.13 (see page 296). This result did not rely on direct estimates of velocities, transactions volumes, and so on, and a modern reader would be right to wonder how much of lasting value was added to it by Fisher's painstaking efforts to construct series for these variables. To be sure, his use of bank clearing data to get at deposit velocities involved a plausible enough approach to the problem, and his actual construction of these series presents an early and important example of the use of benchmarking and interpolation in the construction of a time series. However, Fisher's estimates of currency's velocity were derived from the volumes of wage payments and of withdrawals and deposits of currency with banks, by way of essentially unsupported assumptions about the frequency with which currency turned over between appearing in wage packets and being redeposited at the bank. They are a good deal less convincing. So too are his estimates of real transactions, which attracted explicit criticism from Keynes (1911).

I do not draw attention to these problems to belittle Fisher's work, or to undermine his conclusions about the importance of variations in the quantity of money for the behaviour of the price level. However, they are manifestations of a fundamental problem with the transactions version of the quantity theory, namely that the variables on which it focuses are virtually impossible to measure. The problems that are so evident in Fisher's attempts to overcome these difficulties continued to plague monetary economists working in the transactions velocity tradition well into the middle of this century, and were never really overcome. Indeed, it was these problems as much as anything else that led to the demise of this tradition as an active area of research.[30] There is thus a certain irony in the fact that the greatest protagonist of the transactions approach to the quantity theory was also a committed empiricist, and that these two characteristics of his contribution to monetary economics were in the longer run, to prove incompatible. There is a matching irony in the fact that an alternative approach, far more suitable as a vehicle for systematic empirical work was the product of the Cambridge School. The account of their contribution given earlier in this chapter contains no discussion of statistical work for the simple reason that, although the tools they developed were much better adapted than Fisher's to systematic statistical analysis, the Cambridge School never put them to such a use. It was only much later, with the work of such economists as Clark Warburton, a selection of whose work is collected in Warburton (1966), and Friedman and Schwartz (1963) that the empirical tradition in monetary economics to which Fisher contributed began to rely on an essentially Cambridge approach to monetary theory, and to exploit its advantages for empirical investigation.

Conclusions

The most striking characteristic of the two versions of the quantity theory of money that we have discussed in this chapter is surely their continuity with the classical analysis which preceded them. Both the Cambridge School and Fisher believed that, in the long run 'money is only a mechanism by which [a] gigantic system of barter is carried out' (Marshall, 1926, page 115) and took the explanation of price level behaviour as the central problem of monetary economics.[31] In this respect they placed themselves in the mainstream of a tradition which stretched all the way back to Hume. As we have seen though, they did far more than reiterate classical doctrine. They refined and clarified it, and adapted it to a much changed (and indeed changing) institutional framework.

To begin with, and once and for all, they banished from monetary economics the last vestiges of the classical cost of production theory of value considered as an *alternative* to the quantity theory. To be sure, Senior, Mill and Jevons had moved a long way in this direction, but they had left the connections between the short run in which the quantity theory held, and the long run in which cost of production dominated, unclear. Without a firm grasp of the stock flow distinction, it is hard indeed to put the (rising) marginal cost of extracting new supplies of the precious metals in its proper place among the factors determining the purchasing power of commodity money. Fisher and Marshall alike, not to mention Pigou, tackled this issue each in his own way, and came to the same logically coherent conclusions about it. The quantity theory in their hands became the general explanation of the price level, and marginal costs of production of the precious metals were reduced to one, seldom important, factor affecting the supply of money under a particular set of institutional arrangements. They thus rid monetary economics of the notion that there was something particularly appropriate or 'natural', to use the classical adjective, about the behaviour of the price level under a commodity standard in general, and the Gold Standard in particular.

But the shift away from stressing cost of production effects was only part of their contribution. Classical economists, not least Mill, had great difficulty in adapting the quantity theory framework to the conditions of a modern commercial banking system. Once again, we have seen that the Cambridge School and Fisher, each in their own way, coped well with this difficulty. The latter treated bank deposits as another form of money, and modified the quantity theory accordingly, while the former usually treated them as a means of economising on currency. Both, though, understood the proportinal relationship between currency and deposits which fractional reserve banking and the parallel circulation of currency and deposits introduced into the system, and Marshall, at least, also understood the dynamics of the credit multiplier process.[32] This advance in positive economic understanding thus brought institutional factors, that is things of human design, into the forefront of influences on the price level to replace the natural conditions of production of the precious metals. Marshall and Fisher alike were quite conscious of this shift of emphasis in their theory of the price level, and, as we shall see in Chapter 6, it deeply influenced their attitude towards monetary policy questions.

This chapter has stressed the fact that the neoclassical quantity theory of money was a theory of the general price level. It should not be inferred, however, that price level behaviour was the only problem taken up by neoclassical monetary economists, or that neoclassical monetary theory began and ended with the quantity theory. We have seen that the credit cycle, so-called, was a matter of concern to classical economists, and though secular deflation, followed by slow secular inflation were the dominant features of the monetary history of the four decades prior to World War I, the period was no more free of cyclical fluctuations than were earlier times. It should hardly come as a surprise, then, that economists continued to study the cycle, that their work built upon classical foundations, and that the developments in the theory of the price level which we have described in this chapter informed that work. Neoclassical work on the cycle has been neglected in this chapter, not because it is unimportant then, but because it is important enough to merit separate treatment, to which we now turn.

Notes

1. On the intentions of the founders of the Federal Reserve System to cater to regional diversity, see Welsey C. Mitchell (1914).
2. The reference here is to Wilde's comedy of 1895 *The Importance of Being Earnest* Act II scene i in which Miss Prism orders Cecily, the play's heroine, to her studies in the following terms:

    Cecily, you will read your Political Economy in my absence. The chapter on the Fall of the Rupee you may omit. It is somewhat too sensational. Even these metallic problems have their melodramatic side.

    This nowadays obscure joke obtained a new lease on life from Blomqvist, Wonnacott and Wonnacott (1983) who use it as a motto for their chapter on exchange rates. The American bimetallist controversy also seems to have left its mark on contemporary literature, if Hugh Rockoff's (1990) interpretation of *The Wizard of Oz* as an allegory of that controversy is to be given credence – and the outlines of his case, if not all the details are convincing.

3. The first of these (Marshall, 1871) was eventually published in John Whitaker's 1975 edition of *The Early Economic Writings of Alfred Marshall* and the second is reprinted as ch. 8 of the 1925 *Memorials of Alfred Marshall*.

4. A brief but essentially complete account of Cambridge monetary economics did, however, soon appear in Pigou's *Wealth and Welfare* (1912; pp. 423–38). This book, not as well known as it should be, saw only one edition. The microeconomic analysis contained in it in due course evolved into *The Economics of Welfare* (1919), and the monetary and cycle theory, much expanded, was later incorporated into *Industrial Fluctuations* (1927).

5. This point about the relationship between Marshall's work and that of Mill is made by Whitaker in his commentary on Marshall in *The Early Economic Writings of Alfred Marshall* (1975).

6. As we shall see in Chapter 6, however, the view that Marshall expresses in the following statement was commonly held by bimetallists at the time, and was by no means unique to him. He himself cites the prominent bimetallist Mr Henry Hucks-Gibbs, later Baron Aldenham, a director and sometime governor of the Bank of England as also holding it. It is worth noting that, in his 1893 *Treatise on Money*, Professor Joseph S. Nicholson of the University of Edinburgh, also a convinced bimetallist argued that:

> it is a gross error to say, as Mill does, that 'the value of gold depends, apart from temporary fluctuations, on its cost of production.' . . . the general level of prices rests on many causes, and this general level of prices determines the exchange value of gold coins . . . while the value of coins determines the value of bullion. (pages 70–1)

Compare also the quotation from Henri Cernuschi (1876) in Chapter 6 (page 157–8).

7. Similarly, Wicksell (1898), who was familiar with Marshall's approach, focused upon money's 'interval of rest' rather than its reciprocal, the velocity of circulation, when expounding his version of the quantity theory and for the same reason as Marshall, namely, that to do so enabled the analysis of choice to be brought more easily to bear on monetary questions (see Chapter 5, page 125 below). With hindsight, the distinction here might seem to be a trivial one, but when new theoretical ground is being broken, the convenience of the tools used does matter. Hence this change of focus on Marshall's part was important.

8. The one exception is Appendix C of *Money, Credit and Commerce*

(1923), whose style suggests that it was written at the same time as the unpublished 1871 manuscript.

9. Some commentators on the evolution of Keynesian monetary economics – e.g. Pascal Bridel (1987) and Eprime Eshag (1963) – treat liquidity preference theory as a refinement of earlier Cambridge monetary thought. For arguments to the effect that the refinement in question was of significant proportions, see Patinkin (1973) and Laidler (1987b).

10. Bridel (1987) also cites the above passage, using it as evidence that Pigou did indeed take a portfolio choice view of money holding. He does not, however, note the problem with the time dimensionality of Pigou's formulation pointed to here. Nevertheless, Pigou's approach to these matters was consistently marginalist. For example, in 1912 he talked of agents comparing 'the satisfactions . . . from the nth unit of money and the nth unit of commodities' (page 424) in fixing their money holdings.

11. Indeed Marshall's analysis of this matter does little more than restate the analysis of Cairnes and Mill referred to in Chapter 2, page 18, above.

12. And in publishing it in the *Quarterly Journal of Economics* he presumably intended it for an American audience too. His substitution of the American 'wheat' for the English 'corn' of Marshall's analysis also points to this intention.

13. For a useful account of the history of the use of this expression, see Thomas Humphrey (1984). Bordo (1987a) also deals with this matter.

14. But the monetary system which the Classics dealt with was also muddled. When cheques circulate in the business community with multiple endorsements, the problem of deciding whether the cheque or the deposit on which it is drawn is money has no straightforward solution.

15. For a recent and vigorous statement of this view of Fisher's work, see Harrington (1989). The immediately following pages and page 92ff. of the next chapter explain why I do not share it.

16. There is an element of this characterisation of Fisher in Keynes' (1911) *Economic Journal* review of *The Purchasing Power of Money*. However, if I had to pick a single source that stresses it, I would opt for Mises (1912; 1924, e.g. page 140). The myth, is as much Austrian as Cantabrigian.

17. It is worth noting that Fisher was not consistent in his treatment of the currency–deposit ratio even in the short run. In particular, systematic fluctuations in that ratio play a role in his account of transition periods (see page 78).

18. The target of this last objection of Fisher's was surely J. Lawrence Laughlin, who, notably in 1903 and 1909 attributed an important role to these institutions in creating what we would now call 'cost-push' inflation from the mid-1890s onwards. Earlier, both Laughlin (1887) and Mitchell (1896) had sought to rebut the quantity theory by arguing that, since the price level was a relative price ruling between money and

goods, it must be affected both by factors affecting the value of money and the value of goods. These critics treated the values in question as if they were determined *independently* of one another. Fisher's insistence on the interconnectedness of markets in the general equilibrium system, epitomised in the passage of *The Purchasing Power of Money* quoted from in the foregoing text, is clearly and accurately aimed at this type of confusion. On all this, see also Chapter 6, pages 163–4.

19. Note that Hume (1752, page 319) also uses a hydraulic analogy when dealing with balance of payments effects, arguing that money will be distributed according to relative demands in open economies just as 'water everywhere finds its level'.

20. The reader is referred to Mill (1871, page 509), Walker (1878, page 12) and Wicksell (1915, page 152) for other examples of quantity theorists arguing that money serving a pure store of value role should be regarded as no longer in circulation, and hence irrelevant to the working of the quantity theory.

21. There is more than an echo here of Thomas Nixon Carver's (1897) view that the very fact of changes in the cost of production of gold affecting its purchasing power as money should be regarded as evidence in favour of the quantity theory rather than against it. This view was supported by the argument that the key link between a variation in gold's cost of production and the price level was the effect on prices of a change in the quantity of it circulating as money relative to the demand for it at the initial price level. It is worth noting that Carver's analysis, inasmuch as it uses a supply and demand framework, anticipates that of Pigou (1912, 1917), who did indeed cite it with approval in the latter source.

22. The hydraulic diagram described here is in fact a simplified version of one initially devised by Fisher to analyse the working of bimetallism. This latter diagram which appears in *The Purchasing Power of Money* (1911, pages 116, 119) first appeared in his 1894 *Economic Journal* article on bimetallism, and was later adapted and used by Edgeworth (1895) to compare the working of ordinary bimetallism with Marshall's variation on the arrangement, *symmetallism* as Edgeworth called it. See Chapter 6, page 171, for an account of symmetallism.

23. Compare this passage with that from Wicksell's *Interest and Prices* quoted below (Chapter 5, page 126–7).

24. Note that, although Fisher here shows an appreciation of the influence of expected inflation on money holding, he stops rather a long way short of suggesting that a smooth functional relationship links the variables in question. Once again the reader will note the essential similarity of Fisher's treatment of a topic to that of the Cambridge economists.

25. These matters are discussed in Chapter 4, page 91ff.

26. See 1915, page 128. Note that this phrase of Wicksell's is his complete characterisation of *The Purchasing Power of Money* and not merely one aspect of a longer account.

27. Thus Fisher did not regard the 'neutrality' postulate as one that needed

empirical testing. In noting this fact, I do not mean to imply approval of his judgement here. As should be apparent, Fisher's view of the role of empirical evidence in monetary economics differed from that which informs most recent efforts in this area. The main thrust of his work was to illustrate the validity of, in his word to verify, the quantity theory, not to test it.

28. The target of this remark is surely Laughlin, (e.g. 1887, 1909) or perhaps Mitchell (1896), both of whom did characterise the quantity theory in this way prior to attacking it.

29. See this chapter pages 44–50, and Chapter 6, pages154–6 for accounts of these post-1870 developments.

30. Marget (1938–42) provides a useful survey of much of the work to which I refer here.

31. The phrase quoted here is taken from a question posed to Marshall by Mr D. M. (later Sir David) Barbour, a member of the Gold and Silver Commission. Marshall did however agree that the phrase in question captured his own view 'so far as permanent effects go' (1926, page 115). Note that Barbour plays a peripheral role in our story a little later, see Chapter 6, page 168.

32. Marshall's analysis here was based, as he acknowledged, on a passage in Giffen's *Stock Exchange Securities* of 1877. Eshag (1963) records that Marshall's copy of this book contains a marginal note in Marshall's hand in which the credit expansion process is explicitly formulated as a geometric progression.

4 • The monetary element in neoclassical cycle theory

Introduction

Many, perhaps most, developments in cycle theory during our period had little to do with monetary economics. This was particularly true in continental Europe where the socialist tradition in economic thought was more influential than in the English-speaking world; but even in Britain, a wide variety of non-monetary approaches to the cycle were investigated, including extensions of Jevons' work on the 'sunspot' theory, the archetype of modern 'real' business-cycle theory, and the under-consumptionist analysis of Hobson (1894).[1] There was also Dennis Robertson's (1915) analysis of the difficulties of co-ordinating real saving and investment decisions, in which monetary elements played a much less important role than they would in his later (1926) development of the same line of reasoning.[2] As we saw in Chapter 2, however, classical 'credit cycle' analysis, by its very nature, gave pride of place to monetary factors, sometimes in instigating, but always in propagating and amplifying, fluctuations. It is hardly surprising, therefore, that those who developed and refined the classical quantity theory of money also carried forward the classical monetary approach to cycle theory.

Earlier I characterised classical analysis, as epitomised in Mill's account of the cycle, as being more akin to a description than an explanation of the phenomenon. To be sure, his description was more elaborate than that offered by Lord Overstone in 1837, and as quoted by Marshall and Marshall (1879):

> the state of trade revolves apparently in an established cycle. First we find it in a state of quiescence – next, improvement, – growing confidence, – prosperity, – excitement, – over-trading, – convulsion, – pressure, – stagnation, – distress, – ending again in quiescence

but it did not differ in essentials.[3] Though there is considerable variety among the contributions to the monetary explanation of the cycle we shall consider here, all of them followed the mainstream classical tradition, epitomised by Mill, of stressing the speculative element in business behaviour during the upswing. Those contributions, moreover, took an extremely important step forward by grounding the analysis of speculation in the distinction between the nominal and real rates of interest. Though this distinction does occur from time to time in monetary writings as far back as the eighteenth century, it was left to Marshall and Fisher, not to mention Hawtrey, to recognise and exploit its significance for understanding the cycle.[4]

The nominal–real interest rate distinction

The earliest account of the cycle relevant to this chapter is probably that of Marshall and Marshall (1879), but though this contained, as we shall see below, much that is of interest, it did not touch on the key theoretical insight which was to become central to the analysis of monetary elements in cycle theory, and to which I have just referred, namely the distinction between the nominal and real rate of interest. This distinction seems to have made its first appearance in the writings of Marshall (and indeed in the literature of neoclassical economics) in the 1887 *Contemporary Review* essay 'Remedies for fluctuations of general prices' to which I have already referred on a number of occasions above. The relevant passage is worth quoting at some length.

> We often talk of borrowing or lending on good security at, say, 5 per cent. If we had a real standard of value that could be done; but, as things are, it is a feat which no one performs except by accident. Suppose, for instance, a man borrows £100 under contract to pay back £105 at the end of the year. If the purchasing power of money has meanwhile risen 10 per cent. (or, which is the same thing, general prices have fallen in the ratio of ten to eleven), he cannot get the £105 which he has to pay back without selling one-tenth more commodities than would have been sufficient for the purpose at the beginning of the year. While nominally paying 5 per cent. for the use of his money, he has really been paying 15½ per cent.
>
> On the other hand, if prices had risen so much that the purchasing power of money had fallen 10 per cent. during the year . . . then,

instead of paying 5 per cent. for the loan, he would really be paid 5½ per cent. for taking charge of the money (page 190).

The insight set out here was immediately applied to explaining the very type of speculative boom whose description is a commonplace in the classical literature on the credit cycle.

> The consequence of . . . uncertainty [about price level stability] is that, when prices are likely to rise, people rush to borrow money and buy goods, and thus help prices to rise; business is inflated, it is managed recklessly and wastefully; those working on borrowed capital pay back less real value than they borrowed, and enrich themselves at the expense of the community (pages 190–1).

Marshall attached sufficient importance to the above passages to incorporate them, in a modified but still recognisable form in the first (1890) and all subsequent editions of the *Principles of Economics* with the following sentence interpolated.

> When we come to discuss the causes of alternating periods of inflation and depression of commercial activity, we shall find that they are intimately connected with those variations in the real rate of interest which are caused by changes in the purchasing power of money (1890, page 594).

Marshall, then, provided at least a sketch of an explanation of the speculative price rises which his classical predecessors had often described as characterising the upswing of the cycle, and he accorded these forces a role in the downswing as well. However, he never did fill out this sketch into the systematic account of 'alternating periods of inflation and depression' promised in this last quotation. Fisher (1911) and Hawtrey (1913) did so, however, arguing that inflation and depression were 'intimately connected with those variations in the real rate of interest which are caused by changes in the purchasing power of money' just as Marshall had suggested. Indeed, as we shall see below, they went further than Marshall's Cambridge colleagues thought wise. They used the distinction between nominal and real interest rates not merely to analyse the monetary element in cyclical behaviour, but as a key component of a purely monetary explanation of the cycle as a whole.

Fisher's contribution to our understanding of the factors at work here is significant far beyond the boundaries of cycle theory; and indeed his seminal work on the interaction of inflation and rates of interest, 'Appreciation and interest' (1896), was not mainly about the cycle, but about the secular relationship between price level changes and the level of nominal interest rates. In this study, as notable for its empirical as for its theoretical content, Fisher distinguished carefully – far more so than Marshall – between realised and anticipated changes in the price level. He argued that

> We need not ascribe to the practical man any knowledge of 'absolute' appreciation, but whatever absolute appreciation is, it is included, though unseparated, in the practical man's forecast in terms of money of all the economic elements which concern him – prices of his product, cost of living, wages of his workmen, and so forth (page 36).

Fisher's examination of a wide variety of nineteenth-century data showed that high nominal interest rates had been associated with low real rates and vice versa, but also that fluctuations in 'commodity [i.e. real] interest' had been greater than those in 'money [i.e. nominal] interest'. He concluded that this 'must mean that the price movements were inadequately predicted' (page 67); though he also noted that 'the adjustment of (money) interest to long price movements is more perfect than to short' (page 71). Fisher explained this lagged adjustment, as we would now call it, along the following lines. Beginning with the proposition that 'business foresight exists' (page 36), he went on to argue that not all agents are equally endowed with it: 'Only a few persons have the faculty of always "coming out where they look". Now it is precisely these persons who make up the borrowing class' (page 77). Within this class, however, some are quicker off the mark than others: 'Suppose an upward movement of prices begins. . . . Borrowers can now afford to pay higher "money interest". If, however, only a few persons see this, the interest will not be fully adjusted' (page 75).

Now in 1896 Fisher was, as I have pointed out, mainly concerned to explain the secular characteristics of the data he studied, and it is in this context that the passages just quoted should be read in the first instance. However the information asymmetries and learning lags which figured so prominently in his 1896 secular analysis were later to become central to his monetary theory of the cycle. Though the relevance of this analysis to the cycle was discussed briefly in

'Appreciation and interest', as was its connection to those insights of Marshall's discussed above (see 1896, pages 76–9), it is to Chapter 4 of *The Purchasing Power of Money* that we must turn to find Fisher's monetary theory of the cycle first fully set out, in the guise, as we noted in the previous chapter, of an analysis of 'transition periods', and of the processes whereby changes in the quantity of money work their way through to their ultimate effect on prices.[5]

In 1911 Fisher entertained both the logical and empirical possibility of impulses other than changes in the quantity of money setting the cycle in motion, but nevertheless, when he came to expound his analysis, and needed to postulate a shock that would set the cycle in motion, 'the chief factor which we shall select for study . . . is the quantity of money' (page 55). Taking it for granted that nominal interest rates would fail immediately to adjust fully to inflation, Fisher described the consequences of 'a slight initial disturbance, such as would be produced, for instance by an increase in the quantity of gold' (page 58) in the following terms:

> As prices rise, profits of business men, measured in money, will rise also, even if the costs of business were to rise in the same proportion. . . . But, as a matter of fact, the business man's profits will rise more than this because the rate of interest he has to pay will not adjust itself immediately. . . . Thus the profits *will* rise faster than prices. Consequently he will . . . be encouraged to expand his business by increasing his borrowings. These borrowings are mostly in the form of short-time loans from banks; and . . . engender deposits . . . but this extension of deposit currency tends further to raise the general level of prices (pages 58–9; Fisher's italics).

And so the upswing cumulates, with further complicating factors. 'There are disturbances in the Qs [i.e. in the real volume of transactions]', though this effect is minor because 'the amount of trade is dependent almost entirely on other things than the quantity of currency' (pages 61–2). More important, and in a passage already quoted earlier, Fisher noted that:

> the rise in prices . . . will accelerate the circulation of money. We all hasten to get rid of any commodity which, like ripe fruit, is spoiling on our hands. Money is no exception; when it is depreciating, holders will get rid of it as fast as possible (page 63).

For Fisher then, the economy's progress through successive stages of 'improvement, – growing confidence, – prosperity, – excitement, – overtrading' hinges upon the tendency of the nominal interest rate to lag behind inflation, and that progress gathers momentum because of induced expansion in the quantity of bank money and an associated acceleration of velocity. As he succinctly put in, 'Rise of prices generates rise of prices, and continues to do so *as long as the interest rate lags behind its normal figure*' (1911, page 60; Fisher's italics). But 'the rise in interest, though belated, is progressive' (page 64) and will eventually overtake the inflation rate. It will do so because of decisions taken by the banks. 'The banks are forced in self-defence to raise interest because they cannot stand so abnormal an expansion of loans relatively to reserves' (page 64). Moreover,

> Not only is the amount of deposit currency limited both by law and by prudence to a certain maximum multiple of the amount of bank reserves; but bank reserves are themselves limited by the amount of money available for use as reserves. Further, with the rise of interest, the value of certain collateral securities . . . begins to fall . . . and therefore they cannot be used as collateral for loans as large as before. This check to loans is, as previously explained, a check to deposits also (page 64–5).

Some firms are inevitably unable to renew their loans and therefore fail. This,

> induces fear on the part of many depositors that the banks will not be able to realize on these loans. Hence the banks themselves fall under suspicion, and for this reason depositors demand cash. Then occur 'runs on the banks,' which deplete the bank reserves at the very moment they are most needed. . . . This culmination of an upward price movement is what is called a crisis (1911, page 65).

That a collapse of confidence in the banking system might accompany any economic crisis was, of course, well known to Fisher's contemporaries, particularly in the United States where just such a state of affairs had occurred as recently as 1907.[6] That, however, was not the point he emphasised. Rather it was that this collapse of confidence was itself the consequence of a more fundamental cause, namely 'a belated adjustment in the interest rate' (page 66). During the crisis, 'borrowers, unable to get easy loans, blame the high rate of interest'; but for Fisher, that was not the point, because '[h]ad the previous rate been high enough, the borrowers never would have overinvested' (page 67). There is no need to discuss Fisher's analysis of the downswing phase of the cycle and its trough in any detail. His treatment of the downswing is essentially symmetrical with that of the upswing and peak. A lag in the response of the interest rate to *falling* prices is now at the heart of the matter and 'Owing to this tardiness of the interest rate in falling to a lower and a normal level, the sequence of events is now the opposite of what it was before' (page 68). In Fisher's view, the downswing too was self-limiting, bringing to an end what he termed 'a complete credit cycle . . . [a] swing of the commercial pendulum' whose period was normally ten years.[7]

Though, as I have noted, Fisher did recognise that quantities of goods produced might expand a little during the boom, and contract during the downswing, it was nevertheless for him 'the rise, culmination, fall and recovery of *prices*' (page 70; my italics) that constituted a complete cycle. In his account of it movements of real variables were incidental to, and not of the essence of, the phenomenon. In this, of course, he displayed considerable continuity of thought with his classical predecessors, but he also set himself somewhat apart from a number of his important contemporaries. In particular, Marshall, and later Pigou and Hawtrey, attempted to supplement the analysis of the interaction of inflation and interest rates, which they shared with Fisher, with a treatment of fluctuations in such real variables as output and, in particular, employment. Of this group, moreover, only Hawtrey shared Fisher's view that monetary factors alone sufficed to explain cyclical fluctuations.

Money wage stickiness

Marshall and Pigou did not, strictly speaking, adhere to a monetary theory of the cycle. In particular they did not regard changes in the quantity of money as being empirically important impulses setting cyclical mechanisms to work. For them, monetary elements came into play as factors amplifying cyclical fluctuations in prices; and price fluctuations in turn were important not only in and of themselves, but also as proximate causes of variations in employment, which the Cambridge School recognized as being an integral and important aspect of the cycle.[8] Moreover, since the orthodox microeconomics of the time had the demand for labour depend upon the real wage, it seemed relatively straightforward to explain employment fluctuations as a consequence of price level variation. The key here was the postulate of money wage stickiness, as we shall now see.

The few pages in Marshall and Marshall's (1879) *Economics of Industry* devoted to the cycle begin conventionally enough with a description of the phenomenon which the Marshalls themselves summarise with the passage from Overstone quoted earlier in this chapter. They characterise the upswing as a matter of speculation, followed by a crisis of confidence in commodity and financial markets, during which 'though men have the power to purchase they may not choose to use it' (page 154). Such hoarding is temporary, and caused by 'a want of confidence'. Its cure is a 'renewal of confidence'. A temporary over-supply of commodities is not a manifestation of any general over-production of commodities, for the simple reason that 'what constitutes the means of payment for commodities is simply commodities' 1879 (page 154). As should be evident in the light of the discussion of Chapter 2 above, all this is completely derivative of Mill, including the explicit and quite self-conscious avowal of the truth of Say's Law which is in fact a direct quotation from him. However, the Marshalls' treatment of the downswing and depression phase of the cycle goes beyond Mill. Falling prices are one characteristic of this phase, but the Marshalls introduce a new element into the discussion when they point out that '[t]he connexion [*sic*] between a fall of prices and a suspension of industry requires to be further worked out' (1879, page 155).

With this sentence, the Marshalls placed the question of fluctuations in output and employment on the agenda of cycle theory in a way in which the classical economists did not, and in a way in which Fisher did not more than three decades later. Not only did they pose the question, but, as I have already asserted, they sketched an answer to it based on the postulate of money wage stickiness which was to become central to virtually all discussions of cyclical unemployment until the 1970s:

It . . . very seldom happens . . . that the expenses which a manufacturer has to pay out fall as much in proportion as the price which he gets for his goods. For when prices are rising, the rise in the price of the finished commodity is generally more rapid than that in the price of the raw material, always more rapid than that in the price of labour; and when prices are falling, the fall in the price of the finished commodity is generally more rapid than that in the price of the raw material, always more rapid than that in the price of labour 1879, page 156).

The Marshalls here treat money wage stickiness not as a theoretical possibility but as a fact; and in this they seem to follow such earlier commentators as Jevons (1863, reprinted 1884) who, however, did not work out the implications of this fact for employment during the cycle.[9] In his later writings Alfred Marshall always treated wage stickiness in this way, not only when dealing with the cycle, but also in discussion of secular phenomena. Thus, the relative unconcern which he expressed to the Gold and Silver Commission in 1889 about the then current downward secular trend in prices was based upon his belief that it would benefit the working classes by causing real wages to rise more rapidly than they otherwise would, albeit apparently without leading to depressed output and employment levels; and his 1899 evidence to the Indian Currency Committee leaves the impression that he regarded subsequent events as having vindicated his judgement about this matter.[10]

Like Marshall, Pigou also took the fact of wage stickiness for granted, and he also attempted to explain why it occurred. He devoted a whole chapter, entitled 'The plasticity of wage rates' of his primer on *Unemployment* (1913a) to the question. This chapter begins by setting aside maladjustments (such as minimum wage laws and pockets of labour market monopoly) which might create unemployment in the stationary state, and proceeds to observe that:

In the actual world there is still scope for much additional maladjustment, consequent upon the obvious fact that the demand for labour, in every part of the industrial field, is exposed to fluctuations. . . . There is no *necessity* that such fluctuations should involve unemployment: for the wage-rate that workpeople ask for . . . *might* so vary in response to variations of demand that there were never anywhere more workpeople than employers were willing to engage. . . . In real life, of course, everybody knows that no wage-rates are perfectly plastic . . . and that, as a consequence, fluctuations do involve unemployment (page 75–6; Pigou's italics).

Pigou ascribes this lack of 'plasticity' in wages to two main causes: that 'the great majority of people . . . think in terms of gold and silver, not in terms of what gold and silver will buy' (page 79), and that '[b]oth employers and employed are impelled to strive after greater rigidity than is directly to their advantage, on account of the inharmonious character of their mutual relations'. Even when 'relations are reasonably satisfactory . . . conditions will rarely be found, in which [an agreed mechanism of wage adjustment] can be safely invoked otherwise than at fairly long intervals . . . two or three . . . even . . . five years' (page 81–4). In short the money wage stickiness to which the Marshalls had drawn attention in 1879 as the key cause of cyclical unemployment was, by 1913, being explained by Pigou as the consequence of money illusion and the costs of contracting. This analysis was to be the lynchpin of conventional treatments of this question for the next sixty years.[11]

Pigou did not use the word 'fluctuations' to refer exclusively to the business cycle, but he nevertheless regarded 'cyclical movements in the aggregate wage fund' as being a sufficiently significant source of unemployment to devote a separate chapter of his (1913a) book to explaining them and analysing their consequences. Even though Pigou placed the interaction of prices and money wages at the centre of his treatment of the cyclical behaviour of the labour market, his explanation of the cycle itself, as sketched out in 1912 and 1913a but not fully developed until 1927, was not mainly a monetary one. In 1913a he pointed to two factors, namely real shocks arising from fluctuations in the harvest and changes in business confidence, as being capable of initiating a cyclical fluctuation, and argued that since 'in a considerable number of cases, booms in business confidence have their origin in good harvests' (page 115) they would often operate together. This argument repeats the essentials of one set out in *Wealth and Welfare* (1912). There we read that 'spontaneous variations in the comparative attractiveness of investment – which involves the purchase of labour' (page 453) are the initiating forces of the cycle. This attractiveness in turn depends upon forecasts made by agents concerning the profitability of investment, and these forecasts are subject to error, which is correlated across agents:

> the forecasts made by business men are largely coloured by their
> present fortune. It follows then that interdependence of fortune

carries with it interdependence of forecasts, and, thus, allies itself with the psychology of crowds, as a force tending to promote action in droves (page 461).

Moreover, 'current prosperity or adversity, which originates in the bounty of nature, is one not unimportant cause of variations in the error of business forecasts' (page 471).

As Peart (1990) has pointed out, Pigou's stress on variations in agricultural output as an impulse driving the cycle betrays the influence of Jevons, whose 'sunspot' hypothesis about harvest variations is referred to with cautious approval in 1913a (page 116); and his treatment of the forces propagating the effects of such initial disturbances was equally derivative. It is in its analysis of propagation mechanisms that Pigou's cycle theory admits a monetary element, for it stresses the role of the trade credit system in spreading the effects of shocks throughout the economy and that of the banking system in amplifying (or damping) them. As Pigou put it in *Wealth and Welfare*:

> In the actual world . . . the errors that come into being are not quiescent inert things. Rather, they are . . . self propagating, with a tendency to grow continually larger, till some external force intervenes to destroy them. This peculiar character is imposed upon them by the fact that transactions are conducted in terms of a standard of purchasing power, whose value, relatively to commodities in general, is liable to vary with variations in the demand for it (1912, page 462).

As a result,

> an error of optimism once made . . . is expanded to greater girth. [Businessmen] borrow more money, and, thereby, cause prices to rise still further. By this rise, their fortunes are again improved, and, in consequence, the error of their forecasts is again expanded. The process thus begun tends, if it is not interrupted by an external force, to continue indefinitely (1912, page 463).

The banks can, however, act as that 'external force', because, as Pigou put it in *Unemployment*:

> it is in the power of these institutions either to assist rash speculators along the road to disaster, thus making their ultimate collapse and its consequences to others more serious, or to check them at a comparatively early stage (1913a, page 119).

Here Pigou acknowledges the influence of Bagehot whose advice to the banks to lend freely at high interest in times of crisis 'has probably been responsible, indirectly, for an important limitation in the range of movements undergone by the aggregate wage fund' (page 120). To this forty-year-old influence we may surely add that of Marshall, and particularly the latter's analysis of the real–nominal interest rate distinction. Indeed, Pigou explicitly tells his readers that:

> in periods of boom business men are given an excess of prosperity at the expense of sleeping capitalists; because the real interest which they have to pay on their loans is automatically reduced . . . in times of industrial depression, business men suffer a special loss for the benefit (more or less) of their creditors (1913a, page 121).

Note that there is nothing in Pigou's account of these matters that parallels Fisher's detailed treatment of the creation and destruction of bank money and induced changes in velocity which accompany the cycle. For Pigou, as for Marshall, such monetary fluctuations were not fundamental to the cycle. The Cambridge economists did not, as did Fisher, develop cycle theory as an extension of the quantity theory of money. Rather they treated it as a separate, more complex, piece of analysis of which monetary analysis was but one component. Even so, by postulating money wage stickiness, they showed that price level variations induced, or at least accommodated, by variations in the quantity of money and its velocity might in their turn create variations in real output and employment. Hence, as we shall see in Chapter 6, the design of policies to stabilise prices became one of their central concerns, and such policies were, not surprisingly, monetary in nature.

The Marshallian components of Hawtrey's cycle theory

The work of Marshall and Pigou (in the case of the latter, that completed before 1914) is better thought of as contributing to the understanding of certain characteristics of the upswing and downswing phases of the cycle, and the monetary elements at work in them, than as creating a coherent model of the cycle taken as a whole. It was Ralph Hawtrey, educated at Cambridge to be sure but not really of the Cambridge School, who, in pre-World War I Britain, produced a complete and purely monetary theory of the cycle. He integrated the cash balance approach to the quantity theory with other elements in Cambridge thought, not to mention some acute insights of his own, into a theory of fluctuations which explained turning points as endogenous phenomena. Unlike Fisher, moreover, Hawtrey treated output and employment fluctuations as essential features of the cycle.

Hawtrey's first systematic exposition of his theory of the cycle, *Good and Bad Trade*, was published in 1913, but according to its author, the book was begun in 1909. It is, as Pigou (1913b) noted in his somewhat patronising review of it, an 'ordinary' book rather than an academic treatise, not least in the almost total absence of references to the work of others from its pages. The only other author cited – as Pigou noted – is Irving Fisher (twice), even though – as Pigou also noted – Hawtrey's analysis is heavily dependent upon Marshallian ideas.[12] But *Good and Bad Trade* is much more than the unoriginal compendium of well known ideas put together by a talented amateur for the benefit of the general reader, which the reader of Pigou's review might expect. It is rather a *locus classicus* of monetary explanations of the business cycle, being far more systematic and wide ranging in its treatment of this approach than any other work – *The Purchasing Power of Money* included – appearing in English during our period. Pigou's review stressed that the main components of Hawtrey's analysis were current in Cambridge monetary economics at the time he began to write. That is indeed true, but it is equally true, as the same review failed to notice, that the theory which Hawtrey built from them is nevertheless a most original construction.

First, Hawtrey was an exponent of the Cambridge cash balance version of the quantity theory: 'every man has to keep a greater or less reserve of money, or "working balance", which represents the margin, up to date, of his income over expenditure' (page 11), and not only 'man *qua* consumer and investor, but his position *qua* producer is not in essence different' (page 12). There is no ambiguity about Hawtrey's choice of scale variable for the relationship. In his view the aggregate demand for cash balances depends upon the level of national income, while his assertion that 'Money is merely purchasing power' (page 14) surely indicates at least an informal understanding that the demand for money is indeed a demand for real balances. All this is conventional enough, and does not go beyond what Pigou (1912) had already published.[13] However, it is worth noting explicitly that Hawtrey departed from usual Marshallian conventions in using the word 'money' 'to cover every species of purchasing power available for immediate use, both legal tender money and credit money, whether in the form of coin, notes, or deposits at banks' (page 3). Here perhaps we can see the influence of Fisher (1911), whom Hawtrey had, as we have noted, read.[14]

Hawtrey attached considerable importance to the distinction between real and nominal interest rates, though he did not use this terminology. In his Foreword to the 1961 reprint of *Good and Bad Trade* he claims subjective originality for his treatment of this topic, while acknowledging, as he had in a footnote in the original text (1913, page 44), the priority of Fisher (but not Marshall). Hawtrey's analysis of this matter differs in a noteworthy way from that of these others. He pays particular attention to term structure issues, pointing out that 'the effect of the falling prices of commodities is far greater on the rate of interest for temporary loans than on that for permanent investments' (pages 45–6). Hawtrey may have been a conventional neoclassical quantity theorist in putting the interaction of inflation with the rate of interest at the heart of his analysis of cyclical upswings and downswings, but his insight that short-term variations in inflation expectations, such as might occur within a cycle phase, would have a relatively small effect on the interest rates relevant to long-term investments led him to stress the role of short interest rates and their influence on inventory investment, in this context, in a way that others did not.[15]

The third building block of Hawtrey's cycle theory is the idea of money wage stickiness, which has already been discussed at some length in this chapter. However, his treatment of the phenomenon is not quite the same as that of the Marshalls and Pigou (and not always quite consistent either) inasmuch as he tended to attribute stickiness to prices as well. His initial discussion of the idea occurs as he works out the consequences of a conceptual experiment involving a once and for all cut in the level of the money supply in an economy initially in a state of full employment equilibrium. He notes that:

> if the adjustment could be made entirely by a suitable diminution of wages and salaries, accompanied by a diminution of prices, the commercial community could be placed forthwith in a new position of equilibrium, in which the output would continue unchanged. . . . If customary wages and customary prices resist the change, the adjustment, which is bound to come sooner or later, will only be forced upon the people by the pressure of distress (1913, page 41).

Hawtrey does not speculate on the speed with which equilibrium will be restored in such a case, noting only that it 'will probably depend on the willingness of employees to accept the reduced wages' and that 'the mere presence of a body of unemployed ready to accept work on almost any terms would have a tendency to depress wages' (page 42). However, the conceptual experiment of a once and for all cut in the money supply is only an expositional device deployed by Hawtrey to enable him to make clearly his main and, in the context of this cycle theory, all important point, namely that:

> If for a period the stock of money continuously diminishes, precisely the same causes will be at work as in the period following a sudden diminution. Wages will cling to their customary rate until the stress of unemployment begins to drive them down; they will follow the downward movement of money and prices at an interval; and at last, when the movement of prices stops, there will be an accumulated weight of unemployment only to be relieved by a continuance of the movement of wages (page 42–3).

As this quotation makes clear, Hawtrey should not be thought of as naively postulating that prices are flexible and wages sticky in terms of their levels. He is better interpreted as attributing some stickiness to both variables, but rather more to wages, and stickiness of a type that, when both are varying, causes money wages to *lag behind* prices, rather than remain fixed, or even move more slowly. I do not claim originality for Hawtrey's formulation here. The 'wage lag doctrine' is a time-honoured one which some commentators attribute to David Hume, and it was widely accepted among Hawtrey's contemporaries. Robertson (1915) remarked that 'the lagging of money wages behind prices is now so generally admitted as scarcely to require detailed illustration' (page 215). Nevertheless, Hawtrey did put the idea to one particularly original use. In conventional Cambridge writing, the money wage stickiness postulate exists to explain why unemployment occurs. In Hawtrey's self-consciously dynamic formulation the idea retained its usefulness for this purpose, but, as I shall show later, it is also central to his explanation of cyclical turning points as endogeneous phenomena.

One other factor is crucial to Hawtrey's theory of the cycle, and here too, though the idea itself is a commonplace, the use to which he puts it is original. I refer to the inflow and outflow of reserves of currency to and from the banking system as prices fluctuate, and the effect of such movements on the banks' willingness to lend and hence create deposits. As we have seen in earlier chapters, Marshall made something of this phenomenon when dealing with the transmission mechanism linking imports of gold to an increase in domestic prices. It also played a part in Fisher's analysis of the cycle, being in his view the key mechanism turning the upper turning point into a crisis. Moreover, the phenomenon in question had, under the label 'internal drain' been much discussed for more than a century before Hawtrey wrote, and, as we saw in Chapter 2, was part of the conventional wisdom of classical monetary economics embodied in *Lombard Street*. Hawtrey, however, complemented this idea with some discussion of what we would nowadays term the public's desired currency–deposit ratio. He argued that this ratio would vary systematically with the distribution of national income between wages and profits, rising as the share of wages (and hence the incomes of those most prone to use cash for their market transactions) rose, and vice versa. This mechanism, interacting with lagging money wages, is fundamental to his analysis of cyclical turning points.

Hawtrey's theory of the cycle

The Cambridge quantity theorists treated monetary factors as amplifying disturbances originating elsewhere in the real economy. Hawtrey accorded those factors more importance: noting that 'Trade as a whole is subject to a well-marked though not quite regular wave motion, with a period from crest to crest or from trough to trough, which varies from four or five to about ten years'. He stated the purpose of his analysis in the following unequivocal terms: 'The general result up to which I hope to work is that the *fluctuations are due to disturbances in the available stock of "money"* ' (page 3; my italics).[16] His demonstration of this result begins with a simple closed economy without banks, and he examines in this context the consequences of an exogenous change in the money supply. He then complicates his analysis by introducing a banking system, and, finally, he discusses open economy considerations.

Hawtrey's simple economy consists of workers, producers and dealers, and operates initially at full employment equilibrium with a stable price level. This hypothetical equilibrium is then disturbed by a cut in the money supply so that conventional cash balance mechanics come into play.

> After the withdrawal [of currency from circulation] . . . some . . . members of the community . . . will find they are in danger of a shortage. In the absence (as assumed) of a banking system, it will be necessary for them to restrict expenditure for a time in order to replenish their balances.
>
> But though anyone may replenish his balance by economising, it is clear that no transfers of money from one individual to another can replenish *all* the balances, the total of which has been definitely reduced by a certain amount. A new equilibrium can only be found by a change in incomes which will make a reduced scale of balances sufficient. (page 38; Hawtrey's italics).[17]

Aggregate money expenditure will therefore fall, and

> As less commodities are sold, the retailers will order less from the wholesale dealers, who in turn will order less from the producers. If the producers do not receive sufficient orders to employ their capital and labour at full time, they must either reduce their output, or reduce their prices, or both (page 40).

Even at this early stage in his exposition, and before banks have been introduced, Hawtrey deals with the complications of wage stickiness and the effects of expected deflation on the rate of interest, pointing out that:

> low profits are associated with flagging demand in two quite distinct ways . . . the profits on existing capital are encroached upon through wages resisting the fall which the failure of demand requires . . . the profits on any new instrument in which the *money* value of the

original capital is to be maintained unimpaired are diminished (page 47).

In the absence of banks though, this latter factor simply adjusts the money rate of interest, leaving the real rate unchanged: 'According to theory . . . the prevailing rate of interest should be the rate which existed before the disturbance, as modified by the falling prices of commodities' (page 48). Moreover, the process which Hawtrey here analyses (and the reverse one which follows from an increase in the money supply) converges upon a new equilibrium in which prices and wages are lower (higher) and full employment is restored.

In Hawtrey's view, it is only with the introduction of a banking system whose deposit liabilities circulate as money, and which holds fractional reserves of currency, that the possibility, indeed the virtual inevitability, of a self-generating and repeating cycle arises. Once banks exist, the public can restore any shortfall in their currency holdings by withdrawals from them, thereby creating:

> a depletion of the banks' reserves below the level demanded by their liabilities. This the bankers cannot acquiesce in, and they will proceed to restore their reserves by discouraging borrowers, and in particular by raising the rates of interest which they charge for loans (page 59).

Such an increase in the rate of interest, even though it has been delayed a little, will affect two major classes of borrowers, namely producers and dealers, but it is the latter whose response is crucial:

> One of the special functions of a dealer is to keep a stock or 'working balance' of the goods in which he deals. . . . When the rate of interest goes up he will be anxious to reduce this indebtedness. . . . He can reduce his indebtedness if he can reduce his stocks of goods, and he can reduce his stocks of goods by merely delaying replenishment when they are sold. . . . The effect, from the point of view of the manufacturer, is very nearly the same as that which . . . ensue[s] upon a contraction of the currency in a country without banks. That is to say, he experiences a slackening of demand (pages 62-3).

Though the effect is very nearly the same, however, the transmission mechanism through which a monetary shock takes effect is quite different in this case. It now works not through cash-balance mechanics, but through interest rate variations; and the economy's subsequent path of adjustment is different too:

> the reduction of stocks . . . and the restriction of output . . . will have been accompanied by a diminution of the indebtedness of both producers and dealers to the banks, and this . . . will have been accompanied by a diminution . . . in the supply of credit money . . . in the hands of the public. . . . The result is that as fast as the dealers reduce their stocks at one end . . . they find that their stocks accumulate at the other end in consequence of a flagging of the demand from the consumer. Their stocks, therefore, are on the whole depleted little, if at all, but there is a continuous decline of both wholesale and retail prices . . . and this. . . , involving a fall in the money value of a given stock of goods, helps to maintain the decrease of indebtedness, and therefore of credit money (page 63).

Eventually the banks will succeed in restoring their reserve ratios, they will reduce their lending rate and the money supply will be stabilised. At this stage, however, the economy will be characterised by depressed production and employment:

> productive resources . . . will not be fully employed until the level of prices is reduced in the same proportion [as the fall in the money supply]; prices cannot be reduced until the cost of production is sufficiently reduced; and the cost of production can only be reduced as wages are reduced. Wages, therefore, are the key to the situation (page 65).[18]

Wages do of course fall in the face of unemployment, and as they catch up with prices the share of profits in income, which Hawtrey believed would be falling during the cycle's downswing, now begins to increase again. This latter effect has crucial consequences for the monetary system's behaviour.

According to Hawtrey, workers are inclined to hold their 'unspent margin' of money balances in the form of currency, or 'legal tender money' to use his phrase, while dealers and manufacturers prefer to hold deposits.[19]

> At the stage, therefore, at which the banks become satisfied with their position and no longer think it necessary to curtail loans or to maintain a high rate of interest, a greater proportion of the available stock of legal tender money will be in circulation and a smaller proportion will be accumulated in the hands of the banks than under normal conditions. . . . But as business approaches normal con-

ditions there must be a tendency on the whole for profits to recover at the expense of earnings, and the cash will come back from circulation into the hands of the banks.

Here is a process at work which is likely enough to produce fluctuations. For the bankers will thereupon be ready to *increase* the stock of credit money again, and once they have embarked upon this course they may find it very difficult to stop short of a dangerous inflation (pages 190–1; Hawtrey's italics).

An upswing, to all intents and purposes a mirror image of the preceding downswing, thus ensues. So long as the banks' lending rate fails to keep pace with the rate of profit (Hawtrey's term for the real rate of return on capital adjusted for inflation), and wages fail to keep pace with prices, profits are high, and the economy's demand for cash low. The banks therefore continue to expand credit, and hence the supply of deposits. Eventually wages will begin to catch up with rising prices, and their share in national income will begin to rise too. Therefore, the economy's demand for currency will begin to rise, and the resulting drain of reserves from the banks will now trigger an incrase in interest rates, perhaps a financial crisis, but certainly a downswing in economic activity; and so on.

As we have already seen, Hawtrey began *Good and Bad Trade* by promising his readers that:

The general result up to which I hope to work is that the fluctuations are due to disturbances in the available stock of 'money' – the term 'money' being taken to cover every species of purchasing power available for immediate use, both legal tender money and credit money, whether in the form of coin, notes, or deposits at banks (page 3).

The analysis just described enabled him to claim that 'we have proved that there is an inherent tendency towards fluctuations in the banking institutions which prevail in the world as it is' (page 199).[20] The reference here to the *banking system* is all important: Hawtrey believed that fluctuations could in principle be produced by exogenous monetary changes, but he also believed that 'arbitrary changes in the quantity of legal tender currency in circulation cannot be of much practical importance. Such changes rarely occur' (page 73). Hence, he went on, 'what we are looking for is the origination of changes not necessarily in the quantity of legal tender currency, but in the quantity of purchasing power, which is based on the quantity of credit money' (page 74). His cycle theory therefore stressed the latter changes, and he thought these would be pervasive in a modern economy. For reasons implicit in the foregoing analysis,

> the equilibrium which the bankers have to maintain in fixing the rate of interest is essentially 'unstable', in the sense that if the rate of interest deviates from its proper value by any amount, however small, the deviation will tend to grow greater and greater until steps are taken to correct it (page 76).

Moreover, the economic fluctuations associated with these deviations would tend to repeat themselves. This was not quite inevitable, but almost so. At that moment in the cycle's trough at which currency began to flow back into the banks,

> in order to steer business back into stable conditions they would have to foresee the diminution of cash requirements, and to ease off the rate of interest with graduations so nicely calculated as just to effect the requisite reduction of credit money at the very final stage, when the cash requirements have also reached the normal proportion. In practice it would be impossible to know accurately even in an isolated community, still less in the world as it is, what cash requirements to anticipate or what ultimate volume of credit money to aim at (page 191).

Forty-five years after the publication of *Good and Bad Trade*, Hawtrey gave evidence to the British Radcliffe Committee on the Working of the Monetary System about the crucial role of 'the inherent instability of credit' in generating economic fluctuations, and the importance of using monetary policy, and particularly short rates of interest, to offset its undesirable effects. In the words of Deutscher (1990) 'Hawtrey's economics, articulated over the course of half a century, was remarkably consistent' (page 21), and his 1913 model of the cycle formed the basis of that economics throughout his long and disinguished career. That model, as we have now seen, deals with the workings of a closed economy and concentrates on short-term fluctuations in the market for inventories. However, Hawtrey was by no means blind to the facts of the world around him, and in *Good and Bad Trade* he discussed both open economy considerations, and the behaviour of long-term investment over the course of the cycle. His discussion of both issues, however, involved him in elaborating his basic analysis to cope with extra details, not in changing his view of the fundamental mechanisms driving the cycle.

Hawtrey analysed open economy effects in the context of both flexible and fixed exchange rate systems. In the former case, he noted that the tendency of the bank lending, and hence market, rate of interest to lag behind the rate of profit (the real rate of return on capital adjusted for inflation) would lead to exchange rate overshooting, very much along the lines analysed by Rudiger Dornbusch (1976). He also noted that the effect of this in a downswing would be to 'hasten that general fall of prices which is the necessary condition of equilibrium in [the country undergoing the contraction]' (page 98). However, Hawtrey regarded this as a relatively unimportant complication which made no qualitative difference to the cycle's characteristics in an open economy:

> it will be seen that the mutual influence of two areas with independent currency systems is on the whole not very great. Indeed, the only important consequence to either of a contraction of currency in the other, is the tendency for the first to lend money to the second in order to get the benefit of the high rate of interest. This hastens the movement towards ultimate equilibrium in the area of stringency (page 99).

Hawtrey referred to the case of 'the international effects of a fluctuation experienced in a country using a metal currency common to itself and its neighbours' as a 'much more important case' (page 102) than that of flexible rates, but he meant by this an empirically more relevant case, rather than one in which his basic closed economy analysis needed more radical revision. He deals with the effects of the fluctuation in question on exchange rates (within the gold points) and gold flows, in considerable detail, but he does so along quite conventional lines:

> Gold flows from foreign countries to the area of stringency in response to the high rate of interest, ... While this process is at work the rates of interest in foreign countries are raised. . . . As soon as the bankers' loans have been brought into the proper proportion to the stock of gold, the rate of interest reverts to the profit rate in the area of stringency, but the influx of gold continues from each foreign country until the average level of prices there has so far fallen that its

divergence from the average level of prices in the area of stringency is no longer great enough to cover the cost of sending the gold (page 113).

As should be clear from the relevant sections of Chapter 2 above, all this would be familiar to anyone conversant with Mill or Goschen (1861) or any other standard source of classical balance of payments analysis. Hawtrey's treatment of these issues is in one important respect markedly inferior to that of the classical orthodoxy described there; for he does not consider the possibility that an external drain of specie might trigger the upper turning point of the cycle. Given the central role of this mechanism in classical analysis, Hawtrey's neglect of it in *Good and Bad Trade* is quite remarkable, and strong evidence that open economy considerations should not be regarded as lying at its analytic core.[21]

The same may be said of Hawtrey's treatment of fixed investment. By the time of the publication of *Good and Bad Trade* it was commonplace that fixed investment was particularly prone to cyclical oscillations and that the output of producer's goods was considerably more volatile than that of goods in general. Hawtrey explained this phenomenon, which was first noted by Jevons (1863, reprinted 1884) in terms of an embryonic, but unmistakable, accelerator mechanism:

> it may be that . . . output increases . . . at an average rate of 1 per cent per annum, and that the fixed capital requires renewal after twenty years . . . if there is an expansion of trade which increases the output of this industry in a particular year by 4 per cent . . . the new plant needed will be 9 per cent of the existing plant or no less than 50 per cent more than the average . . . however the full effect of this tendency may be mitigated, it is clear enough that all business connected with investment is in a class by itself so far as its responsiveness to trade fluctuations is concerned (page 207).

Though the accelerator is usually associated with John Maurice Clark (1917), Hawtrey was by no means the only economist to anticipate his development of the idea. In English-language literature Pigou discussed the matter briefly in his primer on *Unemployment* (1913a, pages 110–12) and Charles Bickerdike (1914) devoted a whole article to the mechanism, illustrated with reference to the influence of variations in the demand for shipping services on the output of the shipbuilding industry, as 'A non-monetary cause of fluctuations in employment'.[22] None of these, however, and certainly not Hawtery, made any attempt to integrate such a mechanism into the heart of an analysis of the cycle in a manner which contributes to its self-generating nature. In Hawtrey's case, it was simply added to his exposition to cope with a particular stylised fact, without becoming an integral part of the model which forms the core of that exposition. That perhaps is why, in *Good and Bad Trade*, as well as in his interwar writings, Hawtrey argued against the feasibility of using public works expenditures as a stabilising device, a point on which Pigou (1913b) explicitly criticised him. This matter was not of great policy importance in 1913, perhaps, but the 'Treasury view' implicit in Hawtrey's analysis of the question would attain considerable significance in the 1920s and 1930s.

Concluding comments

There has never existed at any time a single coherent framework to which one might refer as *the* theory of the business cycle. This generalisation is as true of the period under study in this book as any other. Those approaches associated with the quantity theory of money, which I have discussed in this chapter, represent but one strand of a wide ranging and complicated literature; and even among monetary approaches to the cycle there is little uniformity.[23] As we have seen, for Marshall, and even more clearly for Pigou, the impulses driving the cycle did not originate in the monetary sector. Monetary factors complicated and amplified the economy's responses to more fundamental impulses, but monetary fluctuations *per se* were as much a symptom as a cause of the cycle. Indeed, in his Review of *Good and Bad Trade*, Pigou characterised Hawtrey's view that 'the causes of fluctuations are exclusively monetary and banking causes' as 'extremely superficial' (1913b, page 582).

Fisher too took the positon that monetary factors predominated both as impulses and in the working out of the cycle's propagation mechanism, but his conception of the facts which cycle theory had to explain was different from that of his English contemporaries and relatively old-fashioned too. He treated the cycle as a matter of price level fluctuations; and though he was aware that variations in such real variables as output and employment were part of the complete picture, these were peripheral to his vision. That is why, of all those whom we have discussed in this chapter, it is in Fisher's work that the relationship between the quantity theory of money *per se*, and the theory of the cycle is the closest. To be sure he recognised the need to modify the quantity theory as he conceived of it when he came to confront cyclical phenomena. The endogeneity of the quantity of bank money, and of velocity, within the cycle undermined the simple picture of unidirectional causation among the variables in the equation of exchange that he believed characterised their secular relationships; but it is nevertheless the case that, for Fisher, even within the cycle, the predominant channel of causation ran from money, including bank deposits, to prices, rather than vice versa, and that the impulse which usually set the cycle in motion was a change in the quantity of *currency*.

Hawtrey's analysis was, as I have already noted, just as clear as Fisher's in identifying fluctuations in the quantity of bank deposit money as the critical causative factor driving the cycle. Nevertheless, the particular variables whose behaviour needed to be explained as far as he was concerned were not just prices but real output and employment as well. Thus though one might appropriately characterise Fisher's cycle theory as 'quantity theoretic', such an adjective would not come naturally to the mind of anyone seeking a label for Hawtrey's model. The quantity theory, in its Cambridge cash balance form, plays a role, but because of his concern with output and employment, so too does the wage lag hypothesis, which exists quite independently of the quantity theory. Hawtrey, moreover, treats endogenous fluctuations in the quantity of bank money, operating through an interest rate transmission mechanism as the basic factor which *keeps* the cycle going, and hence, except as an expository device, he does not need to look for any exogenous impulse to set it in motion in the first place.

And yet we must be careful not to press any claims to superiority on Hawtrey's part too hard. His analysis of the factors leading to endogenous fluctuations in the quantity of bank money is richer than Fisher's, to be sure. He relies on an interest rate transmission mechanism at all points in his account of how cycles occur in the real world rather than ever falling back on cash-balance mechanics in this context. Hawtrey treats employment fluctuations as an integral part of the story as well, but neither he nor anyone else working during our period got very far with this last issue. It is one thing to say that, because of wage stickiness, output and employment will decrease during the downswing, but it is quite another to explain what will determine the amount of such decreases, or to consider the way in which such fluctuations themselves feed into the mechanism driving the level of demand for output as a whole. The cycle analysis we have surveyed here, that of Hawtrey as much as that of Marshall and Pigou, had nothing useful to say about these last two questions.[24] Though there are traces of an embryonic multiplier process in Hawtrey's work in the 1920s (see Deutscher, 1990, page 103), these do not occur in *Good and Bad Trade*. The observation in Marshall and Marshall (1879) that 'the stoppage of work in one trade diminishes the demand for others' (page 155) is as close as anyone came to recognising the existence of such a process in the period under discussion here. Accelerator effects were analysed more thoroughly, as we have seen, for they seemed to offer an explanation of the observation that capital goods industries were particularly prone to cyclical output fluctuations.[25] They were not, however, integrated into anyone's model, let alone Hawtrey's, as they would have had to be if fluctuations in real variables were to be given what we would nowadays regard as an appropriately thorough treatment.

The monetary approach to cycle theory was thus very much in a state of flux at the onset of World War I and would remain so long after the war had ended. But ideas of lasting importance were nevertheless added to it during our period. First and foremost, the real–nominal interest rate distinction, and the closely associated idea that inflation and deflation of the price level would have important consequences for the time path of bank lending, and hence of bank deposits were both developed and widely deployed by quantity theorists interested in the cycle; while the idea that unemployment was to be explained by variations in real wages caused by a stickiness of money wages relative to prices also became commonplace, at least of the British literature during this period.

Radically different though the details of their various models were, we should not lose sight of the fact that the neoclassical quantity theorists whose work we have discussed in this chapter all produced analyses which seemed to imply that stabilising the price level was the *sine qua non* of stabilising the cycle. If the price level did not fluctuate, real and nominal interest rates would not diverge, and the banking system's capacity for amplifying fluctuations, upon whose importance Fisher and his British contemporaries were entirely agreed, would not come into play. As far as exponents of the wage stickiness hypothesis were concerned, this phenomenon too would cease to matter: in the absence of price level fluctuations, real wages would change inappropriately, and cyclical fluctuations in unemployment would not occur. In short, if the approaches to cycle theory associated with the quantity theory of money were many and various, they all nevertheless pointed to price level stability as an extremely desirable goal. As we shall see in Chapter 6 this key insight yielded by quantity theoretic analysis had a profound influence on its exponents' discussions of the design of monetary institutions and the conduct of policy.

Notes

1. Jevons' hypothesis was that sunspot activity affected the weather, specifically the Bengal monsoon, the rice harvest and, therefore, British exports of industrial output, particularly textiles (see 1884, page 216ff.). Modern work on productivity shocks stems from that of Kydland and Prescott (1982).
2. Robertson's book is less than 300 pages long, and monetary issues are not introduced into the discussion until page 206. On page 211 he remarks:

   > The fact that our long, complicated, and perhaps not unfruitful discussion has been conducted so far without reference to specifically monetary phenomena relieves us of the necessity of a formal refutation of those who, like Clement Juglar and Mr. Hawtrey, find in monetary influences the sole and sufficient explanation of industrial fluctuations.

   In 1915, the monetary element in Robertson's cycle theory was minor, far less important than that played in the approach of Pigou, to be discussed below. That and the fact that his major contributions to monetary economics were made after World War I is why Robertson does not play a large role in the story told here.
3. See the long quotation from Mill given in Chapter 2, page 23 above. This passage from Overstone is quoted by Marshall and Marshall (1879, page 153) and later by Marshall (1923, page 246).
4. Nowadays as noted in Chapter 2 (page 44) we think of Thornton as having originated this distinction in one of his 1811 speeches on the Bullion Report. Fisher (1896), however, lists several other sources for

the idea, including an anonymous eighteenth-century inhabitant of Rhode Island, but does not mention Thornton.

5. Of course the theory in question is also expounded in Fisher's famous paper of 1923 – 'The business cycle – largely a "Dance of the Dollar" ' .

6. The reader's attention is drawn to the fact that it is an internal drain rather than a combination of external and internal drains that precipitates the upper turning point here. This sets Fisher's model apart from earlier English classical treatments, where the external drain was usually viewed as crucial. His model is, therefore, best viewed as one of a closed economy, and its empirical background is surely the history of those post Civil War crises in the United States documented by Sprague (1910) and Friedman and Schwartz (1963) and of which that of 1907 was the last.

7. The ten-year period referred to here was, roughly speaking, the nineteenth-century norm, as first documented by Juglar (1860).

8. In denying money any unique role in originating (as opposed to amplifying) cyclical impulses, the Cambridge economists were simply adopting a position which had been commonplace in the classical theory of the credit cycle, whose exponents were at best eclectic, and more often agnostic, about this aspect of cycle theory.

9. The Marshalls do not explicitly cite Jevons, who concentrated not on downward but upward stickiness of money wages, and concluded that inflation tended to lower real wages, at least until the labour force took measures, including strike action, to remedy matters. See Jevons (1863, reprinted 1884, page 85). I do not mean to suggest that Jevons originated the idea of money wage stickiness. It can be found, for example, in Thornton's (1802) *Paper Credit*. Even so, it was only with Jevons, and particularly the Marshalls, that the hypothesis began to attract the attention which macroeconomists have given it ever since.

10. On these matters see Marshall (1926), for example, pages 19–20, 91 and 286. I can offer no explanation for the apparent logical inconsistency between Marshall's treatment of the cyclical implications of wage stickiness, where he stressed its consequences for employment, and its secular implications, where employment effects were downplayed.

11. Nowadays, of course, it is common to refer to wage stickiness as a Keynesian postulate, despite the fact that Chapter 19 of the *General Theory* makes it quite clear that Keynes thought that his analysis did not depend on this assumption. There is not space here to argue about whether or not he was right in this judgement, but I would, if pressed, tend to argue 'not'.

12. This was not Hawtrey's own view. In a 1963 letter to Claude Guillebaud, made available to me by John Whitaker he claimed that the source of much of his analysis was conventional wisdom circulating in the City, which he traced back to Bagehot. Since Marshall had been teaching his monetary analysis at Cambridge for several decades before 1913, it is quite possible that his ideas had thoroughly penetrated that conventional City wisdom by then.

13. See Chapter 3, page 57 above on this. There is no reason to suppose

that Hawtrey had read *Wealth and Welfare* before completing his own book, however.

14. But as we have seen above (Chapter 3, page 57) Pigou also adopted this usage in 1912. Perhaps there is some influence of Fisher here too, since Pigou explicitly refers to *The Purchasing Power of Money*, though not with reference to this topic, in *Wealth and Welfare*.

15. The Keynesian revolution, with its stress on the role of fixed investment was to shift the emphasis to the long rate of interest. Hawtrey's stress on short rates is, of course, a logical consequence of putting the interaction of cyclically fluctuating inflation expectations with real and nominal interest rates at the heart of the cyclical mechanism.

16. Hawtrey was explicitly criticised for placing such exclusive reliance on monetary factors both by Pigou (1913b) and Robertson (1915) (cf. Note 2, above).

17. The reader's attention is drawn to the similarity between Hawtrey's account of cash-balance mechanics and those of Fisher (see Chapter 3, page 77) and Wicksell (see Chapter 5, pages 126–7). It should be stressed however that he deploys this analysis not as a description of any real world transmission process, but only in the context of a hypothetical expository exercise. For Hawtrey, as we shall see, the transmission mechanism in the real world ran through interest rates.

18. The reader will note that there is at this point a certain inconsistency in Hawtrey's treatment of price–wage interaction. Here we have something which looks very like a suggestion of mark-up pricing, which if taken seriously would be hard indeed to square with the proposition that money wages lag behind money prices over the course of the cycle.

19. 'Legal tender money' was a common synonym for currency in British usage. See for example Pigou (1917) for another example.

20. Hawtrey's decision to stress monetary factors was not taken without a discussion of the possibility that real shocks might be important. He dismissed this possibility on the grounds that real shocks impinge upon particular markets, and that the cycle is an economy-wide phenomenon (see 1913, Chapter 11). In this his reasoning was similar to that of Juglar (1860). Pigou, of course, was well aware of this problem, which was why he spent so much effort establishing the possibility that the forecasting errors of individual businessmen might be correlated with each other. It is also why Pigou was attracted to the Jevonian hypotheses concerning the role of harvests in the cycle. Agriculture was a sector large enough that shocks arising there might be expected to have economy-wide repercussions. On the role of expectations in Jevons' analysis of how cyclical fluctuations, originating in the agricultural sector, could be amplified, and the influence of that analysis on Pigou, see Peart (1990).

21. Here as with Fisher, it is worth drawing attention to this departure of Hawtrey from the standard classical practice of treating open economy considerations in general, and the external drain in particular, as of critical importance to the cycle. Perhaps what we see here is some influence running from Fisher's work to Hawtrey's, or perhaps the

influence of American experience. He does remark in his 1961 Foreword to the book (page vii) that it was the American crisis of 1907 which he had in mind when writing *Good and Bad Trade*.

22. We should note though that the discussions of Carver (1903) and Albert Aftalion (1909) referred to by John Chipman (1987) appear to antedate any English exposition of the accelerator. Robertson's understanding of the mechanism seems to have derived from his reading of Aftalion.

23. Gottfried Haberler's (1937) *Prosperity and Depression* remains a superb survey of cycle theory, including the rich interwar literature, and provides ample evidence to support the claim that monetary theories of the cycle, in the sense that the phrase might be applied to Fisher's or Hawtrey's analysis, were very much a minority taste.

24. As Patinkin (1976) has correctly stressed, it was not until Keynes' (1936) analysis of the equilibrating role of output fluctuations that economics acquired a logically coherent method of analysing these matters.

25. See Jevons' suggestion (1863, reprinted 1884, page 27), that the key to the cycle 'seems to lie in the *varying proportion which the capital devoted to permanent and remote investment bears to that which is but temporarily invested soon to reproduce itself*' (Jevons' italics). He did not follow up this insight in his subsequent studies of cyclical phenomena.

5 • Wicksell and the quantity theory

Introduction

Knut Wicksell's work was seminal to intellectual developments that, in the twentieth century, were to discredit the quantity theory of money among the majority of academic economists. The dynamic economics of the Stockholm School started from his analysis of inflation as a cumulative process; so did the Austrian business cycle theory of Mises, Hayek and Robbins; and Keynes' *Treatise on Money* (1930) betrays an explicitly acknowledged Wicksellian influence, which also marks the *General Theory* (1936). And yet Wicksell himself, in Bertil Ohlin's (1936) words, 'always insisted that this reasoning [the cumulative process model of inflation] did not mean more than an amplification of the old quantity theory' (page viii). Furthermore, and as we shall soon see, the amplified version of the quantity theory which Wicksell developed differs at first sight only slightly from Marshall's. As we shall also see though, if we view Wicksell's work with hindsight informed by knowledge of the above-mentioned subsequent developments in monetary economics, the differences between him and Marshall (not to mention Fisher) turn out to be more important.

Three readily available accounts by Wicksell of his monetary thought are available in English. Of these, two are comprehensive, namely *Interest and Prices* (1898, translated 1936) and *Lectures on Political Economy* Vol. II (revised edn 1915, translated 1935), and the third is a short article in the *Economic Journal* (1907b).[1] The first two form the major sources of this chapter, and differ in that the earlier one is a monograph largely devoted to setting out Wicksell's own ideas, while the latter expounds those ideas in the course of a more general survey of monetary economics. The fact that the analysis of *Interest and Prices* is more detailed and precise than that of the later work is surely mainly explained by this fact, for there is no essential difference between the *theoretical* content of the two books. When it comes to claims about the *empirical* relevance of that theoretical content, however, those made in the *Lectures* are a little more modest. The reasons for this will be discussed in due course; but before we come to the empirical relevance of Wicksell's theoretical ideas, we need to be clear about what they were. The first task of this chapter is to set out Wicksell's views on the quantity theory in relation to the ideas of his contemporaries, paying particular attention to his efforts to remedy what he believed to be its analytic weaknesses.

Cost of production and the quantity theory

Like Fisher and the Cambridge School, Wicksell was acutely aware of the tension inherent in classical monetary economics' simultaneous adherence to two potentially competing theories of the value of money, namely the quantity theory and the cost of production theory of value; and like them he treated the former as the more correct and general theory, within whose framework cost of production effects might have a role to play. Wicksell, however, was working in a German language tradition, where in the work of both Marxians and the Historical School, the cost of production theory of value played a major role.[2] That is why he took very seriously those who treated the two approaches as alternatives, going out of his way to attack:

> Karl Marx and his school who generally carry the classical theory of value to its extreme, and consequently to the point of absurdity, [and who] adhere to the cost of production theory as a simple and tangible explanation of the value of money and oppose it to the Quantity Theory (Wicksell, 1915, page 147).

Chapter 4 of *Interest and Prices* bears the title 'The so-called cost of production theory of money' and begins with the following (implicitly anti-Marxian) assertion:

> No theorist can to-day lend his support to the traditional conception that money possesses in itself an independent, and more or less invariable, intrinsic value, against which the exchange values of real

commodities are, as it were, compared or measured . . . the modern
theory of value must have put a definite end to this approach
(Wicksell, 1898, page 29).

Though Wicksell was willing to concede the logical possibility
implicit in the above-mentioned 'modern theory of value' that the
purchasing power of a commodity money might be given exoge-
nously to the monetary sector because it was 'determined more or
less completely, through the influence of other markets in which it
appears as a commodity proper' (1898, page 29), he immediately
went on to deny the contemporary empirical relevance of this
possibility.[3]

> But the case is a different one where the employment of the money
> commodity as an article of use, and particularly its *actual* consump-
> tion . . . have come to occupy a position altogether secondary to its
> employment as a medium of exchange, and where, in addition, the
> yearly production results only in a relatively slow increase in
> monetary stocks. Such is the case with the precious metals standard
> of today, and with the instruments of exchange that are based upon
> it (1898, page 30; Wicksell's italics).

Here, and in parallel passages in the *Lectures* (pages 146–53), he
cites Senior's (1840) account of the theory of the price level as the
basis of his argument that changes in the cost of production of the
precious metals will, under such circumstances, influence the price
level only to the extent that they lead to changes in the quantity of
money. Furthermore, he notes that to introduce the more precise
concept of marginal production cost into the analysis forces one to
the conclusion that it, and the value of money, are simultaneously
determined endogenous variables, making it impossible to argue
that one variable determines the other. The upshot is that:

> The cost of production theory is thus fully justified as constituting *an
> element* in the Quantity Theory. But only one element. Since the
> annual production of gold, even in the most favourable circum-
> stances, can only increase the existing stocks of gold coin by a few
> per cent, changes in output will only gradually, and as a rule very
> slowly, exert their influence (1915, page 149; Wicksell's italics).

As a practical matter,

it is precisely changes in prices and fluctuations in the value of money

> over relatively *short* periods – ten, fifteen or twenty years – which have the most serious consequences for trade. The more gradual changes . . . are of far less importance . . . it is just when enlightenment is most urgently needed that this [cost of production] theory leaves us sadly in the lurch (1898, page 33; Wicksell's italics).

Nor was Wicksell any kinder to other alternatives to the quantity theory proposed by his contemporaries. Like Fisher, he had no time for the ideas of Laughlin, and in particular Laughlin's denial of the quantity theory's relevance even in the case of inconvertible money based on relating its current purchasing power to 'the hope of the future convertibility of the notes into metal' (1915, page 151). Here he argued, just as did Fisher, that expected appreciation of paper would reduce its quantity *in circulation* and influence the current price levels via this route. What we would now call the 'backing' theory of the value of money was thus treated as encompassed by the quantity theory. As to the Austrian idea, nowadays usually associated with Mises, that:

> it is the image of the actual metallic currency into which the notes were at one time convertible before they were declared legal tender which remains in the mind of the public and thereby to some extent maintains the value of the notes (1915, page 151)

it was placed, along with Laughlin's analysis, in the category of 'most perverse and fantastic explanations' (1915, page 151).[4]
For Wicksell, then,

> The only specific theory of the value of money which has been propounded, and perhaps the only one which can make any claim to real scientific importance, is the Quantity Theory, according to which the value or purchasing power of money varies in inverse proportion to its quantity (1915, page 141).

But in conceding 'scientific importance' to the quantity theory, Wicksell certainly did not also signify wholehearted acceptance of any version of the doctrine. The quantity theory, as he understood it, might provide 'a real explanation of its subject matter . . . but only on assumptions that unfortunately have little relation to practice, and in some respects none whatsoever' (1898, page 41). He identified two problems with the theory in question. First, there was the matter of its all important *ceteris paribus* clause which held equal 'some

of the flimsiest and most intangible factors in the whole of economics
. . . in particular the velocity of circulation of money' (1898, page 42).
Second, there was the question of the transmission mechanism:

> That a large and a small quantity of money *can* serve the same
> purpose of turnover if commodity prices rise or fall proportionately
> to the quantity is one thing. It is another thing to show why such a
> change of price must always follow a change in the quantity of
> money and to describe what happens (1915, page 160).

Because Wicksell was conscious of 'the folly of supposing that
circumstances in which . . . there is an essential relation between two
things – goods and money – can ever be satisfactorily explained from
the point of view of . . . only one of them' (1915, page 151), he saw
that:

> A general rise in prices is . . . only conceivable on the supposition
> that the general demand has for some reason become, or is expected
> to become, greater than the supply. This may sound paradoxical,
> because we have accustomed ourselves, with J. B. Say, to regard
> goods themselves as reciprocally constituting and limiting the
> demand for each other. And indeed *ultimately* they do so; here,
> however, we are concerned with precisely what occurs, *in the first
> place*, with the middle link in the final exchange of one good against
> another, which is formed by the demand of money for goods and the
> supply of goods against money (1915, page 159; Wicksell's italics).

As this quotation shows, Wicksell understood far more clearly than
had Mill (1844), and indeed just as clearly as Patinkin (1956), that
the 'classical dichotomy' between theories of relative prices and the
general price level could not be generally valid, and had to be
abandoned if the causative mechanisms bringing about price level
variations were to be analysed.[5] The mechanisms in question
differed, however, between two theoretically limiting cases, namely
the pure cash economy to which the quantity theory applied, and
the pure credit economy to which it was irrelevant.

The pure cash economy

No modern exponent of the quantity theory can avoid the awkward
question of how to specify empirically the 'money stock' variable
which is so central to that theory, but there is nothing new about

this question. As we have already seen in earlier chapters, it puzzled monetary economists throughout the nineteenth century, because then, as now, the institutional framework of the financial sector was undergoing a process of constant development which clearly influenced the economy's exchange mechanisms.[6] Even as late as the turn of the century, the word 'money' was normally used to refer to what we would now call 'currency' – i.e. notes and coin in circulation – and there was no consensus as to how to modify the quantity theory of money to accommodate the existence of deposit banks and the credit facilities which they made available to the business community. Fisher (1911) recognised that chequable deposits circulated just as surely as did notes and coin, and incorporated their quantity and velocity as separate variables in his formulation of the equation of exchange; while the Cambridge economists (but not Hawtrey nor exceptionally Pigou (1912)), in accordance with traditional usage, more often focused on the supply and demand for a stock of currency, and treated bank deposits as an alternative way of holding 'titles to legal tender' (the phrase is taken from Pigou (1917)), the existence of which would affect the demand for 'legal tender', or currency, itself.

Wicksell took the same line as the Cambridge School but in a more thoroughgoing way. When he analysed what he termed 'a pure cash economy', by which he meant one completely devoid of credit relations, whether direct between buyers and seller, or indirect between the debtors and creditors of a banking system, he defined velocity as 'the average number of times the available pieces of *money* change hands during the unit of time' (1898, page 52; my italics), thus treating 'cash' and 'money' as synonyms.[7] He maintained this usage when he extended his analysis to the cases of 'simple credit' and 'an organised credit economy', remarking with respect to the theoretically limiting case of the latter, in which all transactions are effected through the transfer of bank deposits, that in such circumstances, 'there is no real need for any money at all' and that the banks 'would require *no stock of cash*' (1898, page 68; Wicksell's italics). These matters of usage are worth explicit attention for two reasons. First, and obviously, it is easy to misunderstand much of what Wicksell has to say about the quantity theory of *money* unless one bears in mind what he means by that word. Second, and far more important, Wicksell did not, as did Fisher or Hawtrey, apply the concept of velocity to bank deposits.

That is why, in the above-mentioned limiting case of a 'pure credit economy', the quantity theory of money was presented as irrelevant, rather than merely in need of modification to accommodate a different money concept. The point is semantic, as Patinkin (1965, page 588) noted, but semantics nevertheless affected the substance of Wicksell's analysis.

We will discuss the pure credit economy case below. Here we shall discuss Wicksell's treatment of the quantity theory in the context of the opposite abstraction, namely, the above mentioned 'pure cash economy', where his exposition was based on a version of the cash-balance approach.[8] He began by noting 'that the purely physical conditions under which money can be paid and transported set a definite limit to the magnitude of the velocity of circulation' (1898, page 54), but only as a preliminary step to arguing that:

> [t]here is . . . an important factor which sets both upper and lower limits to the magnitude of the velocity of circulation. It is the time during which each piece of money has to lie unused in the till between two successive payments (1898, page 55).

He made this 'interval of rest' of money, which he explicitly characterised as 'the reciprocal of [the] velocity of circulation' (1898, page 52), the centrepiece of his analysis, picturing it as depending upon three factors. The first of these boils down to what we would now call the 'transactions motive'. In general 'technical and natural features' affect 'the size of the cash holding' (1898, page 56) and in a cash economy 'the most essential cash holdings are those which are destined for definite payments at given points of time in the future' (1898, page 57). Wicksell then proceeded to discuss the influence on money holding of 'those more or less *unforeseen* disbursements which occur in every business' (1898, page 57; Wicksell's italics), and developed a simple analysis of what we would now term the 'precautionary motive', based explicitly on an application of probability theory.

> Suppose that experience has shown that . . . the excess of payments over simultaneous receipts . . . tends to oscillate from year to year about a certain mean value, a. Let the 'probable deviation' be b: this means that the odds are even . . . in favour of payments . . . over the period . . . lying between $a + b$ and $a - b$. If the business man is satisfied with this so-called simple margin of safety, he must have by

him a cash holding of $a + b$. . . . With a cash holding of as little as $a + 2b$, the betting on the total exhaustion of his till over the period in question would, according to the laws of probability, be more than 9 to 1; with a cash holding of $a + 3b$ it would be more than 44 to 1 (1898, pages 57–8).

Though Wicksell conceded that '[t]he business man has never heard of the Calculus of Probability', he also argued that 'his empirical line of reasoning' would lead him to maintain precautionary money holdings whose 'stability becomes even more marked when it is the average of all businesses in a particular field that is under consideration' (1898, page 58).

Wicksell's third factor influencing money's average interval of rest in a cash economy was not, of course, akin to the Keynesian 'speculative motive', because there are no bonds in such an economy; but it did involve the temporary holding by the wealthy of 'considerable sums of money [which] accumulate from time to time . . . as a result of the sale of individual blocks of capital or the like' (1898, page 58), and it was likely to introduce an element of instability to velocity. However, he paid only passing attention to this possibility, concluding that, in the pure cash economy, 'the average interval of rest, and consequently the average velocity of circulation of money, is of almost constant magnitude' (1898, page 59).

The details of Wicksell's theorising about the demand for money in some respects went deeper than those of either Fisher or the Cambridge School. Nothing in their work parallels his analysis of different motives for money holding, particularly his application of probability theory in this context.[9] Even so, the theorising in question yielded nothing new in the way of predictions about the behaviour of velocity, which Wicksell believed would be 'almost constant' in a cash economy. Nor did he add anything to the analysis of the transmission mechanism in such an economy. We might admire the clarity of the following exposition of cash-balance mechanics, particularly given its date of composition, but there is nothing of substance in it that cannot also be found in the works of Fisher and the Cambridge School.[10]

Now let us suppose that for some reason or other commodity prices rise while the stock of money remains unchanged, or that the stock of money is diminished while prices remain temporarily unchanged.

The cash balances will gradually appear *to be too small in relation to the new level of prices.* . . . I therefore seek to enlarge my balance. This can only be done . . . through a *reduction* in my *demand* for goods and services, or through an *increase* in the *supply* of my own . . . or through both together. The same is true of all other owners and consumers of commodities. But in fact nobody will succeed in realizing the object at which each is aiming – to increase his cash balance; for the sum of individual cash balances is limited by the amount of the available stock of money, or rather is identical with it. On the other hand, the universal reduction in demand and increase in supply of commodities will necessarily bring about a continuous fall in all prices. This can only cease when prices have fallen to the level at which the cash balances are regarded as *adequate*. (In the first case prices will now have fallen to their original level.) (1898, pages 39–40; Wicksell's italics.)

If Wicksell had done no more than analyse the quantity theory of money in the cash economy case, he would now be remembered, not so much as an original thinker, but more as a capable exponent of conventional ideas. However, he dealt with this case not as an end in itself, but simply as a starting point for his treatment of an economy characterised by highly developed credit institutions. This matter had of course occupied every monetary economist from Adam Smith onwards, not least Wicksell's contemporaries in England and the United States, but none of them dealt with it with the depth and care which marked his work.

Credit and the velocity of money

Like any other quantity theorist, Wicksell understood that '[e]very change in the normal velocity of circulation of money must . . . be regarded as acting in the same way' on prices as 'a change in the actual amount of money' (1915, page 168), and when he introduced credit into the picture, variations in velocity replaced variations in the quantity of money as the main source of price fluctuations. For him credit was 'the great and principal agent in accelerating or retarding the velocity of circulation' (1915, page 169), whether it was 'simple credit', essentially trade credit arrangements between agents with ongoing commercial relations, or 'organised credit' involving the operations of commercial banks. The former would enable agents to dispense with money held for financing regular and foreseen transactions (cf. 1898, page 57) but its effects were not nearly as significant as those of organised credit. The existence of a banking system gave agents another opportunity to dispense with transactions balances, and also enabled them to avoid temporarily holding large blocks of wealth in the form of money. Indeed, it reduced the significance of any kind of money holding because it also facilitated the reduction of precautionary balances. This latter effect was partly due to 'the regularity of chance, the "Law of Large Numbers", but still more to the real interdependence of firms, a payment by one firm resulting, directly and indirectly, in a corresponding receipt by another' (1898, page 66), and its result was that:

> The greater the number of the bank's customers, and the more diverse their occupations and their positions in life, the smaller is the stock of cash which the bank has to maintain in relation to the total extent of its business; and the greater *pro tanto* is the velocity of circulation of money (1898, page 68).

In the limiting case 'all payments could be effected by . . . bookkeeping transfers, except possibly those for which small change suffices' (1898, page 68), so that '[i]n a developed credit economy . . . the velocity of circulation is *capable* of being increased more or less at will' (1898, page 62; Wicksell's italics).

The italicisation of the word 'capable' here is important. The accounts which Wicksell gave of the workings of 'a developed credit economy', both in *Interest and Prices* and *The Lectures*, show that he sometimes thought in terms of an economy in which bank credit completely replaced what he called money, and that he also treated this case as a practical possibility for the future. However, they also attest to his understanding that:

> a state of affairs in which money does not actually circulate at all, neither in the form of coin (except perhaps as small change) nor in the form of notes, but where all domestic payments are effected by means of the *Giro* system and bookkeeping transfers (1898, page 70)

did not adequately describe the pre-World War I monetary system which he was at pains to understand. He referred the pure credit economy as a 'purely imaginary case . . . a precise antithesis to the equally imaginary case of a pure cash system' and characterised '[t]he monetary systems actually employed in various countries . . . as *combinations* of these two extreme types' (1898, page 70; Wicksell's italics). However, Wicksell went on to argue,

> [i]f we can obtain a clear picture of the causes responsible for the value of money in *both* these imaginary cases, we shall . . . have found the right key to a solution of the complications which monetary phenomena exhibit in practice (1898, pages 70–1).

Hence he treated the pure credit economy case in which the quantity theory was, in his eyes, rendered irrelevant by the complete absence of 'money', in even more detail than its antithesis, and, as we shall now see, with a great deal more originality.

Interest rates and inflation

Wicksell's understanding of the limits to the validity of Say's Law in a monetary economy was exceptionally clear. He saw that, if prices in general were to change, it must be as a consequence of an excess demand or supply of goods in general, and that in the cash economy case, this required that an excess supply or demand for money set in motion conventional cash balance mechanics. In a pure credit economy which he thought of as being devoid of money, however, this cannot work. Some other channel of causation is required to change the nominal prices of goods, and Wicksell sought and found it in an interest rate mechanism. He was well aware that he was by no means the first economist to analyse the interaction of interest rates and prices. Extensive passages in *Interest and Prices* and *The Lectures* deal with the treatment of this matter by English classical economists, notably Ricardo and Tooke.[11] Moreover, Wicksell was familiar with the evidence Marshall presented to the Gold and Silver Commission in 1889 on the role of the interest rate in the 'transmission mechanism'; and he also knew Fisher's (1896) analysis of the influence of expected inflation on nominal interest rates. Nevertheless, it was his knowledge of the capital theory of Jevons and Eugen von Boehm-Bawerk, to whose development he was himself a major contributor, which prompted him to say new and important, though not always entirely satisfactory, things about these matters.[12]

The heart of Wicksell's contribution lies in his distinction between the *market* or *money* rate of interest, that charged by banks on their loans to customers, and the *neutral, normal, real* or *natural* rate of interest, which he defined in a variety of ways. In *Interest and Prices* he characterised it as follows:

> There is a certain rate of interest on loans which is neutral in respect to commodity prices, and tends neither to raise nor to lower them. This is necessarily the same as the rate of interest which would be determined by supply and demand if no use were made of money and all lending were in the form of real capital goods (1898, page 102).

In the *Lectures*, (Volume II) we find this definition:

> The rate of interest at which *the demand for loan capital and the supply of savings* exactly agree, and which more or less corresponds to the expected yield on the newly created capital, will then be the normal or natural real rate (1915, page 193; Wicksell's italics).

And in the *Economic Journal* we are told that 'the profit on capital . . . is determined by the productivity and relative abundance of real capital, or in the terms of modern political economy, by its *marginal productivity*' (1907b, page 214; Wicksell's italics).

Even if we set aside the by now well understood problems of relating an economy-wide rate of profit or interest to the marginal product of some aggregate called 'capital', and Wicksell was well aware of these, there are still difficulties here.[13] Why should flows of saving and investment just be equal at a rate of interest equal to the marginal product of capital per unit of capital? Why should that value of the rate of interest which equates savings and investment in a barter economy also do so in a money economy? And will prices be constant if banks charge this rate for loans, regardless of the pace at which the economy is growing? Wicksell never discussed these questions explicitly, and in his most careful analysis of the interaction of the market and natural rates of interest, that contained in Chapter 9 (Systematic exposition of the theory) of *Interest and Prices*, he made precisely the right set of assumptions to render his potentially incompatible definitions of the natural rate of interest equivalent to one another (and to give the marginal productivity of capital per unit of capital the dimension of a pure rate of flow per unit of time into the bargain!). He also claimed, however, that those assumptions were 'made purely for the sake of simplicity and clarity; not a single one of them is essential to the validity of the general conclusion' (1898, page 136).[14]

Wicksell explicitly told readers of *Interest and Prices* that they could safely omit the above-mentioned Chapter 9 (cf. 1898, page 121), but though it is more difficult than the rest of the book, this chapter also displays more clearly than any other source both the depth of, and limits to, Wicksell's understanding of the interaction of interest rates and the price level, not least the extent to which his notion of the natural rate of interest derives from the capital theory of Jevons and the Austrians (cf. pages 122–34). Moreover, and precisely because its analysis is presented in terms of an explicit model, a modern reader will feel more comfortable with it than with other accounts, which are unacceptably loose by present-day standards (which were *not* however, those ruling at the turn of the century).[15]

Wicksell's model economy is inhabited by no fewer than four types of agent: entrepreneurs who hire labour and fixed capital (including land) to produce output; the owners of those inputs, henceforth subsumed under the label 'workers'; banks, which borrow from capitalists and lend to entrepreneurs; and the just-mentioned capitalists, who in addition act as middlemen in the output market, buying goods from entrepreneurs and selling them to workers. Furthermore:

> capital goods which have been invested for a long time ('rent earning goods') are subject to no other change than the repairs . . . necessary for their maintenance . . . liquid real capital which has to be renewed year by year is maintained by the capitalists at a constant amount . . . the length of the period of production is the same in every business, and amounts to one year . . . production begins everywhere at the same moment of time . . . and . . . the final product, the consumption goods, are not completed or available for exchange until the end of the year (1898, page 136).

The assumption of zero capital accumulation here disposes of those problems, alluded to earlier, having to do with the maintenance of simultaneous stock and flow equilibrium in the capital market, and as we shall see in a moment, it also helps to ensure that zero nominal credit expansion on the part of the banks will produce a constant price level. Moreover, the assumption of a uniform period of production for all types of consumption goods, which also form the stock of liquid capital, eliminates that interdependence between the structure of relative prices and the rate of interest which lies at the heart of the difficulties, also alluded to above, of constructing a single index that simultaneously measures capital and its marginal product.[16]

To complete Wicksell's scheme, it is only necessary to specify the timing of transactions over the period of production. The typical year begins with *last* year's output in the hands of capitalists, and entrepreneurs making their plans for *this* year's activities. The latter decide upon their nominal expenditure on inputs, and take interest-bearing loans from the banks to finance it. Workers (and other inputs) are hired for the year, paid in advance, and immediately purchase from the capitalists the stock of consumption goods which will support them during the period of production. Production then begins with entrepreneurs indebted to the banks, and capitalists holding the matching (and interest-bearing) liabilities. At the end of the period, output is realised in an amount equal to the initial stock of circulating capital plus profits. This is sold to capitalists in exchange for their bank liabilities, gross of interest, which sum is just sufficient to enable entrepreneurs to pay off their loans, including interest charges, to the bank. Capitalists take, for their own consumption, goods equal in value to their interest income, and hold the remainder in anticipation of their sale at the beginning of the next period. Clearly, this scenario leaves entrepreneurs and banks with zero incomes, but, equally clearly, nothing essential to the model hinges upon this assumption, and Wicksell did in fact soften it in the course of his exposition (cf. 1898, page 140).

Wicksell sets his economy going on the assumption that the 'contractual rate of interest' (1898, page 139) which the banks charge entrepreneurs is equal to the natural rate (the ratio of the difference between output and the stock of circulating capital to the stock). A modern economist, versed in the mechanics of rational expectations modelling, would conclude that in such circumstances the price level is indeterminate. The nominal amount which the representative entrepreneur is willing to borrow to finance production will depend upon the revenue expected to be realised from the sale of output at the end of the period; but the model's structure ensures that, in the aggregate, the latter sum will be equal to the former, plus interest. Any agent understanding the model's structure will, then, also understand that any volume of nominal borrowing, and therefore any price level, is sustainable.[17] This, however, was *not* Wicksell's conclusion. Though he understood perfectly well that the borrowing decision depended upon expectations about output price, he anchored the relevant expectations in experience, and assumed that 'entrepreneurs are not reckoning . . . on any future rise in prices' (1898, page 144).

As Ohlin (1936, page xii) noted, 'The assertion that business calculations are as a rule made on the basis of current prices would not have withstood much criticism', but this was always (though often implicitly) Wicksell's assumption when he discussed situations in which the market and natural rates of interest were equal. Moreover, he usually maintained it when he analysed the early stages of the economy's reaction to a discrepancy between the two rates as well. The effect of this assumption was, of course, to select a unique value for entrepreneurs' expected nominal receipts, and to ensure that the volume of nominal borrowing, and hence the price level, would remain constant over time so long as the market and natural rates of interest remained equal to one another. But Wicksell was concerned with the consequences for the price level of a discrepancy arising between the two rates, and in Chapter 9 of *Interest and Prices* he introduced it by postulating an increase in the natural rate of interest. He noted that '[i]n the first place [the gain from this increase] accrues to the entrepreneurs' (1898, page 141). With nothing else changed, all of the transactions that have previously gone through can still be completed, with the extra output implied by an increase in the yield of a (by assumption) given capital stock remaining for entrepreneurs' own consumption. Since this gain in consumption, however, is proportional to the scale of production, each entrepreneur now has an incentive to expand operations, and hence to increase borrowing from the banks in order to bid for extra inputs. In Wicksell's words,

> If entrepreneurs continue, year after year perhaps, to realise some surplus profit of this kind, the result can only be to set up a tendency for an expansion of their activities. I emphasise . . . that . . . it is purely a question of a *tendency*. An *actual* expansion of production is quite impossible, for it would necessitate an increase in the supply of real factors of production. . . . The *tendency* towards an expansion of output . . . brings about an increase in the demand for labour and other factors of production. . . . Money wages and

money rents are forced up, and although there is no general expansion in production, entrepreneurs are obliged to borrow more capital from the banks for the production of the current year (1898, pages 143–4; Wicksell's italics).

As before, a modern economist would attribute an essential indeterminacy to the process under analysis, stemming this time from the fundamental disequilibrium forced upon this economy by the discrepancy between the natural and money rates of interest; but though Wicksell conceded that 'It is impossible to tell directly how much wages will go up, and therefore by how much industrial capital has to be increased' he argued that 'on our assumption it is possible to fix a limit.' It is not clear just which 'assumption' is being referred to here, but perhaps it is that 'entrepreneurs are not reckoning for the moment on any rise in [output] prices' (1898, page 144). Apparently Wicksell believed that this condition was enough to ensure that entrepreneurs would be willing to add to their nominal factor payments no more than the current value of the windfall in consumption goods that the increase in the natural rate of interest has made available, or, in Wicksell's words, 'the upper limit to the possible rise in wages is the fall [sic] in the rate of interest' (1898, page 144).[18]

Wicksell then goes on to show that, because increased nominal payments to inputs find their way into the hands of capitalists in exchange for the stock of consumption goods produced last period, and because the market interest rate which entrepreneurs pay and capitalists receive is still below the natural rate, the former are, at the end of the period, able to sell the same quantity of goods to the latter as they did previously, but at a higher price. He also shows that this higher price enables them to meet their higher nominal indebtedness without being forced to sell the extra output conferred upon them by the higher natural rate of interest. Hence, the incentives that led to credit expansion and inflation in the first place remain exactly as they did at the outset, and the process repeats itself period after period for as long as the discrepancy between natural and market interest rates persists. Indeed, inflation may accelerate as entrepreneurs come to expect output prices to rise and take account of this in their borrowing decisions.

It is possible in this way to picture a steady, and more or less uniform, rise in all wages, rents, and prices (as expressed in money). But once the entrepreneurs begin to rely upon this process continuing – as soon, that is to say, as they start reckoning on a future rise in prices – the actual rise will become more and more rapid. In the extreme case in which the expected rise in prices is each time *fully* discounted, the annual rise in prices will be indefinitely great (1898, page 148; Wicksell's italics).

Wicksell's flirtation in the last sentence of this passage with rational expectations is not the only one to occur in his writings, but neither here nor anywhere else does he make anything of the idea. Backward looking, and indeed static, expectations were enough to generate an ongoing inflationary process in his analysis, and he usually stuck with these postulates.[19]

The cumulative process and the quantity theory

Now the model which Wicksell analyses in Chapter 9 of *Interest and Prices* with, by the standards of his time, such extraordinary care is of a pure credit economy. As we have seen, he regarded such analysis, not as an end in itself, but as a step to understanding a real world in which both money and credit had roles to play. Moreover, though price changes cumulate over time in the pure credit economy, the inflationary mechanism at work there does not, in and of itself, constitute the 'cumulative process' which we associate with Wicksell's name.[20] Rather it is one component of that process. The key insight yielded by Wicksell's analysis is that, in the words of his *Economic Journal* article,

> If, other things remaining the same, all the leading banks of the world were to lower their rate of interest, say 1 per cent below its ordinary level, and keep it so for some years, then the prices of all commodities would rise and rise and rise without any limit whatever (1907b, page 213).

The prediction here is a conditional one, and in the world to which Wicksell wished to apply his analysis, the conditions in question could not be fully met. The economy of that world was (in Wicksell's sense of the word) a 'money' using economy, and under the Gold Standard, a commodity money at that. As a matter of fact then,

> under actual conditions there is a considerable quantity of coin in circulation – or of notes, which under the banking laws of many

countries comes to the same thing. . . . A rise in prices exerts its influence, not only on the relation between the production and consumption of gold, but to a much more important extent on the demands of the monetary circulation. The quantity of coins and notes circulating in the hands of the public is usually much larger than the available reserves of the banks. It follows that quite a small rise in prices may bring about a very significant contraction of the banks' reserves (1898, pages 113-14).

In turn this drain of reserves will induce the banks to raise their lending rate of interest so that '[i]t is thus confidently to be expected that . . . the money rate of interest . . . will always coincide *eventually* with the natural capital rate' (1898, page 117; Wicksell's italics). Thus, for Wicksell, a discrepancy between the natural and money rates of interest sets in motion a 'cumulative process' in which *rising prices induce a tendency for the discrepancy in question to be closed by a rising money rate of interest.*

Now modern economists, equipped with the notions of a stable desired reserve deposit ratio for the banks, and a stable desired currency deposit ratio for the non-bank public, (both of which ideas are to be found in Fisher's *Purchasing Power of Money*) are inclined to see Wicksell's analysis of the cumulative process as being, first and foremost, a useful elaboration of the mechanisms whereby an influx of the money commodity, whether from newly discovered mines in the case of the world economy, or through the balance of payments in the case of a single open economy, would lead on to a new, higher and *stable* equilibrium price level by way of a temporary disturbance to the money rate of interest. Hence they see it as a supplement to the traditional quantity theory particularly relevant to an open economy with a well-developed banking system. That, however, is not quite how Wicksell saw it. He was well aware of the possibilities of this line of reasoning from his studies of the classical literature, and from Marshall's evidence to the Gold and Silver Commission, but he asserted that 'Marshall seems to me to lay too much emphasis on the *direct* influence that he alleges is exerted by the magnitude of banking reserves on the rate of interest and consequently on prices' (1898, page 76; Wicksell's italics).

It is of the essence of the quantity theory that it pictures the typical disturbance to the price level being a change in the quantity of money, or at least the banking system's reserve base. This was certainly Wicksell's interpretation of the theory – 'the explanation suggested by the Quantity Theory [is] that rising prices are due to the excess of money, falling prices to a scarcity' (1898, page 166), but in *Interest and Prices*, he argues that in fact the typical disturbance to the price level arises in the real economy, not in the monetary sector. The quotation used above to illustrate his account of the role of a rising money rate of interest in bringing the cumulative process to an end tells us that 'the money rate of interest . . . will always coincide *eventually* with the natural capital rate' but continues as follows 'or rather . . . it is always *tending* to coincide with an ever-changing natural rate' (1898, page 117; Wicksell's italics). There is no sign in *Interest and Prices* of a postulate that either the banking system's reserve deposit ratio or the public's currency deposit ratio is stable. Moreover, in that book, Wicksell treated the concept of stable equilibrium, which is of course central to the quantity theory as it was (and indeed is) usually expounded, as being *almost* irrelevant to the analysis of price level behaviour once the pure cash economy assumption was abandoned. He is worth quoting at some length on this point.[21]

the movement and equilibrium of actual money prices represent a fundamentally different phenomenon, above all in a fully developed credit system, from those of *relative* prices. The latter might perhaps be compared with a mechanical system which satisfies the conditions of *stable* equilibrium, for instance a pendulum. Every movement away from the position of equilibrium sets forces into operation – on a scale that increases with the extent of the movement – which tend to restore the system to its original position, and actually succeed in doing so, though some oscillations may intervene.

The analogous picture for *money* prices should rather be some easily movable object, such as a cylinder, which rests on a horizontal plane in so-called *neutral* equilibrium. The plane is somewhat rough and a certain force is required to set the price-cylinder in motion and to keep it in motion. But so long as this force – the raising or lowering of the rate of interest – remains in operation, the cylinder continues to move in the same direction. Indeed it will, after a time, start 'rolling': the motion is an accelerated one up to a certain point, and it continues for a time even when the force has ceased to operate. Once the cylinder has come to rest, there is no tendency for it to be restored to the original position. It simply remains where it is so long as no opposite forces come into operation to push it back.

It is, of course, clear that such forces can never be entirely absent, no matter how developed the credit system may be, if a precious metal . . . serves as a monetary basis. The simple quantity theory is no longer adequate to deal with the nature of these reactions, and with the manner of the operation (1898, pages 100–1; Wicksell's italics).

Wicksell's account of this matter in the *Lectures* appears similar at first sight; but closer inspection reveals a subtle, but suggestive, difference of emphasis. The reader who turns to pages 196 of that work will find an explicit reference to, followed by what amounts to a paraphrase of, the above discussion of stable and meta-stable equilibria. Now, however, the concept of a meta-stable equilibrium is said to be relevant not '*above all* in a fully developed credit system' (1898, page 100; my italics) but simply 'on the assumption of a monetary system of unlimited elasticity' (1915, page 197). Furthermore, the paraphrase in question is followed by a passage which begins:

> This conclusion [about the meta-stability of equilibrium in a monetary system of unlimited elasticity] . . . is in full agreement with what would occur if prices rose in consequence of an actual superfluity of gold, if the new gold came into the hands of the public in the form of loans from the banks' (1915, pages 197–8).

This passage then goes on to expound precisely the transmission mechanism, which Marshall had sketched out in 1889 (see page 66 above), whereby such a price increase is brought about, although it also warns the reader that:

> This [i.e. new gold coming into the hands of the public in the form of new loans from the banks] is certainly not usually the case, for gold flows into the country from abroad to some extent directly in payment for goods. In such a case it should immediately give rise to an increase in commodity prices, and this increase may even precede the arrival of the gold, so that in relation to the continually rising price level there may be no excess of gold and consequently no reason for lowering the rate of interest (1915, page 198).

Wicksell had, then, by 1915 become less dismissive of the importance of gold, and hence currency supply changes, as opposed to velocity shifts, as explanations of price level fluctuations, and he also suggested that his cumulative process might be useful as a description of the transmission mechanism whereby gold supply changes (to the extent that they were important) had their effects on the price level. In 1898 he treated changes in the gold supply as empirically irrelevant to explaining price level changes. By 1915 he seemed to be less sure of this. As we shall now see his ambivalence here arose from his beliefs about what empirical evidence had to say about these issues, and his views changed as that evidence accumulated.[22]

Empirical evidence

In 1898, Wicksell explicitly denied the empirical validity of the quantity theory in the light of nineteenth-century history.

> It is impossible to conceive that a change in prices has no connection whatever with the situation in the money market. . . . But the explanation suggested by the Quantity Theory – that rising prices are due to an excess of money, falling prices to a scarcity – does not accord with actually observed movements of the rate of interest. If it were correct, we should expect that at a time of rising prices there would be a temporary reduction in the rate of interest, at a time of falling prices a temporary increase; and that when prices had become accommodated to the change in the stocks of precious metal, the rate of interest would once again return to its normal position. Observation teaches us, however, that when prices are rising there is a continual *rise* in rates of interest, and that when prices are falling, there is a continual *fall* in rates of interest (1898, pages 166–7; Wicksell's italics).

This passage occurs in *Interest and Prices* immediately *following* a discussion of Irving Fisher's (1896) 'Appreciation and Interest', where Fisher advanced what is nowadays regarded by the majority of economists as the correct explanation of the co-existence of rising prices with high and perhaps rising interest, namely the influence (lagged in Fisher's view) of expected inflation on the *nominal* rate of interest.[23] Wicksell, despite his acknowledgements elsewhere that agents might come to anticipate an ongoing inflation, rejected this explanation because its:

> logical basis . . . is that entrepreneurs incur their 'expense' . . . when things are cheap, and dispose of their product after prices have gone up. But it is then necessary to suppose that the rise in prices originates from some quite *independent* cause (1898, page 166; Wicksell's italics).

This, of course, is a version of the objection, also advanced by Keynes in his 1911 review of *The Purchasing Power of Money*, to Fisher's analysis of the behaviour of nominal interest rates, namely, that it is incomplete in that it gives no account of the transmission mechanism by which an increase in the quantity of money *sets prices rising in the first place*. Wicksell's analysis *did* permit him to explain how this would come about, but in his model, as we have seen,

> a rise in prices . . . is usually due to a rise in the entrepreneurs' demand for labour and other productive services. Such a rise in prices is thus the consequence of a previous, no matter how far from uniform, rise in money, wages and rents, and it merely serves to compensate the entrepreneurs for the rise in costs of production. It does not provide them with the means of paying a higher rate of interest – except in the case where the prevailing rate of interest is lower than the *natural rate* (1898, page 166; Wicksell's italics).

Given the simplifying assumptions which Wicksell used in his 'Systematic Exposition', as set out in (1898, Chapter 9) notably those about the timing of market transactions relative to a uniform period of production, which is also the period for which credit is granted, this conclusion is correct. But if consumption goods are storable and credit available for more than one period, to suggest but one possible way of complicating his model, it is not; and if, in such a Wicksellian system, expectations are forward-looking (a possibility which Marshall canvassed in his Gold and Silver Commission evidence) an increase in stocks of gold can simultaneously *raise* the nominal value of the market rate of interest and *lower* it relative to the (inflation adjusted) natural rate.[24] The system envisaged here, though, *is* Wicksellian *not* Wicksell's, and he *did* reject Fisher's analysis for inadequate reasons stemming from an overgeneralisation of the implications of a very special theoretical structure. Instead of deploying the Fisher effect to explain the empirical relationship between price level and interest rate behaviour, then, Wicksell argued that:

> All these difficulties and complications at once disappear when it is changes, brought about by independent factors, in the *natural rate of interest on capital* that are regarded as the essential cause of such movements. These changes can be regarded as the cause, not only of the movement of prices, but indirectly of the analogous but somewhat later alteration in the money rate of interest. Abundance or

scarcity of money . . . are to be regarded as consequences of changes in the demand for instruments of exchange brought about by changes in the level of prices. . . . [H]owever . . . they *may* take their origin in independent causes . . . and . . . they then have an independent significance in regard to . . . prices, in so far as they accelerate or retard the movement of the money rate of interest to the new position of the natural rate (1898, page 167; Wicksell's italics).

Wicksell does here acknowledge the *logical* possibility of independent changes in the quantity of money having an effect on prices, but his subsequent interpretation of the history of price level behaviour in the nineteenth century accorded them little *practical* significance. Inflation during the Revolutionary and Napoleonic wars is presented as due to upward pressure placed on the natural rate of interest by a war-induced scarcity of capital; falling prices after 1815 as due to capital's relative post-war abundance. As to the 'upward movement of prices [which] started in the fifties' and 'the gradual fall in prices' which began in 1873 'and has continued up to the present time . . . [t]he explanation seems to me completely analogous to that of the movement of prices in the years 1790–1815 and 1815–1850' (1898, pages 173–4). The Crimean War, the American Civil War, Prussia's wars with Denmark, Austria and France, the 'general progressive movement of industry' and 'the freezing of enormous quantities of liquid capital as a result of the completion of the west European railway system' had all driven up the natural rate of interest after 1850. The 'large increase in the production of gold, and the issue of paper money in America, in Austria and finally in France' might have been 'partly' responsible for the failure of the money rate of interest to keep pace with the natural rate, but that was all (cf. 1898, page 171). As to the period after 1873, 'the economic depression which for more than twenty years has provided a constant source of complaint . . . must be regarded as the cause rather than the effect of the fall in prices' (1898, page 194).

The above-mentioned account of the behaviour of prices during the nineteenth century shows Wicksell to have rejected almost entirely the explanation which Fisher (following Jevons, whose interpretation of events Wicksell also explicitly discussed and rejected) was later to advance in *The Purchasing Power of Money*.[25] For Wicksell, writing in 1898, the dominant factor at work in driving prices throughout the preceding century was not variations in the quantity of money (i.e. currency). It was variations in the natural rate of interest; and price level movements were *accommodated* either by fortuitous variations in the quantity of money, or, and mainly, by changes in its velocity associated with the failure of the banking system immediately and completely to adapt its lending rates to changed circumstances. In the *Lectures* this stance is softened. Empirical evidence about the co-existence of rising prices with high interest rates is still taken seriously, and in the edition that was to be ultimately translated into English, is systematically presented in a chart covering the years 1850–1913. Moreover the evidence in question is still treated as problematic for the quantity theory (cf. 1915, pages 164–5, 202, etc.). There is no sign of any acceptance of Fisher's (1896) analysis, which is not referred to in the *Lectures*; while the less detailed account of the 'cumulative process' given there generally pays less attention to endogenous inflation expectations than does that of *Interest and Prices.*[26]

Not surprisingly, then, variations in the natural rate of interest are still accorded an important role by Wicksell in the *Lectures* as independent impulses affecting prices, but now it is not all price level fluctuations which are explained in this way, but rather '[t]he fluctuations in commodity prices which are not directly caused by *changes in gold production*' (1915, page 205; Wicksell's italics). And, in non-gold producing countries, changes in gold production do not have to work on prices solely, or even mainly, through the banking system. They can influence the quantity of money directly through the balance of payments without the intervention of any fall in the money rate of interest. Moreover, the 'quantity of gold may in general have no influence on prices if the demand for money has simultaneously increased owing to the growth of population or to a more widespread social division of labour or a more extended use of money' (1915, pages 204–5). Though it is still problematic, the empirical association between rising prices and high interest is no longer presented by Wicksell in the *Lectures* as it was in *Interest and Prices* as being *logically* incompatible with an explanation of price level behaviour that relies, in part at least, on variations in the quantity of money.

The probable source of Wicksell's shift towards an eclectic explanation of price level behaviour between the publication of *Interest and Prices* and the edition of the *Lectures* which we have in English is not hard to track down. When the former work was published, the 'Great Depression' of prices had just given way to inflation, but this fact was not then obvious. It was by 1915, as was its most likely cause, namely, the gold discoveries made and quickly exploited in the Transvaal and the Yukon. Wicksell's comments on these discoveries, and their consequences are worth quoting at some length, for they show that he did indeed attribute the mild inflation that preceded World War I to an increase in money, and not to an upward shift in the natural rate of interest.

> If the experience of the last seventy years does not seem to confirm this [the powerlessness of existing stocks of gold to buffer the price level against the impact of the discovery or exhaustion of gold fields] to the degree one might expect, it is due entirely to the fact that the great discoveries of gold and silver in the latter part of the nineteenth century occurred simultaneously with a great increase in population in most countries and a transition from trade in kind to trade in money . . . and, more important still, these discoveries were accompanied by the almost universal adoption of the gold or some cognate standard. . . . These factors, however, are of a more or less accidental nature and their combination in the desired direction cannot always be counted upon, *as the much higher price level during the decade 1893–1913 clearly shows* (1915, page 125; my italics).

Wicksell on the cycle

As we saw above, Wicksell usually resisted the incorporation of the Marshall–Fisher nominal–real interest rate distinction into his analysis of the cumulative process of inflation and deflation. Even so, important similarities remain between this analysis and Fisher's treatment of transition periods. Both discussions were self-consciously concerned with the way in which money and prices would interact in the wake of a disturbance to the equilibrium relationship between them; both put a discrepancy between the rate of interest which borrowers were willing to pay and that which banks were willing to charge at the centre of things; and both regarded the consequent endogenous expansion and contraction of bank credit as playing an important part in amplifying the effects of any disturbance. To be sure the reasons which Wicksell gave for the origin of the interest rate gap differed from Fisher's – shifts in the productivity of capital as opposed to monetary disturbances – and he implicitly accorded a purely passive role to the bank money created as a by-product of bank lending, rather than an active one in generating further price increases as did Fisher. But both Fisher and

Wicksell gave falling reserve ratios a key role in bringing an inflationary process to an end, and both emphasised their influence on the interest rates charged by the banks. A 'Wicksellian' cycle model, with a family resemblance to Fisher's would, therefore, be easy to construct; but Wicksell did not do so, and it is worth asking why.[27]

The key here lies in the fact that interest rate–inflation rate interaction postulated by Wicksell involved the money rate of interest rising to the level of the natural rate, credit creation ceasing, and the price level coming to rest at a new, higher, meta-stable equilibrium value. He did not permit variations in inflation expectations to become involved here.[28] Fisher, on the other hand, saw the effects of rising lending rates slowing down inflation and simultaneously driving up the perceived real costs of borrowing via this very channel. His vision of the dynamics involved here had the interest rate overshoot the value compatible with a new equilibrium price level and hence precipitate a downturn. Because it did not endogenise the influence of inflation expectation on the real rate of interest, Wicksell's cumulative process analysis, taken in isolation, could at best have been put to use to account for the upswing and downswing phases of the cycle, but not its turning points. Fisher's parallel treatment of the same phenomena, because of its emphasis on endogenous inflation expectations, was capable of creating a richer dynamic framework.

There is, though a deeper reason than this for Wicksell's failure – or rather unwillingness – to develop a monetary model of the cycle, namely that his view of the facts that any cycle theory had to explain was not the same as Fisher's. The latter, as we have seen followed classical tradition in treating the cycle as principally a matter of price level fluctuations. For Wicksell the cycle was a matter of the alternation of ' "good" and "bad" times' (1915, page 209), by which he meant fluctuations in the level of output, but also and crucially in the proportion of output devoted to fixed capital formation. That there was a monetary element involved here he did not dispute: 'changes in the purchasing power of money caused by credit are under existing conditions certainly ultimately bound up with industrial fluctuations and undoubtedly affect them, especially in causing crises' (1915, page 211). However, he immediately qualified this judgement as follows: 'though we need not assume any necessary connection between the phenomena'. Moreover, the second paragraph of Wicksell's most systematic treatment of the topic, namely 'The enigma of business cycles' (1907a) begins: 'In order to better delimit my subject, I must first ask leave to exclude from the field of my observations everything that has to do with the influence of monetary and credit systems on crises' (1898, page 223). Discussion of a factor is only omitted for the sake of simplicity if it is regarded as peripheral to the main topic, and it was indeed Wicksell's explicit view that:

> Since rising prices almost always accompany prosperous times and falling prices times of depression, it is natural – *though in my opinion wrong* – to regard such a rise in prices as the cause of good times, and falling prices as the cause of depression (1915, page 209; my italics).

On the contrary he believed that:

> The principal and sufficient cause of cyclical fluctuations should rather be sought in the fact that in its very nature technical or commercial advance cannot maintain the same even progress as does, in our days, the increase in needs . . . but is sometimes precipitate, sometimes delayed (1915, page 211).

Wicksell characterised a specifically Marxist vision of the cycle (as expressed by Engels) as 'economic romanticism, not to say an adventure story' (1898, page 226); but his basic view, that the social role of 'overproduction' in bad times of slow technical advance and investment, was to create the inventories of producer goods which would in due course be available for investment in fixed capital during good times, places him far closer to the Marx–Schumpeter tradition in cycle theory than to any monetary tradition. Even so, he did in one place entertain the possibility that the banking system could conceivably act so as to turn the cycle into a phenomenon of variations in the *structure* of relative prices and *composition* of output alone, rather than also in their levels. During periods of technical advance:

> such goods (raw materials) as serve in the construction of fixed capital – bricks, timber, iron, etc – would be in great demand and rise in price, and . . . in a period of depression they would be in slight demand and fall in price. But this rise or fall in price should under ordinary conditions be accompanied by a movement in the opposite direction of the price of other goods, so that the average level of prices would remain unchanged. This would probably be the case if the banks at the beginning of a boom raised their interest rates

sufficiently and on the other hand finally lowered them at the beginning of a depression. In that case presumably the real element of the crisis would be eliminated and what remained would be merely an even fluctuation between periods in which the newly formed capital would assume, and, economically speaking, should assume, other forms (1915, page 212).

Such a successful stabilisation policy, though, would supplement forces already at work, namely the tendency of producers to 'work for stock' during bad times in response to the incentive of low wages and expected higher prices when good times return, and would not alter the essential nature of the cycle as involving fluctuations in the rate of fixed capital accumulation.

Note that the fluctuations in question here were desirable in Wicksell's eyes. Mises (1924) and Hayek (1931) were in due course to combine Wicksell's cumulative process analysis with the classical idea of forced saving to produce a monetary theory of the cycle in which fluctuations in fixed investment induced by bank credit expansion distorted the time structure of production in an undesirable, and indeed unsustainable, way. In so doing, they produced a monetary theory of the cycle which dominated academic discussion prior to the publication of the *General Theory*. Wicksell himself considered extending his analysis along just these lines, albeit in the context of rising prices caused by increased gold production, and dismissed its potential as follows:

> But if the formation of the real capital . . . is only based on the rise in prices itself, i.e. is due to diminished consumption on the part of those persons or classes of society with fixed money incomes, then the increased prosperity could scarcely be very great or enduring (1915, page 209).

Wicksell was, in short, so impressed by the real elements in cyclical fluctuations, and in particular those involving investments activity, that he treated monetary aspects of the cycle as peripheral. In this, he was probably closer to the centre of contemporary professional opinion about the cycle than Fisher or Hawtrey.

Wicksell's legacy

As we noted at the outset of this chapter, Wicksell always regarded himself as a (far from uncritical) exponent of the quantity theory of money. Even so, his work was, in due course, to do more to undermine than strengthen the central position of the quantity theory in monetary economics. The reasons for this lie in a combination of circumstances, some inherent in the work itself and some arising from developments in the real world economy.

The fact that its outlines are clearly evident in Marshall's Gold and Silver Commission evidence, which Wicksell had read, precludes us from classifying Wicksell as a co-discoverer of the cash balance version of the quantity theory, but in *Interest and Prices* he developed it well beyond anything available in the then published literature. He also paid particular attention to what we would now call the transmission mechanism, and here too there is similarity between his analysis and Marshall's earlier work. Both relied on 'cash balance mechanics' in an economy devoid of banks, and both argued that, once these institutions became important, then so did interest rates. Wicksell, though, did far more to analyse the micro-foundations of the transmission mechanism. He was self-conscious in a way that Marshall was not about placing limits upon the validity of Say's Law in a monetary economy, and he paid much more attention to analysing the real determinants of what he called the 'natural' rate of interest. The post-1898 softening of his view of this matter notwithstanding, Wicksell was also more inclined than Marshall (let alone Fisher) to seek the sources of price level movements, not to mention cyclical fluctuations, in the real economy, rather than to locate them in the monetary sector.

Marshall and Fisher believed velocity changes, particularly those brought about by the secular evolution of the banking system, to be important for explaining variations in the price level, and Wicksell recognised these effects too.[29] In this, all three were simply reflecting views which had long been commonplace in the classical quantity theory tradition. But Wicksell went further than Marshall and Fisher. He postulated that a modern banking system had capacity to render the velocity of currency a passive variable in the face of real shocks. This postulate underlay his idea that price level equilibrium was meta-stable, and led him to stress (even in the *Lectures*) fluctuations in the natural rate of interest as the main factor causing the price level to fluctuate. From the point of view of the monetary economics of the first decade or so of the twentieth century, the importance of this difference in emphasis between Wicksell and his contemporaries does not seem critical. The

Cambridge School in particular would have found little difficulty in assimilating the idea that the velocity of currency might have a passive element to it, because, unlike Fisher, they did not attribute stability to reserve–deposit and currency–deposit ratios.

Viewed with hindsight, however, the difference was important; and partly for no better reason than that Wicksell never extended his careful analysis of the motives which prompted the holding of currency in a pure cash economy into a parallel model of the demand for bank deposits in a pure credit economy. The very precision with which he analysed the credit economy in Chapter 9 of *Interest and Prices* ruled this out. In the model developed there, a pure asset demand for bank deposits could not arise, since large capital items did not change hands. More crucially, although Wicksell himself did not explicitly discuss matters in such terms, the pattern of payments and receipts which he imposed there led to a mechanically determined income velocity of deposits of one per period of production (and a transactions velocity of five). It left no room for uncertainty about the timing of those payments and receipts, and hence precluded an associated precautionary demand for bank deposits. There is no logical reason why Wicksell could not have gone on, in less formal treatments, to note that any relaxation of his rigid assumptions would tend to give bank deposits the same role in the credit economy as currency in the cash economy; and then to note that deposits, generated as a by-product of credit creation, would have, by way of cash balance mechanics, their own influence on the economy over and above that stemming from direct credit market effects. He did not take these steps, however.

Thus it came about that the monetary economics which Wicksell bequeathed to his Swedish successors lacked the notion that chequable bank deposits were a form of money whose velocity was susceptible to economic explanation, and as Johan Myhrman 1991 has pointed out, in the interwar years the Stockholm School explicitly rejected as outmoded and irrelevant the quantity theory of money, which they identified with the stable velocity of currency construction of Wicksell's pure cash economy special case. They also followed Wicksell in failing to develop any theory of the demand for bank deposits, and their monetary economics became identified with an extreme anti-quantity theory stance. Keynes was also directly influenced by Wicksell. This influence is more readily discerned in the *Treatise* than the *General Theory*, but Axel Leijonhufvud (1968) makes a compelling case that it is there too. And the very speed with which the Swedish economists assimilated the *General Theory* suggests a strong affinity between Stockholm and Keynesian tradition.[30] Keynes himself, of course, paid careful attention to the role of the quantity of money, including bank deposits, in the economy, but not all of his colleagues and followers adopted this position. Is it an accident that Wicksell's translator, Richard Kahn, was later the main originator of that view of money's essential irrelevance expounded by the Radcliffe Committee in their 1959 *Report*, a view which has come to be identified as that of 'Keynesian' monetary theory? If it is not, then Wicksell, who usually defended the quantity theory, was the seminal contributor to the development of that theory's main twentieth-century rival.

Notes

1. It is usual to date Volume II of Wicksell's *Lectures* as 1906. This is indeed the date of the publication of its first Swedish edition. However, the English translation (1935) of Volume II has been taken from the *second* Swedish edition of 1915, not the first. In what follows, Volume II of the *Lectures* is cited as Wicksell (1915).
2. On the monetary thought of the older German Historical School, see Haim Barkai (1989).
3. As we shall see, the question of the relative importance of the monetary sector as a source of demand for, and hence influence on the price of the precious metals, was important during the debate about bimetallism. Consistent with his empirical judgement that the demand for the precious metals *qua* money was dominant, Wicksell judged bimetallism to be a viable system, though by the time his commentary on this matter in the *Lectures* (pages 34ff) was written, bimetallism was of mainly historical interest.
4. Wicksell refers to and quotes Laughlin explicitly in the relevant section of the *Lectures*, but Mises is not named as the originator of the idea we nowadays associate with him. The latter is left unattributed.
5. It is worth noting that the analysis of such mechanisms involves the existence of a disequilibrium, inherent in which are equilibrating forces that come into play. A devotee of modern equilibrium macroeconomics in the style of Robert Lucas Jr (1972) would not regard the question of the limits on the validity of the classical dichotomy as interesting.
6. And of course Tooke (1844) paid particular attention to this question during the Currency School–Banking School debate. It is no accident

that Wicksell's analysis of the role of banks led him to doubt the usefulness of the quantity theory in the presence of a well-developed banking system, a position with strong Banking School overtones, because he was a careful and sympathetic reader of Tooke's work, as Arnon (forthcoming) notes.

7. The choice of words here, is of course, that of Wicksell's translator Richard Kahn. Kahn's translation is, however, careful and accurate. I am grateful to Mr Horst Raff for advice on this matter.

8. Wicksell had, however, read Marshall's Gold and Silver Commission evidence with considerable care, and we must not therefore treat him as an independent originator of this approach. In turn, it is presumably from his reading of Wicksell that Mises (1912) got the cash-balance approach. Israel Kirtzner (1987) errs in attributing originality to Mises on this matter.

9. Wicksell explicitly acknowledges Edgeworth (1888) as having made an earlier application of probability theory to monetary issues. For a further discussion of Edgeworth's contribution and its influence on Wicksell, see Chapter 6, especially pages 184–7.

10. Compare the passage from *The Purchasing Power of Money* quoted on page 77 above.

11. Wicksell was quite unaware of the contributions to this issue made by Henry Thornton (1802) when he wrote both of these books, though later in his life, Thornton's work was drawn to his attention, cf. Carl Uhr (1960).

12. Wicksell's own contributions to capital theory are to be found in *Value, Capital and Rent* (1896) and volume 1 of the *Lectures* (1905). Thomas Kompas (1989; ch. 4) contains a recent and most useful account of this aspect of his work.

13. cf. *Lectures*, volume 1, (1905, 1911, translated 1935) pages 202–3. See also Kompas (1989) Chapter 4.

14. I suspect that this claim should not be taken at face value. The fact that Wicksell found just the right set of assumptions to rule out the problems in question in his most rigorous exposition of his theory, and the fact that his later discussions of the cumulative process, both in the *Lectures* volume 2 and (1907b) are sufficiently vague to enable him to evade them, point rather to his knowing that a set of problems which he could not solve nevertheless existed. One way of reading the subsequent contributions of both Austrian business cycle theorists and the Stockholm School to monetary economics is to regard them as self-conscious attempts to solve these problems of Wicksell's. On this see Laidler (1991) in Lars Jonung (ed.) (1991).

15. Patinkin (1965) apparently does not share my view of the importance of this particular chapter in *Interest and Prices* for a full understanding of Wicksell's views, and does not refer to it in detail. Note that in an earlier study of Wicksell (Laidler, 1972) my account of the model set out in this chapter is not always clear, a matter on which Roy Bailey (1976) comments helpfully.

16. Wicksell was aware of the impossibility of constructing an aggregate

measure of capital that does not depend on the structure of relative prices in a more general case than this, as Kompas (1989) has shown: hence, in part, my suspicion that his claims to be making only simplifying assumptions here are disingenuous (see Note 14 above).

17. See Anthony Cottrell (1989) and Peter Howitt (1989) who argue, correctly in my view, that much more than matters of semantics are at stake when modern economists attempt to force Wicksell's analysis into an equilibrium framework.

18. Wicksell's discussion here is sufficiently vague, and falls sufficiently short of precisely stating the interpretation which I put upon it, that one is naturally led to wonder about the quality of the translation at this point. However, Mr Horst Raff has checked this matter, and assures me that Kahn's rendering is accurate. The most likely interpretation, then, of Wicksell's confusing exposition is that he was indeed confused on this point. Note also that Wicksell's reference to a 'fall' in the rate of interest is not compatible with his starting assumption that the natural rate of interest has risen. Perhaps he meant the *shortfall* of the money rate from the natural rate, but again, Mr Raff tells me that Kahn's translation is accurate.

19. Consider for example, Wicksell's ironic comparison of those who believe in the beneficial consequences of inflation with people who keep their watches running a little fast to be sure of never missing their trains (1898, page 3). By and large, however, Wicksell pays less attention to endogenous, let alone rational, expectations in his later expositions of the cumulative process than in *Interest and Prices*. Indeed, in his *Economic Journal* piece (1907b), which one might regard as expounding what Wicksell thought of as the essence of this analysis, the possibility that inflation expectations might be endogenous is never mentioned.

20. This point has been particularly stressed by Patinkin (1965, pages 590–7).

21. Note that a state of affairs which, to Wicksell, produces a meta-stable equilibrium, generates in the context of a modern rational-expectations equilibrium model an indeterminate price level (cf pages 132–4 above, and Note 17). The difference here of course arises from Wicksell having assumed static expectations about the level of prices.

22. Note also that in 1904 Gustav Cassel had published, in Swedish, an empirical study of the relationship between gold supplies and the price level that was very much an application of the quantity theory. Perhaps this study also had some influence of the softening of Wicksell's stance on these matters between *Interest and Prices* and the *Lectures*. For a modern and accessible account of Cassel's study, in which his conclusions are explicitly compared to Wicksell's, see Jonung (1979). Note also that, in some unpublished writings after World War I, Wicksell appears to have become an unequivocal advocate of the quantity theory. Thus Jonung (1988) quotes an unpublished 1920 manuscript on 'The effects of the increase in interest rates' as follows: 'To search for *any other* cause behind the decline in the value of money than the

abnormal size of the volume of notes is unnecessary' (Jonung, 1988, page 506; Wicksell's italics).

23. Note that I refer here to 'the majority of economists'. There have been some eminent dissenters from the Fisherine view, including Keynes (1936), Sir Roy Harrod (1969) and Sir John Hicks (1989).

24. See, Marshall (1926) *Official Papers* page 52.

25. And of course, Cassel's (1904) study referred to above (Note 22) is also in this tradition.

26. The account is also notably less careful in specifying a set of assumptions that will just render Wicksell's, in general incompatible, ideas about what constitutes a neutral value for the rate of interest consistent with one another (see Note 14 above).

27. It was Mises (1924) who combined Wicksell's analysis with the idea of forced saving to produce the prototype of Austrian cycle theory. Note that this particular contribution of Mises does not appear in the first (1912) edition of his *Theory of Money and Credit*, and hence falls outside of the time period to which this study is devoted. Only the second edition of Mises' book is available in English translation, and I am indebted to Mr Horst Raff for reading the first German edition and confirming this for me.

28. This matter is discussed in detail on pages 139–40 above.

29. And indeed it was Wicksell's comments on these matters that provided the impetus to Bordo and Jonung's (1987) study of the importance of institutional change for the determination of velocity.

30. Thus Eric Lundberg (1937) was able to assimilate Keynes' analysis of the equilibrating role of real income changes into his celebrated PhD thesis within months of the publication of the *General Theory*. I find it hard to believe that he could have done so with such rapidity had this idea not fitted in easily to his already well established analytic methods. Jonung (ed.) (1991) contains a series of papers documenting the views and achievements of the Stockholm School. As to the Wicksellian influence on the *General Theory*, quite apart from this being readily documentable by way of the explicit references to Wicksell there and in the *Treatise*, it is generally acknowledged that Richard Kahn was by far the most influential of Keynes' younger colleagues during the book's composition; but Kahn's own translation of Wicksell's *Interest and Prices* appeared in 1936. This is not to deny the extraordinary originality of Keynes, or that that originality took him well beyond Wicksell. It is simply to claim for Wicksell an important influence on Keynes' thought.

6 • Neoclassical monetary theory and monetary institutions

Introduction

It was argued at the beginning of Chapter 3 that the development of neoclassical monetary theory before World War I could be expounded and understood independently of the debates about reform of the monetary system which provided its background, and I hope that this has now been demonstrated. Even so, the economists whose work I have discussed did contribute to those debates, and the nature of their contributions was largely determined by the theoretical understanding of monetary mechanisms described in the three previous chapters of this book. I have already suggested that the pioneers of neoclassical monetary economics were far from being defenders of the policy orthodoxy of their time. I am now in a position to demonstrate this, and to suggest why this state of affairs arose.

I shall begin with the bimetallic controversy that marked the first half of our period. The quantity theorists discussed earlier understood bimetallism far better than did its active opponents, and indeed than many of its supporters too, but they did not advocate it. This lack of support, however, stemmed not from any commitment to prevailing orthodoxy, but rather from a conviction based explicitly on their theoretical work, that it was possible to design monetary arrangements superior to any that rested simply on the fixed price convertibility of money into one or more precious metals. This conviction marked their treatment of bimetallism itself, and was implicit in their advocacy of a wide variety of other schemes for achieving price stability or mitigating the consequences of its absence. Though none of them went as far as Herbert S. Foxwell, an active supporter of bimetallism, who (1886, pages 52–3) referred to 'our present money system as a most triumphant

153

proof of the barbarism of the 19th Century,' they were far from being apologists for the Gold Standard.

The spread of gold monometallism

As was explained in Chapter 2 and as Leland Yeager (1966, Chapter 14) has also argued, the international monetary arrangements prevailing during the first seven decades of the nineteenth century had been, in essence, bimetallic. The 'Law of the Year Eleven (1803)' established bimetallism in France, with the relative mint price of silver to gold set at 15½ to 1. Britain was, after 1816, formally on a gold standard, and most other countries – for example, India, and the various states that were eventually to form the German Empire – on silver. The nominally bimetallic *antebellum* United States had set her mint price ratio at 16 to 1, thus overvaluing gold relative to the price prevailing in the then more important French monetary system. Gresham's Law had placed her on a *de facto* gold standard, a fact which Laughlin (1885) was to cite, unfairly, as evidence of the inherent impracticality of bimetallism. Even so, between 1803 and 1873 the relative market price of gold and silver on international markets never deviated by more than 2 per cent from the French mint price, hence ensuring a high degree of exchange rate stability between gold and silver using countries. As was also explained in Chapter 2, the Californian and Australian gold discoveries of 1849–51 put a severe strain upon the system, but it survived with relatively little inflation. In their wake gold largely replaced silver in France, this effect acting as a 'parachute' to use Chevalier's (1859) word, against a precipitate fall in its purchasing power.

The 1870s brought new pressures to bear, however, and this time the system was unable to withstand them. After the Franco–Prussian War, the newly created German Empire switched from a silver standard to a gold standard, and in the United States, where specie convertibility had been given up during the Civil War, legislation of 1873, part of that which laid the ground for the restoration of convertibility in 1879, discontinued the coinage of the standard silver dollar. The combined effects of these measures were to be decisive for the evolution of the international monetary system, but neither of them seems to have been taken for any good economic reason. The 'crime of 1873', as the American measure came to be known among American bimetallists, was committed for no better reason than that the standard silver dollar had not circulated since 1836. As Friedman and Schwartz (1963, page 114) put it 'In 1873 it seems to have been generally accepted that the demonetization of standard silver dollars simply gave recognition to that fact'. In the case of the German Empire, the main reason for adopting gold seems to have been a desire to achieve the same, or perhaps a greater, degree of power and prosperity as Britain by emulating her monetary system. In Horton's words 'As the chief financial, industrial, commercial, monetary power, England's policy, sound or unsound, has for the heedless world a perilous prestige' (1887, page 52). The fact that as Walker later noted, 'The assertion that England owes her prosperity to the single gold standard is weak and superficial' (1897, page 82) did not prevent such arguments carrying great weight in the later years of the nineteenth century.

The German demonetisation of silver had an immediate effect in driving down that metal's market price, and this at a time when newly discovered and rich sources of the metal were being developed in the western United States. France was thus faced with a choice between giving up the system instituted in 1803, or moving rapidly to a *de facto* and potentially inflationary silver mono-metallism. She moved to limit the coinage of silver in 1874 and closed her mints to silver in 1878, as, in short order, did the other countries of the Latin Union (Italy, Belgium and Switzerland). The Scandinavian countries quickly followed suit. By the end of the 1870s then, the western world was well on its way to having transformed its international monetary system from bimetallism to gold monometallism, and in the process the exchange rate regime prevailing between the West (notably Britain) and the monometallic silver standard economies of the East (notably India) shifted from a pegged arrangement maintained inadvertently by the French Mint, to a fluctuating one.

The 1870s and 1880s were decades of rapid real growth, both in Europe and the United States, and by then the output of the Australian and Californian gold fields was well past its peak. These factors combined with the continued spread of gold monometallism to generate a slow but steady fall in the gold price level which persisted until the mid-1890s. The silver price level on the other hand rose, and, important in the case of Britain, the Indian silver rupee therefore depreciated against the gold pound sterling. Then (as now) it was easy (though not for that reason correct) to argue that price deflation would cause real stagnation, and that a rising exchange rate would lead to a loss of competitiveness on the part of domestic industries. It was hardly surprising that, from the 1870s onwards, the spread of the Gold Standard met vociferous opposition, and that much of that opposition centred around proposals to re-establish an international bimetallic monetary system.

The mechanics of bimetallism

A bimetallic system is exactly what its name implies, namely one in which money consists of, or is convertible into, either or both of two precious metals rather than one. A crucial characteristic of the system is that the relative price of the metals in their monetary use be fixed. As is generally the case, so in this particular instance, it is one thing to put in place a law establishing a relative price, and quite another to have that price be effective in the market place. The central question which a bimetallic system poses for monetary theory is to describe the circumstances (if any) under which a *de jure* bimetallic system will be so *de facto*. A secondary, but also important, question is whether, on the assumption that such a system is indeed viable, it will deliver a greater or lesser degree of price level stability than either gold or silver monometallism.

In order to answer these questions with theoretical rigour, one needs a supply and demand apparatus modified to incorporate the stock flow distinction. As we have seen, just such an apparatus was developed by Marshall and Fisher during our period. As we have also seen, before the advent of that apparatus bimetallism had been analysed by, among others, Chevalier (1859), Cairnes (1860) and Jevons (1863) in the course of their discussions of the consequences for the international monetary system of the Australian and Californian gold discoveries of 1849–51; and Jevons had concluded, correctly, that its viability was an empirical matter. Even so, because of his commitment to the cost of production theory of the long-run value of gold and silver, Jevons had in fact analysed a rather special theoretical case in which their relative price was parametric to the monetary system. A more general analysis would have recognised that their productivity in non-monetary uses, as well as their marginal production costs, would be functions of quantities, and hence open to influence from the rules governing the metals' monetary roles.[1]

The essence of Jevons' analysis can be captured by imagining an economy in which the monetary uses, actual and potential, of the two precious metals have a negligible influence upon their market prices as commodities, and then supposing that a bimetallic monetary system is instituted, but with the relative mint price (i.e. price *qua* money) of the metals differing from their relative market price. Then coin made of metal undervalued at the mint will be melted for use as a commodity, and the overvalued metal will be brought in for coining. If instead of metal coins, we have paper money convertible into the metals, then the overvalued metal will be exchanged through the monetary system for its undervalued counterpart as a preliminary to the conversion of the latter into metal marketable as a commodity. In either case, however, the process will continue until the only metal in use in the monetary system is the one overvalued there. 'Bad' (i.e. overvalued at the mint) money thus will drive 'good' (i.e. undervalued at the mint) money out of circulation. Jevons understood that if shocks to their conditions of production were relatively evenly spread between the two metals, the 'parachute' effect could enable bimetallism to deliver a more stable price level than either gold or silver monometallism. However, he also noted that if most shocks were concentrated on silver production, its presence in the monetary system would destabilise prices, relative to what could be achieved under gold monometallism. Because he believed, as an empirical matter, that silver production was likely to be subject to relatively more disturbance in the foreseeable future, Jevons was a strong advocate of gold monometallism.

Even in the 1870s, the assumption that the relative price of gold and silver was indeed parametric to the monetary system was explicitly denied by many bimetallists. Thus, the French commentator Henri Cernuschi asserted (1876, page 25).

C'est la fonction légale de monnaie qui donne grande valeur au métal; c'est le législateur qui attribue au métal cette fonction. C'est donc le métal qui doit obéir au législateur et non le législateur au métal. [It is its legal function as money which imparts great value to the metal; it is the legislator who bestows this function on the metal.

It is, then, the metal which must obey the legislator, not the legislator
the metal.] (my translation)

This argument, loose though it may be, is very much in line with the
explanation of the value of the precious metals which follows from
the neoclassical quantity theory of money whose properties we
described in Chapter 3. Indeed, by 1889 Walras had developed a
correct quantity theoretic analysis of bimetallism's properties in the
special case, the polar-opposite of that dealt with by Jevons, in
which quantities, rather than prices, of the two metals were given,
Walras showed that, where the relative price of the metals in non-
monetary uses varies inversely with their quantities, bimetallism is
viable over a range of mint prices.[2]

To see that this conclusion is correct, suppose that bimetallism is
introduced with a mint price that differs from the metals' relative
market price. As the initially undervalued (overvalued) metal leaves
(flows into) the monetary sector, its price in non-monetary uses is
driven down (up); and the 'bigger' is the monetary use of the metal
relative to others, the more likely is it that the relative market price
of the metals will be brought into equality with their mint price
while both remain in circulation. Moreover, a disturbance to the
conditions of supply and demand for the metals in non-monetary
uses, will, provided it is not 'too big', change their proportions in
the monetary system and the quantity of money overall, but still
leave both in circulation with their relative price unchanged. As
Walras (1889) put it:

> *Bimetallism will . . . work on condition that the price of the silver
> franc in the form of both bullion* [i.e. *qua* commodity] *and coin is
> higher than the price of the gold franc in the form of bullion alone
> and on condition that the price of the gold franc in the form of both
> bullion and coin is higher than the price of the silver franc in the
> form of bullion alone* (1954, page 356; italics in original).

Fisher's (1894, 1911) treatment of bimetallism went beyond that of
Walras, by allowing for new production of the metals at rising
marginal cost, but his conclusion about the system's viability was
essentially the same:

> The conditions of production and consumption under which
> bimetallism can succeed are therefore (1) that under silver mono-

metallism a gold dollar would in equilibrium be cheaper than a silver dollar, and (2) that under gold monometallism silver would be cheaper than gold. A bimetallic level, therefore . . . must always lie between the levels which the two metals would have assumed under gold monometallism . . . and . . . between the levels which the two metals would have under silver monometallism . . . There will always be two limiting ratios between which bimetallism is possible (1911, pages 123–4).

Walras and Fisher's analysis of bimetallism is more formal and rigorous than that of other quantity theorists of the period, but Marshall and Wicksell, for example, shared their understanding of the system. As we have already noted, however, none of these creators of the neoclassical quantity theory supported bimetallism's reinstatement. They took this position, not because they thought bimetallism unworkable, but because they did not think that it offered enough promise of improvement over monometallism to be worthwhile. Walras' (1889) views are typical:

> *The bimetallic standard preserves a certain relative stability of value in cases where the monometallic standards would have varied in opposite directions. It varies as much as these monometallic standards in cases where they would both have moved in the same direction.*
> In short, bimetallism is as much at the mercy of chance as monometallism so far as the stability of value of the monetary standard is concerned; only bimetallism has a few more chances in its favour (page 359; Walras' italics).

Bimetallism's main opponents, were gold monometallists, whose objections were firmly rooted in the policy orthodoxy that had developed by the 1870s, and whose characteristics were described in Chapter 2. I shall discuss their position and the reasons why it carried the day in the form of the Gold Exchange Standard, which became firmly entrenched by 1914, before dealing with the more radical policy proposals of the quantity theorists whose theoretical contributions were discussed in the three preceding chapters.

Arguments for gold monometallism

Jevons' work, discussed in Chapter 2, and referred to above, showed that a coherent case against bimetallism can begin with a claim that the relative market price of the precious metals is, in fact, parametric to their monetary use, and hence that *de jure* bime-tallism might *de facto* degenerate into unstable alternating monometallism, or perhaps an inflationary silver monometallism. The late nineteenth-century defenders of orthodox gold mono-metallism did indeed assert the parametric nature of the relative price of the metals; but, they supported their claims to this effect with analysis that was old-fashioned and incomplete, sometimes being based on a blind application of the cost of production theory of value discussed in Chapter 2, and sometimes being incoherent into the bargain. A few examples, drawn from their writings, will support this assertion.

In analysing the determinants of the relative price of gold and silver, Professor Bonamy Price of Oxford relied on the above-mentioned long-run cost of production theory of value, modified in the short run by supply and demand considerations.[3] As Price put it in a letter to Mr H. R. Grenfell on 12 November, 1882 (reprinted in Hucks-Gibbs and Grenfell 1886, pages 323–4).

> I did say, and do say, that the value of money is determined by the cost of production of the metal, like the value of a loaf of bread is determined by what it costs to produce. And I say further, that, at particular times, the state of supply and demand will alter the value of the metal in exchange, precisely as the character of the seasons may largely affect the price of wheat in a particular year.
>
> By cost of production I meant the cost of production on an average of years. A farmer may, under the influence of the season, get more or less than the cost of production of his wheat; but, as a rule, and upon the average, he sells his wheat for its cost of production, profit included, or else he will cease producing wheat.
>
> There is, in this, no affirming and denying at the same moment that cost of production governs price. There is merely a statement that the state of supply and demand at particular moments will make value vary from cost of production . . ..
>
> You . . . ask me to enter upon a 'discussion as to the degree in which demand so affects the value of the precious metals as to neutralize the absolute doctrine of cost of production.' I am very sorry to have to say that I do not understand the question . . .. I dare say I am very stupid: if so, pray forgive me.

Price was, perhaps, an intelligent man, but his old-fashioned theory of the long-run value of money was incomplete. It did not enable him to see that the long-run *marginal* cost of producing the precious metals is not determined until the demand for them is brought into the picture, and that their demand *qua* money must indeed influence it, perhaps to an important degree if marginal cost increases rapidly with output, and if the volume of output is small relative to existing stocks. Marshall's supply and demand apparatus of 1871, described in Chapter 2 above, (and indeed Walras' analysis of 1886, 1889) enables this to be seen clearly, but of course even Marshall's results were not generally available in 1882; and it must be admitted that Price's correspondent, Grenfell, though closer to a correct position in asserting that a monetary demand for silver could affect its long-run price relative to gold, was far from clear in the analytic arguments he advanced to support this position (see e.g. Hucks-Gibbs and Grenfell, 1886, pages 324-6).

The leading British proponent of gold monometallism was not, however, Price but Giffen. Though an able statistician and an effective advocate of orthodox classical positions on matters of policy, the record nevertheless shows him to have been a mediocre monetary theorist.[4] He believed that 'the State may properly interfere, for some purposes, at least, in matters of coinage' (Giffen, 1886, page 44) but only in a very limited way. Governments might be able to perform the 'easy function' of 'stamping . . . bits of metal so as to give the requisite guarantee as to weight and quality' (page 45). They might also:

> say in what way their own accounts are to be kept . . . declare in what form taxes are to be paid, and in what form payments by the State are to be made. As a convenience for legal interpretation, also, it is obviously proper enough that a Government should say what a contract in money means . . .. But beyond this, I am not aware that Governments do any good, or very much good, by a declaration of legal tender (page 47).

All this was conventional enough nineteenth-century wisdom, very much in the vein of the orthodoxy described in Chapter 2, as was Giffen's avowal that he 'consider[ed] a managed currency to be an unsuitable business for a State to undertake'. However, he based his argument against bimetallism on the judgement that 'a managed currency . . . [was] involved in bimetallism', since it amounted to 'the management of a coinage with a view of artificially keeping a standard stable from period to period'. He therefore went on to condemn bimetallism as 'a departure from the Free Trade principle

which Governments ought to follow in all commercial matters'
(page 49). In order to sustain this position, while simultaneously
supporting a monometallic system, Giffen was forced to argue that
the use of a single metal in the monetary system did not, as
bimetallists constantly urged, have an equally 'artificial' effect on
the value of the single metal in question, because, in the absence of
such an argument, the choice between bimetallism and the Gold
Standard became one between two equally artificial systems, both
of which violated the 'Free Trade principle'. To concede that would
have been, for Giffen, to concede the central element in his case for
sound money.

Giffen devoted an 1889 essay (reprinted as Chapter 3 of 1892a)
entitled 'A problem in money', to this question, arguing that the
value of the precious metals as commodities was parametric to their
use as money under both bimetallism or monometallism. However,
unlike Price, he did not attempt to derive this view from a cost of
production theory of long-run 'natural' value.[5] Giffen's argument
was more direct and down to earth, but no more satisfactory for
that reason. In his words,

> The precious metals . . . have an extensive non-monetary use. They
> are merchandise as well as money. But few people perhaps realise
> that probably this non-monetary use is *preponderant* over the
> monetary use itself. The assumption to the contrary is, in fact, made
> by bimetallists . . . as if there could be no question of it (page 83;
> Giffen's italics).

The bulk of the essay from which the above passage is quoted is
devoted to arguing the case, not only that 'the mass of the precious
metals in an uncoined form must be enormous' (page 83), but also
that it is appropriate to treat the demand for even coined metal held
as reserves by the banking system or 'in private hoards' as
representing a demand for the metals *qua* commodities rather than
money proper: 'the demand for the precious metals as reserves, like
the demand for them for other monetary purposes, is thus, in fact, a
demand for them as merchandise; and in all respects accordingly
the precious metals are merchandise only' (page 94). According to
Giffen, it followed that:

> There is absolutely no difference in gold and silver from any other
> merchandise, and the theories which presuppose some special and

peculiar difference, because the precious metals are used as money is a palpable delusion . . . the money demand proper . . . can hardly ever be the regulator [of the ratios between the precious metals and other commodities]. . . . Gold and silver, therefore, while used as money, are not only merchandise, but the regulator of the ratio between them and other articles must almost necessarily be some other than the money use (pages 94–5).

One can make some sense of Giffen's logic here by attributing to him the empirical judgement (extremely unlikely to be true) that the quantity of a precious metal held by banks and in individual balances is independent of that metal's status in the monetary system, but the reader will search in vain for so clear cut an argument in his essay. Be that as it may, Giffen concluded, as a result of this reasoning, that as an explanation of the value of money, 'the quantitative [*sic*] theory of money . . . is obviously not true' (page 95) but since he regarded that theory as 'really the basis of the whole bimetallic structure' (page 82) that structure could not be true either.

The tactic of attacking bimetallism by way of the quantity theory was not confined to the European debate. It was also deployed in the United States, not least by Laughlin, the most notable American advocate of 'sound money'. The most readily accessible account of his views is in his comprehensive treatise on monetary matters, *The Principles of Money* (1903).[6] Laughlin characterised the quantity theory, not altogether unfairly as has already been noted, as 'the essential basis of bimetallism' and told his readers that 'wherever we find discussions in favor of bimetallism, there we shall find the quantity theory of money' (page 281).

Laughlin's objections to the quantity theory were comprehensive. In the case of metallic money, actual or immediately convertible, he argued that the general laws of value applied, and these he saw as encompassing the forces of demand on the one hand, and production costs on the other. However, because Laughlin understood (correctly) that value was a relative phenomenon, he went on to argue that one must consider factors affecting the demand for and costs of production of goods as well as those of the precious metals. He then went on (erroneously) to treat these two sets of influences as completely independent of one another, and hence characterised what we would now term 'cost-push' forces as important potential determinants of the level of money prices: 'The general level of prices, then, supposing that the agencies directly touching gold are constant, is governed by the high or low expenses of production of goods' (page 355). Even in the case of inconvertible paper – not directly relevant to bimetallism, to be sure – Laughlin would have none of the quantity theory. In this case, where many earlier nineteenth-century economists who had regarded the quantity theory as misleading in convertible conditions had recognised its validity, Laughlin argued bluntly that 'The explanation of the fact that paper which cannot be converted into gold has any value whatever is to be found in the possibility of redemption' (page 530).[7]

The arguments advanced in favour of 'sound money', during and in the wake of the bimetallism debates, all too often amounted to something like the following syllogism: The validity of the quantity theory of money is necessary for the validity of the case for bimetallism; the quantity theory of money is not valid: therefore the case for bimetallism is not valid. The reasons given for the theory's invalidity differed among authors, but on the alleged fact of the invalidity in question they all agreed. Orthodox monometallists were quite right, as a debating tactic, to attack the quantity theory. As we have already seen, it did indeed suggest that bimetallism adopted on a wide enough basis could lead to the demand for the metals as money dominating the determination of their values, and hence to making the maintenance of a stable relative price between them feasible in the face of a range of disturbances to their supply conditions; and bimetallists could, and incessantly did, point to the example of France accomplishing this on behalf of the whole world between 1803 and 1873, during which time there were indeed severe shocks on the production side.[8]

The Gold and Silver Commission, the official body which in 1888–9 considered the possibilities of introducing bimetallism in Britain, and recommended against it, earned a scolding from Giffen for nevertheless conceding just this last point, because it was implicit in such a concession that to adopt bimetallism was a feasible option. The Commission's main argument against the system, namely that the tendency towards alternating mono-metallism which they believed to be inherent in it would be inconvenient to British money users, who were accustomed to gold, could hardly have seemed compelling to anyone concerned about the Gold Standard's then proclivity to deliver falling prices. Never-theless, despite the absence of any intellectually compelling case to keep the Gold Standard in place (other than that it was already in place and seemed to some to be working tolerably well), the Commission did, as I have noted, recommend that it be maintained in Britain. In the United States a similar outcome was presaged by the election of 1892 and confirmed by those of 1896 and 1900. The populist William Jennings Bryan, whose commitment to the free coinage of silver was expressed in the still famous phrase 'Thou shalt not crucify mankind upon a cross of gold', was decisively defeated in the second and third of them.

It is worth a few words of speculation as to why the gold standard carried the day when intellectual support for it was so weak. First, responsible bimetallists, Europeans as much as Americans, recognised that, to be successful, bimetallism had to be established as an international system. Though they held a number of international conferences to promote their ideas, international monetary agreements proved no easier to reach in the late nineteenth century than they are nowadays. Second, closely related, in the United States in particular, the main political support for bimetallism came from those who wished to establish it unilaterally, and at an unreasonably high price for silver into the bargain. Though bimetallism had good arguments on its side, such support for good reason embarrassed its responsible exponents. According to Walker (1897):

> three classes of persons . . . have been wont to call themselves bimetallists. We have first the inhabitants of the silver producing states . . . silver coinage is with them not a financial but an industrial issue . . . the second . . . consists of those . . . in favor of super-abundant and cheap money . . . they are for depreciated silver, because . . . it is the next best thing (by which they mean what we should call the next worst thing) to greenbacks . . . what they really want is silver inflation.
> The third element . . . believe that the system will at once avoid the evil of a restricted money supply, secure an approximate par-of-exchange between gold countries and silver countries, and promote stability of value in the money of the commercial world (pages 217–19).

Though, as we have seen, this third group had good arguments, their inability to disassociate themselves from the first two ensured their political defeat. Third, after 1896 the newly discovered gold reserves of the Transvaal and the Yukon began to come onto the market, and these combined with the simultaneous spread of the

Gold Exchange Standard, a set of institutions well calculated to economise on the use of monetary gold, to turn the previous twenty years' mild deflation into a mild inflation that continued until the outbreak of World War I. Its greater capacity to avoid falling prices was the very foundation of the more responsible (i.e. non-inflationist) case for bimetallism, and this foundation was removed after 1896.[9] We may let Keynes (1913) have the last word on the matter:

> The choice of one metallic standard rather than another for any individual country is rightly guided by historical circumstances; it is not a matter on which theory as to what would make the best universal standard should count for much. In the 'eighties bimetallism must have seemed worth fighting for. But the course of events – American politics, South African gold, and so forth – defeated it. The wise bimetallist should have hastened to acknowledge defeat (page 393).

The international dimension

Economists' understanding of balance of payments and exchange rate issues was, as we noted in Chapter 2, well developed by the 1870s, and the years before World War I brought no notable advances in international monetary theory. Discussions in this area involved the application of existing and well understood principles to new policy problems, both those generated by events, and those inherent in monetary reform proposals of one sort or another. We have already mentioned the depreciation of the silver rupee in the 1870s and 1880s in the wake of the closure of the French mints to silver. This generated widespread concerns that Indian exporters were gaining a permanent competitive advantage over their British competitors. Marshall addressed this issue in his evidence to the Gold and Silver Commission, evidence which, on this point, is notable for its clarity, but not for its originality; and indeed Marshall himself claimed to be doing no more than reiterating 'Ricardo's reasoning . . . [as] developed by Mill, Mr Goschen, Mr Giffen, Professor Bastable, and others' (1926, page 170), the general thrust of which may be summarised in his own words as follows:

> Let two countries A and B trade with one another. Let A have throughout a gold currency.
> I. Let B also have a gold currency. Then trade tends so to adjust the supplies of gold relatively to the demands for gold in the two

countries as to bring gold prices at the sea-boards of the two countries to equality (allowance being made for the carriage). . . .

II. Let B have an inconvertible paper currency (say roubles) . . . The gold price of the rouble will be fixed by the course of trade just at the ratio which gold prices in A bear to rouble prices in B (allowing for the cost of carriage) . . .

III. Let B have a silver currency. This case differs from the preceding one only in consequence of the fact that silver is, and roubles are not, an exportable commodity. Trade tends so to adjust the supplies of gold and silver in the two countries relatively to the demands, as to bring gold prices in A to bear to silver prices in B (after allowing for carriage) a ratio equal to the gold price of silver (1926, page 191–2).

The specific implications of this analysis for the question of whether the depreciation of silver conferred any advantage upon Indian exporters followed immediately:

If we divide gold prices in A by the gold price of silver, we get what we may call *silver prices* in A . . . and we may say that trade tends to make silver prices equal in the two countries. If they are higher in A than in B, there will be a *temporary* bounty on exportation from B to A . . . This *temporary* bounty cannot be large: because silver prices in A cannot rise by more than a very small percentage above silver prices in B without causing a violent movement of silver from A to B (1926, page 192; first italics Marshall's, thereafter mine).

In short, conventional economic theory predicted no real long-run consequences for the pattern of Anglo–Indian trade arising from the demise of the fixed exchange rate between the two economies that the closing of the French mints to silver had precipitated.

But of course the fact that, as we might nowadays put it, the choice of exchange rate regime has no effect on the long-run workings of the real international economy is not the only one pertinent to discussions of the relative merits of alternative regimes. If, earlier in the nineteenth century, both price level and exchange rate stability were regarded as desirable, this seemed to create no conflict. With stability in the purchasing power of gold taken for granted, and the gold price of silver pegged by France, unilateral adherence to either gold or silver convertibility seemed capable of generating both outcomes simultaneously for any country. By the 1880s matters did not look so simple. Gold Standard countries were then experiencing falling prices and appreciation against Silver

Standard countries, and vice versa; and it was apparent, at least to more thoughtful observers, that the most widely touted solution to this problem, namely orthodox bimetallism, would require an explicit (but unattainable) international agreement if it was to have a good chance of being effective. By the 1880s, then, the choice of monetary arrangements, as faced by an individual country, seemed to present a dilemma. Either they could be chosen with a view to providing domestic price stability, or of promoting stability in exchange rates, but not necessarily both. As Marshall put it (1887, page 206, Footnote 2) 'Every plan for regulating the supply of currency, so that its value shall be constant, must, I think, be national and not international.'

There was no consensus among contemporary commentators as to how the twin goals of domestic price and exchange rate stability should be weighted. There was, though, widespread agreement on the desirability of ultimately achieving a sufficient degree of international co-operation that price stability could eventually be pursued on a world-wide basis; we have seen in Chapter 2 how proposals for an international gold money had attracted much support, including that of Jevons, in the 1870s. And the most able bimetallists in the 1880s and 1890s always promoted their scheme as being consistent with what Walker referred to as 'The immortal verity of a world's money as wide as the world's trade' (page 231). As it happened, however, the creation before 1914 of that international gold-based monetary system, to whose stability we nowadays look back with so much nostalgia, took place without the benefit of any prior planning by economists. The Gold Exchange Standard was analysed *ex post*, among others by Keynes in *Indian Currency and Finance* (1912), and also, more briefly, by Irving Fisher in *The Purchasing Power of Money* but it evolved piecemeal. It was not designed *ex ante* by anyone.

The details of the evolution of the Gold Exchange Standard need not concern us here, and differ from country to country. In the case of India, described briefly by Barbour (1912, Chapters 16–17), who was involved in the administration of the system there, and more thoroughly by Keynes, the mints were closed to silver in 1893 when it became clear that bimetallism was not likely to be instituted in the near future, and paper currency substituted for metal.[10] Thereafter '[b]y withholding new issues of currency, the government . . . succeeded by 1899 in raising the gold value of the rupee to 1s 4d, at which figure it . . . remained without sensible variation' (Keynes, 1912, page 1). This exchange rate was prevented from rising further by making sterling legal tender in India and convertible into rupees at this price, and prevented from falling by an administrative practice, backed by no legal requirement, but nevertheless always adhered to, whereby 'the government will sell in Calcutta, in return for rupees tendered there, bills payable in London in sterling at a rate not more unfavourable than $1s\ 29/32d$ per rupee' (page 5). The latter practice rendered India's system a gold exchange standard rather than a gold standard proper, for it involved the Indian monetary authorities holding their foreign exchange reserves not in gold, but in interest-bearing assets denominated in a gold-backed currency.

Keynes described the generic properties of the Gold Exchange Standard as follows:

> The gold-exchange standard may be said to exist when gold does not circulate in a country to an appreciable extent, when the local currency is not necessarily redeemable in gold, but when the government or central bank makes arrangements for the provision of foreign remittances in gold at a fixed maximum rate in terms of the local currency, the reserves necessary to provide these remittances being kept to a considerable extent abroad (pages 21–2).

Thus defined, the Gold Exchange Standard was in no way a uniquely Indian phenomenon. In Europe, Austro–Hungary and to a lesser degree Germany, had all adopted it by 1912, thereby achieving considerable economies relative to holding non-interest-bearing gold, and also, according to Keynes, obtaining a higher degree of flexibility and speed in managing their exchanges than would have been possible had they, as debtor nations, relied solely on bank rate and bullion shipments. And in Asia, Africa and Central America, largely under the influence of colonial powers, including the United States, the system was, in the years immediately prior to World War I, spreading rapidly.

As far as Keynes was concerned, 'in her gold exchange standard, and in the mechanism by which this is supported, India, so far from being anomalous, is in the forefront of monetary progress' (page 182). Even so, as he also pointed out, the Gold Exchange Standard was not really a new system. It was essentially similar to that which had been in place in Scotland in the eighteenth century, when the local banks had held reserves against their note issue and deposit liabilities not primarily in gold, but in bills drawn on London; and in relying on paper rather than the monetary metal itself for domestic currency, the system had an important characteristic in common not only with Ricardo's 1816 *Proposal for an Economical and Secure Currency* but also with Marshall's symmetallism scheme of 1887, which I shall discuss below.

Variations on bimetallism

We have seen earlier that Walras understood the mechanics of bimetallism perfectly, and thought that, on balance, it offered a somewhat better chance of achieving price stability than gold monometallism. However, in common with the other pioneers of neoclassical monetary theory whose work has been discussed in earlier chapters, he did not regard that as sufficient reason for supporting its reintroduction. As he put it (1889, pages 360–1):

> The moment we attempt to inject considerations of the degree of stability of the monetary standard into the applied theory of money, why should we be satisfied with an uncertain and imperfect stability? Why not aim at an assured and perfect stability? . . . This will result not from bimetallism, but from a gold monometallism coupled with a silver billon [token coinage] . . . which is alternatively issued and retired in such a way as to keep the multiple standard from fluctuating.

Such an arrangement, a version of which Walras (1887) also offered to a British audience as a remedy for Anglo–Indian monetary problems, amounted, of course, to a primitive form of managed money. As was noted by Fisher (1911, pages 328–9) it also represented a version of what he, following Horton (1887), called a 'limping standard' under which a gold-based system was supplemented by a substantial coinage of silver.[11] But what would happen under Walras' scheme if the maintenance of price stability required a reduction of the money supply in excess of the amount of silver coin outstanding, or an increase sufficient to drive up the value of silver bullion to its value as coin, and hence to shift the system towards an inconvertible (into gold) silver standard? Fisher raised these questions, and concluded, surely correctly, that Walras' variation on orthodox bimetallism presented problems of its own. Marshall also proposed a variation on orthodox bimetallism in 1887. Like Walras, he understood the mechanics of bimetallism perfectly. However, like Jevons earlier, Marshall opposed its reinstatement on empirical grounds. His judgement about the likely future course of gold and silver production, and the industrial demands for the metals, led him to conclude that, were bimetallism to be adopted on an international basis, at the relative price of the metals then usually envisaged, that is in the region of 16 to 1,

> it is not very improbable that after a few years . . . either the international mintage convention would be dissolved or gold would disappear from circulation. In the latter case the currency would thereafter fluctuate with . . . silver alone. We [Britain] should be landed with a paper currency on a silver basis (*Memorials of Alfred Marshall*, page 202).

Nevertheless, in 1887 he also expected continued deflation under the gold standard, and he therefore suggested its replacement by what he called 'a stable bimetallism' (*Memorials of Alfred Marshall*, page 204), or, to use the word coined by Edgeworth (1895), a system of *symmetallism*. This scheme would, as Marshall said, differ from Ricardo's 1816 *Proposal*:

> only by being bimetallic instead of monometallic. I propose that [paper] currency should be exchangeable at the Mint or Issue Department [of the Bank of England] not for gold, but for gold and silver . . . at the rate of one pound for 56½ grains of gold, together with, say, twenty times as many grains of silver . . .. There would be, as now, token coins of silver and bronze, but none of gold (*Memorials of Alfred Marshall*, pages 204-5).

This scheme of Marshall's amounted, in modern terminology, to one of pegging the domestic currency to a basket of (two) precious metals. Its purchasing power would vary with a weighted average of those of the metals. With gold appreciating and silver depreciating, it promised the benefit of greater price stability than a monometallic standard without the risks of orthodox bimetallism. Among the scheme's advantages, according to Marshall was that '[i]t could be begun at once and without risk by any nation'; although any country adopting it unilaterally would of course (as

Edgeworth (1895) explicitly pointed out) experience exchange rate movements against monometallic countries. Also '[i]f adopted by several nations, it would constitute at once a perfect international basis of currency and prices' (page 206). Indeed, this capacity to form the basis of an international currency was important to Marshall. He understood perfectly well that, if a purely national point of view was taken, schemes with a better capacity for delivering price stability could be devised, but he rejected them precisely because he valued stability in international monetary arrangements.[12]

Marshall's 1887 essay was entered as written evidence to the Gold and Silver Commission, but they gave short shrift to his version of bimetallism:

> To this proposal . . . we have not thought it necessary to give a prolonged consideration. Any scheme which involves so great an alteration in our system of currency would be so opposed to the traditions and prejudices of the people of this country that we think some considerable period of time must elapse before it will have gained that amount of support among the public which will entitle it to be considered as a practicable proposal. (Gold and Silver Commission, 1889, Part I, paragraph 168, page 74)

Thereafter Marshall ceased actively to argue for his scheme, and though it attracted the support of Edgeworth (1895) who provided a far more elaborate defence of its virtues than had Marshall, it made no further headway. As with any scheme designed to introduce silver into the monetary system primarily as a means of bringing about an end to deflation, it was rendered irrelevant by the fact that the deflation in question came to an end in the mid-1890s. That fact was, as I have already suggested, quite extraneous to the development of economics or the conduct of policy, but it probably had more to do with securing gold's status at the centre of the international monetary system than any other factor.

Indexation

In the first half of the nineteenth century it was obvious that prices fluctuated during the course of the 'credit cycle', but not that the 'natural' value about which they moved might itself vary. It was usual, indeed, to treat stability of the value of money relative to gold as essentially the same thing as secular stability in the value of money in general. Two developments of the 1850s and 1860s changed this. First, and best known, the discovery and exploitation of new sources of gold in California and Australia beginning between 1849 and 1851 ushered in a decade of secular inflation. Second, and in direct response to these events, the theory of index numbers was developed, mainly by Jevons, to the point at which serviceable measures of the purchasing power of money over goods in general could be constructed. Though the inflation of the 1850s was mild enough that practical commentators could treat it as presenting 'more scientific than practical' problems, Jevons' (1863) study of what he termed, with some exaggeration 'A serious fall in the value of gold' and his subsequent work on extending his price indices back to the beginning of the century had made it quite plain that secular price stability and gold convertibility were far from the same thing.[13] To those who understood this, and regarded price stability as the critical goal, the policy orthodoxy of the 1870s, as enshrined in *Lombard Street*, and discussed in Chapter 2 above was bound to appear, at best, incomplete.

We have already seen in Chapter 2 that though Jevons himself was a staunch supporter of that orthodoxy he was also a critical and well informed supporter. He favoured gold monometallism over bimetallism because of an empirical judgement that the relative price of silver was likely to be sufficiently volatile in comparison with that of gold as to render the bimetallism an inferior guarantor of secular price level stability, not because he regarded bimetallism as inherently flawed. More important, he was not content to rest with the policy framework proposed by Bagehot, much as he admired it. He proposed to supplement it with an important institutional innovation, namely the 'Tabular Standard of Value'. In *Money and the Mechanism of Exchange* (1875) he expressed the view that price level fluctuations 'would be a matter of comparatively minor importance were money used only as a measure of value at any one moment, and as a medium of exchange' (page 38), but, as he noted, money also fulfilled a third function:

> Every person making a contract by which he will receive something at a future day, will prefer to secure the receipt of a commodity likely to be as valuable then as now. This commodity will usually be the

current money, and it will thus come to perform the function of the *standard of value* (page 14; Jevons' italics).

The 'tabular standard' was a proposal to index money in its role of standard of value, or as we would nowadays express it, to introduce the institution of indexed contracts. The scheme was not original to Jevons, for both Poulett Scrope and Joseph Lowe had proposed similar measures earlier in the century, but Jevons' work on index numbers made it an altogether more practical proposition than it had been earlier. Indeed, once proposed, Jevons thought it would be adopted voluntarily and rapidly, with government's role in the matter limited to publishing index numbers regularly, and, as the scheme became widely adopted, taking measures to have the law recognise indexed contracts. Jevons saw the tabular standard as adding 'a wholly new degree of stability to social relations, securing the fixed incomes of individuals and public institutions from the depreciation which they have often suffered', but he thought it might also make a contribution to stabilising the cycle:

> Speculation, too, based upon the frequent oscillations of prices, which take place in the present state of commerce, would be to a certain extent discouraged . . .. Periodical collapses of credit would no doubt occur from time to time, but the intensity of the crises would be mitigated, because as prices fell the liabilities of debtors would decrease approximately in the same ratio (page 333).

The claim here is a relatively modest one, as befits an author who pioneered, in the form of his celebrated 'sunspot theory', what we nowadays refer to as 'real business cycle theory'.[14] Foxwell, who in 1884 edited Jevons' posthumously published *Investigations in Currency and Finance* which included some of his work on the sunspot theory, was also careful not to claim too much for indexation. Though in 1886 he offered the idea qualified support, he thought that bimetallism would do more to promote monetary stability (see Foxwell, 1886, pages 51-6). However to anyone holding a monetary theory of the cycle of the type described in Chapter 4, indexation naturally appeared to be a much more powerful stabilisation device.[15] That is surely why both Marshall and Fisher, each in his own way, took up and developed Jevons' proposal, despite the fact that it had proved far less attractive among the general public than Jevons had hoped.

Marshall's 1887 *Contemporary Review* essay 'Remedies for fluctuations in general prices', to which I have made frequent reference in this book, is essentially a piece of policy advocacy. Its (rather awkward) opening sentences are as follows:

> The purpose of this paper is to enquire whether the greater part of the fluctuations of general prices are not of such a nature as to be incapable of being materially diminished by the adoption of two metals instead of one as the basis of our currency. I shall argue that they are; that the only effective remedy for them is to be sought in relieving the currency of the duty, which it is not fitted to perform, of acting as a standard of value; and by establishing, in accordance with a plan which has long been familiar to economists, an authoritative standard of purchasing power independent of the currency (*Memorials of Alfred Marshall*, page 188).

In short, the essay's principal theme is that, contrary to the views of bimetallists, such as Foxwell (whose work is not cited), bimetallism (or indeed symmetallism) at best will contribute only a little to price stability and that the problems generated by price fluctuations would be better remedied by other means. The 'long familiar' remedy in question, moreover, is nothing other than the adoption of a tabular standard of value, or as Marshall called it, the 'standard unit of purchasing power' or 'for shortness simply THE UNIT' (page 197; Marshall's capitals)

The originality in Marshall's proposal lay not in his advocacy of indexation *per se* but in his linking its, as he saw them, beneficial effects far more explicitly to the cycle than had Jevons or indeed Foxwell. His reasons for concluding that 'The precious metals cannot afford a good standard of value' are that although 'long period fluctuations . . . are chiefly caused by changes in the amounts of the precious metals relative to the business . . . to be transacted' short-run 'fluctuations are but to a very slight extent caused by variations in the production of gold and silver' (pages 192–3), and that it is the latter which generate those, as we would now say cyclical, 'uncertainties of business which are the cause of so large a share of human suffering and degradation,' (page 193). Under indexation, according to Marshall:

> The borrower would not be at one time impatient to start ill-considered enterprises in order to gain by the expected rise in general prices, and at another afraid of borrowing for legitimate business for

> fear of being caught by a general fall in prices . . . Salaries and wages
> . . . could be fixed in units, their real value would then no longer
> fluctuate constantly in the wrong direction (page 198).

Its introduction, then, 'would be a powerful remedy for a great evil'
(page 199) and, relative to the maintenance of monometallism or
the adoption of bimetallism, would be:

> an advance of the same kind, though not nearly as great, as the
> advance of substituting a yard [sic] measure for the length of the foot
> of one judge, or for the mean between the lengths of the feet of two
> (page 211).

In 1887 then, Marshall was an enthusiastic advocate of indexation, and indexation had other supporters too. In the *Economic
Journal* for 1892, Aneurin Williams suggested an extension of
Jevons' and Marshall's scheme to currency itself.[16] Under Williams'
proposal, gold coin would be withdrawn from circulation, and
(again along lines originally suggested by Ricardo (1816)) replaced
with paper convertible into bullion. However, the rate of conversion would vary in accordance with an index of gold's price
relative to goods in general in such a way as to maintain the
purchasing power of currency over goods constant. This proposal,
which was certainly unrealistic in proposing that the relevant price
index be computed and acted upon daily, drew an angry response
from Giffen under the title 'Fancy Monetary Standards'.

As a result of Giffen's apparently considerable influence with the
Editor of the *Economic Journal* (Edgeworth), his piece was
published in the company of a reprint from *The Economist* of 1875
of Bagehot's (initially anonymous) attack on Jevons' proposals for
a tabular standard. Neither piece does anything to enhance its
author's claim to be regarded as a competent monetary theorist, but
there is more to be said in favour of Giffen's comments of the
difficulties inherent in selecting and then constructing an appropriate and acceptable index number on which any indexation scheme
could be based. Though he was named in neither of them, perhaps
the publication of these articles induced in Marshall a fear of
ridicule. Whatever the reason, however, he subsequently refrained
from any public advocacy of monetary reform.[17] It was left to
Fisher to keep the idea of indexation alive, with his celebrated
'compensated dollar' proposal. As we shall now see this was similar

in its essentials to Williams' scheme of 1892, although set out as a proposal for international rather than domestic monetary reform.

Fisher briefly analysed the mechanisms of the Gold Exchange Standard in *The Purchasing Power of Money*, identifying as its advantages those same characteristics subsequently to be enumerated and analysed in more detail by Keynes, namely, its capacity to economise on the precious metals, and provide an efficient mechanism for coping with balance of payments problems as and when they arose. To these, however, he added another, namely its compatibility with the institution of indexed currency. There is no evidence that Fisher was familiar with Williams' proposal, or indeed with Marshall's (1887) footnote mention of what was essentially the same device for ensuring stability in the domestic purchasing power of money, but his proposal for a 'compensated dollar' represents a version of the same extension of Jevons' tabular standard from money as a standard of deferred payment to its means of exchange and unit of account roles as well.

Fisher regarded the indexation of money as being easy to implement by countries on the Gold Exchange Standard:

> It is a little anomalous that . . . gold exchange standard countries now have a power to regulate their price level, which is not possessed by the gold standard countries themselves. The latter are, by their present system, kept absolutely at the mercy of the accidents of gold mining and metallurgy, while the former can keep or change the par of exchange at will (pages 340–1).

In order that the benefits of indexed money could be extended to the world as a whole, Fisher proposed the following reform, assuming, for the sake of the argument that the system might be based on the Austrian currency:

> In order that such an international system should work, we might imagine three separate functions: (1) the function of maintaining an exchange par with the Austrian gulden to be performed by Foreign Exchange Offices exactly as at present in the Philippines under the gold-exchange system; (2) the similar function of regulating the currency in at least one country, say Austria, by a Bureau of Currency Regulation through buying or selling gold, at the option of the public, at an official price, changing from time to time according to the decisions of the Statistical Office about to be mentioned; (3)

the function of fixing this official price of gold according to the price level [to be measured in turn by the statistical bureau] (page 342).

Though Marshall did not comment on Fisher's scheme, it received some attention in Britain, Keynes (1911) called it an 'admirable proposal'; Pigou offered it cautious support in his monograph *Wealth and Welfare* (1912, pages 437–88); and Hawtrey discussed it in *Good and Bad Trade* (1913, pages 256–8) arguing that 'In principle this proposal is thoroughly sound. In practice, however, there are very serious difficulties to face' (page 257). These included the problems involved in securing international agreement to implement the scheme, in the construction of appropriate index numbers, and so on.

Wicksell on managed money

Wicksell also commented on Fisher's scheme in the 1915 edition of his *Lectures*, and though he too was relatively unenthusiastic about it, it was for reasons different from Hawtrey's. As Fisher had noted, there was nothing essential about gold in his scheme. Silver or anything else would do just as well in principle, though '[t]he less variable the commodity relative to commodities in general, the less would be the readjustments needed and the less active the buying or selling of that commodity by the government' (1911, page 345). Wicksell noted this point too and, characteristically, pushed its logic a step or two further.

> The real advantage of Fisher's method is that, externally, everything would continue as at present, so that the general public would not even notice the change. Such an *argumentum ad ignoratum* seems, however, of doubtful value. The very substance of the proposed reform is to raise something *else* to the position of a *measure of value*, and not gold, as is now the case. Why not, therefore, go the whole way, and choose something different by which the goal in view, a stable price level, may be secured with reasonable certainty? (1915, page 228; Wicksell's italics).

The 'something different' was an institutional framework that would enable the insights yielded by Wicksell's cumulative process analysis to be put to work, and whose nature he had already clearly outlined in *Interest and Prices*. From the perspective of the cumulative process, the central point of all schemes designed to ensure price level stability was that:

> they can attain their objective only in so far as they exert an indirect influence on the *money rate of interest*, and bring it into line with the natural rate, or below it, more rapidly than would otherwise be the case. . . . The question thus arises whether the object in view could not be obtained far more simply, and far more securely through the monetary institutions of the various countries agreeing among themselves to undertake *directly* that alteration in their rates of interest which is necessary and which alone is effective (1898, pages 188–9).

Now Marshall had noted the possibility of using an interest rate policy to stabilise prices in 1887, but had stopped short of advocating this since it could, he believed as a practical matter, only be implemented on a national basis. That too was Hawtrey's view of the matter, though the embryo of many a later discussion of the merits of a managed domestic currency combined with a flexible exchange rate is to be found on page 256 of *Good and Bad Trade*. Wicksell, however, was much more optimistic (perhaps naive is a better word) about the prospects for international monetary co-operation,

> Co-operation between the banks of a single country for the regulation of rates of interest is already, of course, a matter of everyday procedure. Co-operation between the banks of different countries could easily take place, at any rate in times of peace, as soon as it was clear what objective was being aimed at (1898, page 192).

and the procedure in which the banks were expected to co-operate was presented in a disarmingly simple way[18]:

> *So long as prices remain unaltered, the banks' rate of interest is to remain unaltered. If prices rise, the rate of interest is to be raised; and if prices fall the rate of interest is to be lowered; and the rate of interest is henceforth to be maintained at its new level until a further movement of prices calls for a further change in one direction or the other* (1898, page 189; Wicksell's italics).

Wicksell's proposal was then explicitly one for the establishment of 'an international paper standard', to which he referred as 'an ideal standard of value' and the first step to setting it up was to be *'suspension of the free coinage of gold'* (Wicksell's italics). In 1898, he was confident that the propsect for its introduction:

> need not . . . provide cause for consternation. On the contrary, once it had come into being it would perhaps be the present system which would sound like a fairy tale, with its rather senseless and purpose-less sending hither and thither of crates of gold, with its digging up of stores of treasure and burying them again in the recesses of the earth (1898, page 193).

By the time he came to write the 1915 version of *Lectures*, Wicksell was more circumspect, if only because the apparent need for monetary reform was less pressing than it had seemed in the mid-1890s:

> If gold production should again be reduced, or the excess of gold is absorbed – as happened in the nineties – by the countries which have not yet found it necessary to acquire large stocks of gold, and if in consequence commodity prices in the immediate future only show a small or uncertain change, then perhaps it would be folly to attempt to reform the existing monometallic gold system, which is without doubt theoretically the most simple and has great and real advant-ages in practice (1915, pages 224–5).

Nevertheless, if the need for reform was not pressing, Wicksell at the beginning of World War I still described a paper standard, regulated along the lines described above, as 'undoubtedly the ideal which currency systems should endeavour to approach' (1915, page 224).

Central banking

As we have now seen, neoclassical quantity theorists went far beyond the orthodoxy of the 1870s in their discussions of monetary policy, but their schemes for indexing contracts, or money itself, or setting up a managed international paper currency remained just schemes, and the cycle persisted as a policy problem. The question of how the monetary institutions of particular countries should be designed, and how they should behave to cope with financial crises, therefore remained on the agenda throughout our period. The issue was, of course, more pressing in the United States, which under the National Banking System lacked a central bank, than in Britain, where the problem facing Bagehot in 1873 had been to persuade the Bank of England that it was indeed a central bank and should behave like one, notably in holding an adequate reserve of specie, and then being willing to act as a lender of last resort in times of crisis. Issues concerning the 'elasticity' of the currency, both in response to seasonal fluctuations largely driven by the harvest and in response to demands arising from fluctuations in the public's confidence in the monetary system, had been thoroughly thrashed out in Britain in the 1860s and earlier. They were discussed incessantly, and at great length in the United States during our period.

A brief description of certain salient developments in the evolution of central banking in both Britain and the United States is in order here.[19] Though Bagehot was hardly to know it at the time, the last financial crisis involving major insolvencies in the financial sector (that of 1865) had already occurred in Britain before *Lombard Street* came to be written, and in 1890, the potentially extremely serious Baring Crisis was, by general agreement, well handled by the Bank of England. The crisis, moreover, had a lasting effect on the financial system. In the words of its historian, Leslie Presnell (1968, page 168), it:

> accelerated the amalgamation and strengthening of banks . . . encouraged the keeping of higher and more stable cash ratios; . . . emphasised . . . the primacy of the Bank of England, and encouraged grudging bankers to recognise their own and the national interest in co-operation with the Bank.

In short, actual experience after the publication of *Lombard Street*, gave practical and effective incentives for the British financial system to develop along exactly the lines that Bagehot, not to mention Jevons, had hoped for and urged.

It is in the light of this experience that we should read Marshall's evidence to the Indian Currency Committee of 1899. There he expressed the view, which as we have seen also marks his work of the 1880s, that smoothing out price level fluctuations is the key to stabilising the cycle. He thus accorded monetary policy a much more active counter-cyclical role than did conventional Bagehotian wisdom. However, in 1899 Marshall made no mention of indexation, and only one (in passing) of bimetallism (1926, page 286). Perhaps the conservatism of his 1899 views, relative to those he had espoused in 1887, stemmed in part from his fear of ridicule alluded to earlier, but it surely also reflected a growth in his satisfaction with the resilience of the British monetary system over the preceding ten years, a growth in satisfaction easily justified in the light of experience. The fact was that growing public confidence in the banking system engendered by that resilience made the occurrence in Britain of an internal drain, which could turn a crisis into a panic, less and less likely.

The 1899 Commission was, however, dealing with Indian problems, and in that poorer country with its less developed banking system, the internal drain was still a danger in Marshall's view. To cope with it, he recommended institutional reform 'on the lines of the 1844 [Bank Charter] Act, somewhat modified as in the Reichsbank Act' (1926, page 284). The point here was as follows. The Bank Charter Act imposed a 100 per cent marginal specie reserve against the country's stock of currency. To ensure that sufficient currency might always be made available to ward off an incipient panic in Britain, therefore, relatively large and expensive specie reserves had to be held. The German act 'enable[d] the Reichsbank to increase its [note] issues to meet any emergency, whether due to the variations from one part of the year to another, or to a variation in one particular year of the general course of business' (1926, page 283). Marshall thought that such arrangements were more appropriate for a poor country that was less able to afford the luxury of a large stock of bullion, and indeed he was no supporter of the particular regulations governing the note issue that imposed the latter expense on Britain.

It was not just India whose banking system's capacity to deal with financial crises lagged behind those of Britain and Western Europe in the eyes of contemporary observers. The United States system was fragmented, partly as a result of the country's sheer size, but also because of legal restrictions, both federal and state, on consolidation and branching. Moreover, as we have already noted, the United States lacked a central bank. To be sure there was a tendency for the country's specie reserves to become concentrated in New York, but there they were held by a group of banks even less willing than the Bank of England had ever been to accept ongoing responsibility for the stability of the monetary system as a whole. Moreover, the importance of agriculture in the economy placed the same 'autumnal pressure' on the demand for currency there as Jevons (1866, reprinted 1884) had earlier diagnosed in the case of Britain, and with the same result. Any untoward event that put pressure on the banks at the centre of the system in the autumn could turn a normal seasonal drain into a panic, as agents in agricultural areas tried to ensure themselves a ready supply of currency with which to carry out transactions associated with moving the harvest. Acute financial crises were well on their way to being a thing of the past in Britain by the 1870s, but not in the United States, where they persisted on a roughly eleven-year pattern from 1873 till 1907.[20]

Each crisis was met by *ad hoc* measures on the part of clearing house associations, both in New York and elsewhere, not to mention the US Treasury, which towards the end of our period began, quite self-consciously, to behave like a Bagehotian central bank; but the verdict of this period's first historian, Sprague (1910) was that 'It is impossible to escape the depressing conclusion that the banking situation in 1907 was handled less skillfully and boldly than in 1893, and far less so than in 1873'. Sprague's conclusion about the US system was conventional enough, but surely no less correct for that reason:

> Somewhere in the banking system of a country there should be a reserve of lending power, and it should be found in its central money market. Ability in New York to increase loans and to meet the demands of depositors for money [i.e. currency] would have allayed every panic since the establishment of the national banking system. Provision for such reserve power may doubtless be made in a number of different ways. This investigation will have served its purpose if in showing the causes and consequences of its absence in the past it brings home to the reader the need not only of this reserve power, but also of the readiness to use it in future emergencies (page 320).

The study of Sprague's from which the above quotation is taken was, of course, carried out on behalf of the National Monetary Commission, whose deliberations were to lead, in 1913, to the creation of the Federal Reserve System. The system was intended to provide elasticity to the United States monetary system, and to act as a lender of last resort too, just as conventional wisdom required. To be sure, the system was not intended to be centred on New York as Sprague suggested, but rather on the Board of Governors in Washington; and it was supposed to provide not one national, but a federation of regional central banks overseen by the Board. It nevertheless represented a conscious attempt by the United States to adapt and apply widely accepted precepts about central banking to the special circumstances of the United States.[21]

There is much irony here, because those precepts are associated above all with Bagehot (1873); but Bagehot had thought he was writing about how the British system could be made to function better, and as we have seen in Chapter 2, he regarded that system as the unnatural product of historical accidents. An 1870s American style system, under which each commercial bank would hold its own reserves, rather than a British one with a central bank managing a centralised reserve, was in his view the 'natural' one; and yet a mere forty years after he wrote, as he thought about peculiarly British problems, his solution to them had been adapted and applied in order to replace a system which Bagehot himself, in the abstract at least, had thought more viable.[22] The explanation of this curious state of affairs is straightforward: Bagehot had completely failed to recognise a key element in the nature of banking, and it was this element, at work on a practical level, which provided the driving force behind not just the setting up of the Federal Reserve System, but also the development of the Gold Exchange Standard on which we have already commented.

Edgeworth on banking

The gap in Bagehot's analysis to which I refer above was filled by Edgeworth's (1888) 'Mathematical theory of banking'. Though this paper is even now not nearly as well known as it deserves to be, and had little influence among his contemporaries, it is worth discussing in some detail here if for no other reason than that it filled a gaping hole in orthodox classical monetary theory. However, to say that it had little influence, is not to say that it had none. It did influence Wicksell, as we shall see.[23]

The fundamental proposition of Edgeworth's theory is that 'Probability is the foundation of banking' (1888, page 113) and he systematically worked out the major implications of this insight, using as a basic tool of analysis what he called the 'law of error', or as we should now call it, the law of large numbers. Edgeworth first illustrates the usefulness of that law (pages 120ff.) with reference to a 'game' in which each player receives 'a disposable fund of 100 counters' which may be invested in illiquid securities bearing 5 per cent per ten minutes, call notes bearing 2 per cent, or may simply be held as non-interest bearing form. Every two minutes, a random drawing following a well specified rule determines how many counters the player is liable to provide immediately. If they are provided from reserves, the operation is costless, if call notes have to be cashed, a cost proportional to the amount (10 per cent in Edgeworth's example), is incurred, 'But if the demand is so great that he cannot even thus meet it, then he incurs an enormous forfeit, say 100 *l* or 1,000 *l*'. The player's initial fund is replenished every two minutes, but for the sake of simplicity interest earned is not allowed to be added to it. The player's problem, then, is essentially one of portfolio allocation of the type that we might nowadays model under the heading 'precautionary demand for liquid assets'.[24]

Edgeworth answers the 'nice question [of] how far this image of banking business idealises the original' (page 121), with the conjecture that it 'may be applicable to the reserve, at least of quiet banks in ordinary times', but not immediately to the Bank of England which may be 'pulled down by the panic-stricken public acting, not "independently", but like sheep'. However, referring to Mill who distinguished drains of reserves due to 'bad harvests, rise of cotton, &c, from drains due to overspeculation', Edgeworth suggested that those in the first category might be generated by a process which would make them behave in a fashion 'conforming to the law of error', and that their quantitative analysis, if this proved feasible, might enable to Bank to 'fix the reserve at such a point that it would not be likely from ordinary causes to fall below what Mr Bagehot calls the "apprehension minimum" ', (page 122).[25]

Remarkable though it is in its own right, given its date of publication, this application of probability theory to banking problems is not the most important contribution of Edgeworth's paper. He went on to describe how that same body of theory carried with it the implication of what we would now term economies of scale in reserve holding. The analysis was presented 'in a parable. A banker may be compared to a manager of a club who undertakes to supply dinner to as many members as present themselves any evening' (page 123). The manager of such a club would have to hold a reserve of provisions in such circumstances. However,

> Suppose now the number of members in the club to be doubled or trebled, while their habits are unaltered. At first sight it might appear that the reserve . . . should increase proportionately. But the corrected theory is that the ratio of the new reserve to the old should not be two or three, but the *square root* of two or three (page 124; Edgeworth's italics).

Moreover, if the managers of several clubs collude, they may achieve further economies, both because the economies yielded by the law of large numbers can be further exploited, but also because there might exist an interdependence among the demand for meals at their establishments 'in so far as part of the unusually large attendance at the one club is made up by members of another club invited as guests' (page 125). The moral of the parable then was obvious. Not only was there no necessary cause for concern in the fact that the Bank of England's reserve ratio had fallen between 1844 and 1873; but more generally, as far as bankers' balances were concerned:

> if n banks become co-ordinated by keeping their reserve in one prime bank, the reserve which is now required to meet their liabilities tends to be less than n times the previous average reserve for two reasons. First, in so far as payments by one bank are payments to another, cancellation may be substituted for cash payments. But, secondly, the reserve is reducible, not only in virtue of this interdependence of the banks, but also in virtue of their independence (page 126).

The economies of scale that can be realised by replacing a system of competing banks each holding its own reserve, with one based on a central bank, whose theoretical nature Edgeworth so clearly analysed, were not widely understood by economists even after the publication of his paper. However, on the practical front, it was surely those economies that, before World War I, led the United States Bank System to concentrate its reserves in New York even before the setting up of the Federal Reserve, and which also impelled a large number of smaller countries to economise on gold holdings by substituting for them bills drawn on London or New York. Edgeworth himself did not draw implications about the scope for concentration of reserves from his analysis, but Wicksell, who as we have seen earlier (Chapter 6, page 150) cited Edgeworth's paper as the source of a 'fuller account' of the role of the law of large numbers in the monetary system, did (cf. 1898, page 66, footnote 1). In his view it was logically possible that, if all the banks of a single country were connected by a common clearing house, 'they would require *no stock of cash* – not at any rate for purely domestic business' (1898, page 68; Wicksell's italics). Hence Edgeworthian analysis of the independence and interdependence of banks as factors influencing their demand for reserves became, for Wicksell, a key ingredient in establishing the logical possibility of 'a pure credit economy'. Although he knew well enough that such a system did not exist in practice, he was nevertheless willing to argue that in countries where specie did not circulate as coin, 'so far as purely domestic business is concerned . . . cash [hard currency] reserves . . . are now nothing more than a matter of tradition' (1898, page 69). And we have already seen how Wicksell's vision encompassed the possibility of extending such a system to the world as a whole and led him to advocate the establishment of an international paper standard.[26]

Concluding comment

The history of monetary policy discussions, and their interaction with the evolution of policy problems and the development of institutions has never been tidy, and, as we have seen, the period 1870–1914 provides no counter-example to this generalisation. Nevertheless one continuous thread runs through the discussion of this chapter, namely, the tension existing between, on the one hand, the quantity theory of money and theoretical ideas associated with it, and on the other hand, the theoretical basis of the then existing, and indeed spreading, monetary system based upon gold. At the very outset of the period, the supply and demand apparatus developed by Marshall, and deployed (though not clearly exhibited) by him in his contributions to policy debates, showed that the notion that gold had a stable 'natural' value which pinned down the purchasing power of gold-backed currency was simply false. The importance of the demand for gold in monetary uses relative to the *total* demand for it, combined with the very small ratio between current output and existing stocks, meant that the monetary value of gold was as 'artificial' as that of anything else upon which the monetary system might be based. In particular, the quantity theory could be, and was, used to demonstrate the viability of bimetallism, and to argue that a properly designed bimetallic system might be preferable to one based on gold alone.

Moreover, the quantity theory as it was developed during our period seemed to imply that price level fluctuations, particularly in the short run, presented serious problems, while simultaneously pointing to an array of potential remedies technically superior to bimetallism, which included indexed contracts, indexed money and, in the case of Wicksell at least, a completely managed paper money that dispensed entirely with gold. Marshall, Fisher, Hawtrey and other leading quantity theorists also understood how a managed currency could be made to work, but unlike Wicksell, they stopped short of advocating it. Their reasons for doing so, however, did not stem from doubts about the technical viability of such a system. Rather they feared the discretionary power that its introduction might give to policy-makers. But of course, in advocating indexation and international co-operation on monetary reform, they were already conceding that governments might be trusted to improve the system after all. An advocate of sound money like Robert Giffen may not have been a very good monetary theorist, but his political instincts led him to regard bimetallic systems, or indexation schemes, as the thin end of a (to him) dangerous wedge, and to oppose them. If his economic analysis was inferior to that of the neoclassical quantity theorists, his political judgement was perhaps more consistent than theirs.

Notes

1. The reader who is interested in a modern account of the system's properties is referred to Bordo (1987b) and Chen (1972). Walker (1878; Chapters XII–XIII), Walras (1886, 1889) and Fisher (1894) contain contemporary accounts of the system, and the latter paper was later incorporated with very little modification into Chapter VII of *The Purchasing Power of Money*.
2. The essentials of Walras' analysis of bimetallism are developed in 1886, though with less formality than in 1889. The quotations from Walras' *Élements* in the discussion that follows are from William Jaffé's (1954) translation, which is, of course, of the posthumus (1926), so-called

definitive, edition of that work. The text of Leçon 31 of the latter edition is, however, according to Jaffé, comparable with the text of the corresponding Leçon 34 in the 1889 second edition. There is no discussion of bimetallism in the first edition of *Élements*.

3. In short, the value theory he applied was essentially that of Adam Smith, though he cited Mill as its source, because he associated Smith with a specifically labour cost theory of long-run value. See Hucks-Gibbs and Grenfell (1886, page 307). (Note that this book is sometimes, misleadingly, catalogued under Hucks-Gibbs' later name, Baron Aldenham.)

4. Roger Mason (1989) presents a more favourable view of Giffen than emerges from the following discussion of his work. That is, I think, because Giffen's contributions to monetary economics were not only a small part of his total output, but also probably his least competent. Nevertheless, Mason does treat Giffen's contribution to the debate about bimetallism as enhancing his reputation, a judgement which I find it impossible to share. I do not mean to suggest here that the logic of the case put by bimetallists was in every respect beyond reproach. For example, J. S. Nicholson, whose 1893 *Treatise on Money* shows him to have been an able monetary economist on the whole, argued that the existence of widespread customary prices in India would induce sufficient rigidity into the purchasing power of silver as to force *down* the price level in terms of gold in gold standard countries in the face of a decline in silver's relative price. He also argued that the depreciating rupee would confer a long lasting competitive advantage on Indian producers, thus supporting a position against which Marshall was to argue in his Gold and Silver Commission evidence. (see pages 166–7).

5. As I noted earlier, the passages from Price which I quote were written before Marshall's monetary analysis (which clearly brought out the essentially endogenous nature of a commodity money's marginal cost of production) had made its appearance in print. There can be no such excuse for Giffen's neglect of this contribution.

6. Laughlin's *Principles* was of course published at a time when bimetallism was a dead issue. However, it is cited here as the source of his views on the matter because of its comprehensiveness. The views themselves had permeated his writings for the previous two decades.

7. This particular view of Laughlin's was explicitly taken up and rebutted by Fisher (1911, pages 261–2) and Wicksell (1915, page 152). See above Chapter 5, page 122). In its stress on money's future 'backing' as the source of its current value, Laughlin's analysis is similar to that of Thomas Sargent and Neil Wallace (1983), though it differs to the extent that it is the prospect of gold convertibility, rather than of sound fiscal policy, that provides the backing in question.

8. Even now, certain facts of French experience are somewhat obscure. As we have noted earlier, the market price of the metals never deviated by more than 2 per cent away from the mint parity which overvalued gold before about 1850, and silver thereafter. Even now, therefore, as

in the 1880s and 1890s, those sympathetic to bimetallism (such as Friedman, 1990) can point to the French experience as an example of the system's success in stabilising the monetary system. Moreover, data cited both by the Gold and Silver Commission in their *Report* of 1889, and by Giffen (1892a) do show that, in every year between 1803 and 1873, some coins were struck of both metals, and this is prima-facie evidence that a bimetallic circulation was maintained in France. However, the amounts of gold minted before 1850 and of silver thereafter, were very small, so it can be argued that the system was really one of alternating monometallism, and hence to that limited extent inconvenient and a failure. This was Jevons' view and Giffen's too.

9. Not that to contemporaries the mid-1890s appeared to mark the end of bimetallism as a political force. The Bimetallic League actually founded a new journal *The Bimetallist* in 1895, with a lead article by its president, Henry Hucks-Gibbs, in which he proclaimed:

> [our statesmen] see the picture in its true colours, and its aspect is so dreadful to them that they are determined to have it altered. It is that which makes our prospect bright – that will insure us success in the near future (page 2).

10. Sir David Barbour was in fact responsible for closing the Indian mints to silver in 1893. He had been a bimetallist in the 1880s, and a member of the Gold and Silver Commission, so this action involved him in a significant switch of position. Keynes (1913) praised the 'statesmanlike opportunism' which he displayed, and compared it favourably to 'the dogmatism of, for example, Sir Robert Giffen' (page 393).

11. Such a system was in place in the United States by the beginning of the twentieth century. The silver component of the currency was not, however, there to be used for stabilisation purposes as Walras had suggested. Rather, it simply existed as a legacy of earlier political debates about bimetallism in particular and the place of silver in the United States monetary system in general. The Bland Act of 1878 and the Sherman Act of 1890 had resulted in substantial coinage of token silver dollars, but the practice had been suspended in 1893. Silver certificates backed by treasury holdings of the metal were also in circulation. As Fisher (1911, page 144) commented 'The idle silver in the treasury vaults represents mere waste, a subsidy given by the government to encourage silver mining'. See Fisher (1911, pages 143ff) for a contemporary commentary on the US Monetary System, and Friedman and Schwartz (1963 Chapters 3 and 4) for a more recent description.

12. And in 1887, in a footnote later cited by Keynes (1925), he outlined two of these. The first amounted to symmetallism modified so that the rate at which paper money was convertible into the metals would vary with their value relative to goods, and was therefore the prototype both of Williams (1892) scheme, discussed below (page 176), and Fisher's compensated dollar discussed on pages 177–8. The second involved

adopting a paper currency, and stabilising its value by manipulating the rate of interest, and is essentially the same as that proposed for the international monetary system by Wicksell (1898) discussed on pages 178–80. Marshall, however, discussed this second scheme in the context of a single open economy, and in this respect his speculations are closer to those of Hawtrey mentioned on page 179. Though Marshall outlined these schemes, he explicitly declined to advocate them.

13. I have discussed Jevons' analysis of these matters in Laidler (1982). The comment that they presented 'more scientific than practical' problems is cited by Fetter (1965, page 248) as that of an anonymous contributor to the *Westminster Review*.

14. Let it be explicitly noted that I am not one of those who regards the sunspot theory as ridiculous. For a fuller account of the matter see Laidler (1982).

15. And indeed it generated sufficient interest for the British Association for the Advancement of Science to set up a Committee to investigate its feasibility. Edgeworth's important contributions to the theory of index numbers grew directly from his work as secretary of that committee. They are collected, along with a short piece prepared for the Committee by Giffen, also prepared for this Committee, in Edgeworth (1925) Volume 1. The relevant Committee's reports appear in the British Association for the Advancement of Science's *Reports* for 1887, 1888 and 1889.

16. Williams was, at the time of writing this article, a director of the Linthorpe iron works at Middlesbrough, and had been mentioned by Walras (1886) as 'un de mes correspondents anglais'. He was a prominent member of the Co-operative Movement, and the author of a monograph on *Co-operation* for the Home University Library, the same series in which Pigou's (1913a) *Unemployment* appeared. He was also a Justice of the Peace in Middlesbrough, and later a Labour Member of Parliament.

17. I base this conjecture on Keynes' (1925) suggestion that it was an attack by *The Economist* on his monetary reform proposals that unnerved Marshall. It seems more likely to me that it was these *Economic Journal* publications that had this effect, not least because Giffen's piece, ostensibly an attack on the non-academic Williams, does warn 'some of our younger economists' (left unnamed) not to become impractical in their treatment of monetary issues. One must also note the Gold and Silver Commission's summary treatment of symmetallism as a possible factor here. However, it is also the case that, by the end of the 1890s when Marshall next pronounced on monetary policy issues, the British monetary system had weathered the Baring Crisis, and seemed to be functioning far better than could have been hoped even a decade earlier. Marshall's loss of interest in promoting monetary reform may also be related to these developments (see pages 181–2).

18. Wicksell was quite innocent of the potentially destabilising influence of lag effects on the type of feedback mechanism he here described. It

should be noted that the policy regime he sketched in 1898, however other-wordly it must have seemed at that time, is nevertheless the recognisable prototype for many of the proposals made by the Stockholm School in the 1920s and 1930s, and of much utterly conventional wisdom of the 1950s and 1960s that is more often associated with Keynesian economics.

19. The reader seeking a more detailed account of these matters is referred to Goodhart's excellent (1985) monograph, particularly Annex B.

20. The monetary history of this period is dealt with both by Oliver Sprague (1910) and also, of course, by Friedman and Schwartz (1963).

21. Once again, the reader is referred to Friedman and Schwartz (1963) for an account of the evolution of the Federal Reserve System, and how that differed in practice from the intentions of its architects.

22. And of course modern advocates of 'free banking', such as Kevin Dowd (1989), George Selgin (1988) and Glasner (1989), are essentially repeating Bagehot's views. This is not the place to become embroiled in this latest round of an old debate. Suffice it to note that I believe modern advocates of free banking pay insufficient attention to the implications of the analysis of Edgeworth (1888) and Wicksell (1898), to be discussed below.

23. The paper is cited neither in Edgeworth's entry in the *International Encyclopaedia of the Social Sciences* nor that in *The New Palgrave* (see Charles Hildreth (1968) and Peter Newman (1987), respectively). Its importance is, however, acknowledged in another paper which has attracted far less attention than it deserves, namely Malcolm Gray and Michael Parkin (1973), where it is correctly characterised as the starting point for all subsequent analysis of what we now call the precautionary motive for maintaining liquidity.

24. It should be said that Edgeworth asserts the general nature, rather than derives the precise form, of the solution to this problem. (See 1888, pages 120–1).

25. See Chapter 2, page 38 above for a brief discussion of Bagehot's treatment of this concept.

26. See above, Chapter 5, page 128, and this chapter, pages 178–80 for further commentary on Wicksell's treatment of these issues.

7 • A summing up

Monetary theory on the eve of World War I was very a different body of doctrine from that of the early 1870s. In the forty-five-year period covered by this book the following advances had taken place. The transactions version of the quantity theory had received a systematic algebraic formulation and its implications had been worked out with a degree of clarity that has no parallel in the literature of earlier classical orthodoxy. The alternative Cambridge supply and demand for money formulation of the theory had also been completely worked out (as had its Walrasian variant), though a fully fledged account of it was not to be published until 1917. The operations of a modern commercial banking system had been integrated into the quantity theory framework, with a sureness of touch that economists of an earlier generation had failed to attain. In the hands of Wicksell this latter development had led on to his analysis of the 'cumulative process', a piece of theorising which even today receives and merits respectful treatment from textbook writers. Fisher and the Cambridge School had, between them, ensured that the influence of inflation expectations on interest rates had been put at the centre of a monetary explanation of the business cycle. Finally the analysis of the cycle had been broadened to incorporate output and employment fluctuations associated with wage stickiness, not to mention, in the hands of Hawtrey, systematic variations in the public's demand for currency relative to bank deposits arising from the distributional effects of those fluctuations.

In the policy area too, things had moved far beyond Bagehot. Edgeworth and Wicksell had developed analytic tools with which to show that, far from being an unnatural product of particular historical circumstances, central banking was in fact the outcome of the economies of scale implicit in the operations of any monetary system based on commercial banks. And if the analysis in question was not yet either widely read or understood, the forces with which it dealt had been at work in the world for all to see. The US banking system, which Bagehot had thought 'natural' had moved towards centralising its reserves on a group of New York Banks, and had shown itself prone to the type of financial instability which by the end of the nineteenth century had become a thing of the past in Britain. This instability had given a powerful impetus to the creation of the Federal Reserve System which began its operations in 1913. On the international front, the same forces underlay the spread of a Gold Exchange Standard under which reserves were becoming centralised in particular financial centres, notably London, but also to a lesser extent New York. The development of the Gold Exchange Standard was largely spontaneous, and, along with increased gold supplies coming from the Transvaal and the Yukon, appeared in the first decade of the twentieth century to be producing a degree of monetary stability, both national and international, which twenty years earlier had seemed unattainable.

Experience prior to the mid-1890s nevertheless left its mark on the literature dealing with monetary policy. In the first half of the nineteenth century, conventional English classical wisdom had it that gold, if not utterly stable in value, was nevertheless more stable than other commodities, and therefore the appropriate basis for the monetary system. The mild inflation of the 1850s, and Jevons' response to it notwithstanding, the orthodoxy of the 1870s, at least as represented by Bagehot, still incorporated this view. The international spread of the Gold Standard, and the deflation of the 1870s and 1880s that accompanied it, however, led monetary economists to pay more attention than they had in earlier times to devising and debating schemes other than specie convertibility for providing price stability. As I have tried to show in the preceding chapters the most interesting of these schemes were not *ad hoc* measures devised for the moment. Rather, they were explicitly based on the theoretical developments described in earlier chapters. In particular, it was the development of the neoclassical quantity theory which finally undermined the idea that there was something 'natural' about the market value of gold rendering it specially suitable as a basis for the monetary system; and it was the neoclassical monetary theory of the cycle which made short-run price stability, and hence indexation, seem so attractive.

There was nothing new, in and of itself, about monetary reform being proposed and debated, of course. Such debate had come and gone from the early eighteenth century onwards. Far more so after 1870 than in earlier times, however, quite radical proposals came not from fringe groups but from the intellectual leaders in monetary economics. It was, after all, Marshall and Edgeworth who advocated symmetallism; Jevons, Marshall and Fisher who proposed various degrees of indexation; and Wicksell who recommended a managed international paper standard. The intellectual stature of their supporters, however, did not mean that such proposals got anywhere on the practical front, and the very success of the Gold Exchange Standard in the latter part of our period was associated with a considerable lessening of pressure for monetary reform. Nevertheless, whatever the actual state of the monetary system in 1914, the idea that its performance as regards both secular and, far more important, cyclical price stability could be improved by conscious manipulation, had gained a currency and degree of intellectual respectability which it had not had earlier; and which, once established, did not fade away again.

The changes in monetary thought discussed here did not come into being by way of any sudden intellectual revolution. Provided continuity is not confused with mere repetition, it is easy to defend the claim that there was considerable continuity between classical and neoclassical monetary economics. Marshall's development of the supply and demand approach to the quantity theory was the result of a self-conscious effort to clarify what Mill had to say about the respective roles of cost of production and the quantity of money in determining the price level; though the fact that Mill was also open to the type of interpretation that, say, Nicholson or Price put upon him surely shows that such clarification was badly needed.[1] Wicksell's cumulative process was in many respects a revival of ideas that Thornton (1802) had developed in *Paper Credit*. Though this work had more or less dropped from sight by the 1870s, traces of its analysis were still present in the classical analysis of that time, and Wicksell himself was quite conscious that he was building upon the work of his classical predecessors. And Fisher, as we have seen, was explicitly attempting to restore the intellectual reputation of what he characterised as the monetary theory of Ricardo and Mill.

In short, there is hardly an idea among those discussed in this book which cannot be, and indeed has not been, shown to be linked to a component of the earlier orthodoxy. Perhaps Edgeworth's application of probability theory to the analysis of banking and the Cambridge deployment of the idea of money wage stickiness as an explanation of cyclical employment fluctuations are the main exceptions here. But the fact remains that, if an existing body of knowledge undergoes enough clarifications, and enough shifts of emphasis, an essentially new doctrine is the outcome; and though monetary economics moved in a series of small steps, it nevertheless travelled a long way between 1870 and 1914. Even so the neo-classical theory of 1914, say, was in its own way incomplete and full of tensions whose resolution was to occupy the attention of economists in the interwar years.

Neoclassical monetary economics' handling of output and employment fluctuations was particularly weak. That such fluctuations were an important integral part of the cycle was clear enough to the Cambridge economists, who, among monetary theorists, made most of the running in this area during our period. But their explanation went almost completely in terms of the influence of real wage fluctuations on the demand for labour. Such analysis, as Keynes (1936) in particular was later to make clear, involved applying, and perhaps misapplying, partial equilibrium tools that were appropriate enough for dealing with a single market to the economy as a whole. By later standards, neoclassical analysis of unemployment was, to say the least, primitive and incomplete. Though the relevant literature does contain references to quantity spillover effects which, with benefit of hindsight, look like hints at the multiplier process, not to mention a number of rather full expositions of the accelerator mechanism, none of these was integrated into a coherent cycle theory. Neoclassical cycle theory recognised the explanation of quantity fluctuations as an important problem, but it did not provide a satisfactory solution to it.

Neoclassical economists' failure fully to appreciate that the theory of the demand for money could be developed into a theory of portfolio selection was surely an important factor preventing progress towards a more satisfactory explanation of real fluctu-ations. I have already described and attempted to explain the incompleteness of the Cambridge theory of the demand for money in this respect (cf. Chapter 3, pages 60–4) and there is no need to repeat that discussion here. Suffice it to note that with the work of Frederick Lavington (1921), Keynes (1930) and Hicks (1935), this deficiency was repaired, financial assets came to be regarded as alternative stores of value to money, and their rate of return recognised as the opportunity cost of holding it and hence as an argument in a demand for money function. Once this matter was clarified, it became possible to argue that the interest rate had, as it were, too much work to do in a monetary economy. It now seemed to be required both to equilibrate portfolios, and co-ordinate intertemporal choices concerning the allocation of resources. That output fluctuations provided an alternative equilibrating mechanism here was of course, the central theoretical contribution of Keynes' *General Theory*.

Leijonhufvud (1981) has noted that doubts about the smooth functioning of the intertemporal allocation mechanism, and hence about the capacity of a market economy to deliver steady full employment growth, were already implicit in Wicksell's work. Those same doubts informed the work of the Austrian theorists, who in the 1920s combined Wicksell's cumulative process analysis with the classical forced saving doctrine to produce Austrian cycle theory, and of Wicksell's Swedish followers too. However, to repeat, it was the theory of liquidity preference, as developed by Keynes and Hicks from Cambridge monetary theory, that enabled a coherent analysis of the potential for failure inherent in the intertemporal choice mechanism of a monetary economy to be constructed by Keynes and his followers. These theoretical developments of the interwar years, and others of less central importance, would in due course transform neoclassical monetary economics into what came to be called Keynesian macroeconomics. But the creation of Keynesian economics, like that of neoclassical economics before it, was, on this reading, a matter of responding to the gaps and tensions inherent in an already existing body of knowledge; it was not a matter of sweeping aside all that had gone before and starting afresh, as the leaders of the 'Keynesian revolution', including Keynes himself, so often and so misleadingly were to claim.

If Keynesian theory evolved from, rather than overthrew, neo-classical monetary theory, so too, did the Keynesian attitude to policy evolve from early doctrines. It is the hallmark of that attitude to doubt the efficacy of unregulated markets, and to intervene at strategic points with a view to improving their performance. In the macroeconomic area, this general concern translates into a belief that full employment is likely to be the outcome of a careful programme of fiscal and monetary intervention, rather than the automatic product of market forces. It is well known that in the 1920s, and thus before the *General Theory* provided an intellectual basis for such advocacy, the majority of neoclassical economists were recommending 'public works' as a cure for unemployment.[2] In this book I have tried to show that, even before World War I, the whole tenor of neoclassical discussions of monetary reform, dealing as they did with schemes for replacing the Gold Standard, the introduction of indexation and so on, involved the subjection of a hallowed institution to intellectual scrutiny with a view to improving it. Those discussions also established that the way in which that institution worked was itself the result of human intervention.

I am not here suggesting that Marshall, Pigou, Fisher, or anyone else was a Keynesian in any detail of their specific policy recommendations of course, but I am suggesting, more generally, that there is far less difference between neoclassical and Keynesian attitudes to policy intervention, particularly in the monetary area, than is commonly believed. The economists whose contributions I have analysed in this book did not regard any particular set of monetary arrangements as sacrosanct. For most of them, the acid test of any system was its capacity to deliver price level stability and hence, they believed, output and employment stability too. As I have already noted, the Gold Exchange Standard was working well enough in 1914 that advocacy of its reform or replacement was then at a low ebb. World War I changed all that. If, in the war's aftermath, the restoration of the Gold Standard became simply one possibility on a menu for political choice, finally to be rejected in 1931 once the attempt at restoration had clearly failed to produce the desired outcome of economic stability, that is surely partly because neoclassical monetary economics had long taught that such matters should be dealt with in just this way. As to the subsequent adoption of Keynesian policy doctrines, that too was the natural product of treating the choice of economic institutions as a political one, to be made on pragmatic grounds.

The neoclassical economists were, to repeat, not Keynesians, but the intellectual environment in which Keynesian ideas flourished was, to an important extent, the product of the work which they did before World War I. This book makes only part of the case for this conclusion; because, although it attempts to document certain important changes in monetary thought which took place before

1914, an equally detailed treatment of the evolution of economic doctrine in the interwar years is required to complete it. I hope to provide such a treatment in a successor to this volume.

Notes

1. See Chapter 6 above, page 160, 189; *see also* Chapter 3 above, page 85.
2. And indeed, it should be noted that as early as 1886 (pages 58-9) Foxwell recommended public works expenditures as a device for mitigating unemployment. The view that such measures could be effective was widely enough held by the end of our period that, as I noted in Chapter 4, Pigou (1913b, page 581) took Hawtrey to task for arguing against it.

References

Aftalion, A. (1909) 'La réalité des surproductions générales 3me installment', *Revue d'Economie Politique* 23 (Mar.), 201–29.

Arnon, A. (forthcoming) *Thomas Tooke – Pioneer of Monetary Theory*, Aldershot, Hants; Edward Elgar.

Bagehot, W. (1873) *Lombard Street: A Description of the Money Market*, London: P. S. King (reprinted 1962, F. C. Genovese (ed.), Homewood, Ill: Richard Irwin).

Bagehot, W. (1875) 'A new standard of value', *The Economist*, 20 Nov., reprinted 1892, *Economic Journal* 2 (Sept.), 472–7.

Bailey, R. E. (1976) 'On the analytical foundations of Wicksell's cumulative process', *Manchester School* 44 (Mar.), 52–71.

Barbour, D. (1912) *The Standard of Value*, London: Macmillan.

Barkai, H. (1989) 'The old historical school: Roscher on money and monetary issues', *History of Political Economy* 21, No. 2, 179–200.

Becker, G. and Baumol, W. (1952) 'The classical monetary theory: the outcome of the discussion' *Economica* NS 19 (Nov.), 355–76.

Bickerdike, C. F. (1914) 'A non-monetary cause of fluctuations in employment', *Economic Journal* 24 (Sept.), 357–70.

Blomqvist, Å., Wonnacott, P. and Wonnacott, R. (1983) *Economics*, Toronto: McGraw-Hill.

Bordo, M. (1975) 'John Cairnes on the effects of the Australian gold discoveries 1851–72: an early application of the methodology of positive economics', *History of Political Economy* 7, No. 3, 337–59.

Bordo, M. (1987a) 'Equation of exchange' in Eatwell, J., Milgate, M. and Newman, P. (eds) *The New Palgrave – A Dictionary of Economics*, London: Macmillan.

Bordo, M. (1987b) 'Bimetallism' in Eatwell, J., Milgate, M. and Newman, P. (eds) *The New Palgrave – A Dictionary of Economics,* London: Macmillan.

Bordo, M. and Jonung, L. (1987) *The Long-run Behaviour of the Velocity of Circulation*, Cambridge: Cambridge University Press.

Bridel, P. (1987) *Cambridge Monetary Thought*, London: Macmillan.

Cairnes, J. E. (1860) 'Essays towards a solution of the gold question' (reprinted 1873, Cairnes, J. E.).

Cairnes, J. E. (1873) *Essays in Political Economy*, London: Macmillan (reprinted 1965, New York: Augustus Kelley).

Cannan, E. (1919) *The Paper Pound 1797-1821 (The Bullion Report of 1810)*, London: P. S. King and Son (reprinted 1969, New York: Augustus Kelley).

Cantillon, R. (1734) *Essai sur la nature du commerce en général*, edited with English translation, H. Higgs, 1931, London: Macmillan.

Carver, T. N. (1897) 'The value of the money unit', *Quarterly Journal of Economics* 11 (July), 429-35.

Carver, T. N. (1903) 'A suggestion for a theory of industrial depressions', *Quarterly Journal of Economics* 17 (May), 497-500.

Cassel, G. (1904) 'Om förändringar i den allmänna prisnivån' (On Changes in the Price Level), *Ekonomisk Tidskrift* 6, 311-31.

Cernuschi, H. (1876) *M. Michel Chevalier et le Bimétallisme - Articles Publiés dans le Siècle en Avril et Mai 1876*, Paris: Librairie de Guillaumin et Cie.

Chen, C. N. (1972) 'Bimetallism: theory and controversy in perspective', *History of Political Economy* 4 (Spring), 89-112.

Chevalier, M. (1859) *On the Probable Fall in the Value of Gold*, translated by R. Cobden, New York: D. Appleton.

Chipman, J. (1987) 'Bickerdike, Charles Frederick' in Eatwell, J., Milgate, M. and Newman, P. (eds) *The New Palgrave - A Dictionary of Economics,* London: Macmillan.

Clark, J. M. (1917) 'Business acceleration and the law of demand: a technical factor in economic cycles', *Journal of Political Economy* 25 (Mar.), 217-35.

Corry, B. A. (1962) *Money, Saving and Investment in English Economics 1800-1850*, London: Macmillan.

Cottrell, A. (1989) 'Price expectations and equilibrium when the interest-rate is pegged', *Scottish Journal of Political Economy* 36 (May), 125-40.

Deutscher, P. (1990) *R. G. Hawtrey and the Development of*

Macroeconomics, London: Macmillan.

Dornbusch, R. (1976) 'Expectations and exchange rate dynamics', *Journal of Political Economy*, 84 (December), 1161–76.

Dowd, K. (1989) *The State and the Monetary System*, Hemel Hempstead: Philip Allan.

Edgeworth, F. Y. (1887) 'Memorandum by the Secretary, Attendant to Report on Variations in the Value of the Monetary Standard', *Report of the British Association for the Advancement of Science*, pages 254–301.

Edgeworth, F. Y. (1888) 'The mathematical theory of banking', *Journal of the Royal Statistical Society* 51 (Mar.), 113–26.

Edgeworth, F. Y. (1895) 'Thoughts on monetary reform', *Economic Journal* 5 (Sept.), 434–51.

Edgeworth, F. Y. (1925) *Papers Relating to Political Economy*, 3 vols, London: Macmillan for the Royal Economic Society.

Eshag, E. (1963) *From Marshall to Keynes*, Oxford: Blackwell.

Fetter, F.W. (1965) *Development of British Monetary Orthodoxy*, Cambridge, MA: Harvard University Press.

Fetter, F. W. (1968) 'The transfer problem: formal elegance or historical realism' in C. R. Whittlesey and J. S. G. Wilson (eds.) *Essays in Money and Banking in Honour of R. S. Sayers*, Oxford: Clarendon Press.

Fisher, I. (1894) 'The mechanics of bimetallism', *Economic Journal* 4 (Sept.), 341–55.

Fisher, I. (1896) 'Appreciation and interest' *AEA Publications* 3 (11) (Aug.), 331–442.

Fisher, I. (1911) (Revised 1913). *The Purchasing Power of Money*, New York: Macmillan.

Fisher, I. (1923) 'The business cycle – largely a "Dance of the Dollar" ', *Journal of the American Statistical Association* 18 (Dec.), 1024–8.

Foxwell, H. S. (1886) *Irregularity of Employment and Fluctuations of Prices*, Edinburgh: Co-operative Printing Co. Ltd.

Friedman, M. (1990) 'Bimetallism Revisited', *The Journal of Economic Perspectives* 4 (Fall), 85–104.

Friedman, M. and Schwartz, A. J. (1963) *A Monetary History of the United States 1867–1960*, Princeton, NJ: Princeton University Press for the National Bureau of Economic Research.

Giffen, R. (1877) *Stock Exchange Securities*, London: G. Bell.

Giffen, R. (1886) 'On some bimetallic fallacies', (Reprinted in

Giffen, R. (1892a)).

Giffen, R. (1889) 'A problem in money', *The Nineteenth Century*, (reprinted in Giffen, R. (1892a)).

Giffen, R. (1892a) *The Case Against Bimetallism* (2nd edn), London: G. Bell and Sons.

Giffen, R. (1892b) 'Fancy monetary standards', *Economic Journal* 2 (Sept.), 209–38.

Glasner, D. (1985) 'A reinterpretation of classical monetary theory' *Southern Economic Journal* 52 (July), 46–67.

Glasner, D. (1989) *Free Banking and Monetary Reform*, Cambridge: Cambridge University Press.

Gold and Silver Commission (Royal Commission Appointed to Enquire Into Recent Changes in the Relative Values of the Precious Metals) (1889) *Final Report*, Washington: Government Printing Office [*sic*].

Goodhart, C. A. E. (1985) *The Evolution of Central Banks*, London: London School of Economics.

Goschen, G. J. (1861) *The Theory of Foreign Exchanges*, London: Effingham Wilson.

Gray, M. and Parkin, J. M. (1973) 'Portfolio diversification as optimal precautionary behaviour', in Morishima, M. (ed.), *Theories of Demand, Real and Monetary*, London: Oxford University Press.

Haberler, G. (1937), *Prosperity and Depression*, Geneva: League of Nations; 6th edn (1964), Cambridge, MA: Harvard University Press.

Harrington, R. (1989) 'The classical quantity theory', in Cobham, D. Harrington, R. and Zis, G. (eds), *Money, Trade and Payments*, Manchester: Manchester University Press.

Harrod, R. (1969) *Money*, London: Macmillan.

Hawtrey, R. (1913) *Good and Bad Trade*, London: Constable.

Hayek, F. A. von (1931) *Prices and Production*, London: Routledge and Kegan Paul.

Hayek, F. A. von (1932) 'A note on the development of the doctrine of forced saving' *Quarterly Journal of Economics* 47, 123–33.

Hegeland, H. (1951) *The Quantity Theory of Money* (reprinted 1966, New York: Augustus Kelley).

Hicks, J. R. (1935) 'A suggestion for simplifying the theory of money', *Economica*, NS 2 (Feb.), 1–19.

Hicks, J. R. (1983) 'From classical to post-classical: the work of J.

S. Mill', in *Classics and Moderns*, Cambridge, MA: Harvard University Press.

Hicks, J. R. (1989) *A Market Theory of Money*, London: Oxford University Press.

Hildreth, C. (1968) 'F. Y. Edgeworth', in *The International Encyclopaedia of the Social Sciences*, New York: Macmillan and the Free Press.

Hobson, J. A. (1894) *The Evolution of Modern Capitalism*, London: Walter Scott.

Hollander, S. (1979) *The Economics of David Ricardo*, Toronto: University of Toronto Press.

Hollander, S. (1986) *The Economics of John Stuart Mill*, Toronto: University of Toronto Press.

Horton, S. D. (1887) *The Silver Pound and England's Monetary Policy Since the Restoration*, London: Macmillan.

Howitt, P. W. (1989) 'Wicksell's cumulative process as non-convergence to rational expectations equilibrium', London Ontario: University of Western Ontario (mimeo).

Hucks-Gibbs, H. and Grenfell, H. R. (eds) (1886) *The Bimetallic Controversy*, London: Effingham Wilson.

Hume, D. (1752) 'Of Money', 'Of the Balance of Trade' and 'Of Interest' in *Essays Moral, Political and Literary*, (reprinted 1963, London: Oxford University Press).

Humphrey, T. M. (1984) 'Algebraic quantity equations before Fisher and Pigou', *Federal Reserve Bank of Richmond Economic Review* (Sept./Oct.), 13–22.

Jevons, W. S. (1862) 'On the study of periodic commercial fluctuations', (reprinted in Jevons, W.S. (1884)).

Jevons, W. S. (1863) 'A serious fall in the value of gold ascertained and its social effects set forth,' (reprinted in Jevons, W. S. (1884)).

Jevons, W. S. (1866) 'On the frequent autumnal pressure in the money market, and the action of the Bank of England', (reprinted in Jevons, W. S. (1884)).

Jevons, W. S. (1868) 'Gold and silver: a letter to M. Wolowski', (reprinted in Jevons, W. S. (1884)).

Jevons, W. S. (1875) *Money and the Mechanism of Exchange*, London: C. Kegan Paul and Co. (reprinted 1877 New York: D. Appleton).

Jevons, W. S. (1881) 'Bimetallism', (reprinted in Jevons, W. S. (1884)).

Jevons, W. S. (1884) *Investigations in Currency and Finance* edited by H. S. Foxwell, London: Macmillan.

Jonung, L. (1979) 'Knut Wicksell and Gustav Cassell on secular movements in prices', *Journal of Money, Credit and Banking* 11 (May), 165–81.

Jonung, L. (1988) 'Knut Wicksell's unpublished manuscripts – a first glance', *European Economic Review* 32, March 505–11.

Jonung, L. (ed.) (1991) *The Stockholm School of Economics Revisited*, Cambridge: Cambridge University Press.

Juglar, C. (1860) *Des crises commerciales et leur retour périodique en France, en Angleterre et aux Etats-Unis* 1st edn, (5th edn, 1938, Paris, reprinted 1969, New York: Burt Franklin).

Kemmerer, E. W. (1909) *Money and Credit Instruments in their Relation to General Prices*, New York: H. Holt.

Keynes, J. M. (1911) 'Review of Irving Fisher: *The Purchasing Power of Money*', *Economic Journal* 21 (Sept.), 393–8.

Keynes, J. M. (1912) *Indian Currency and Finance*, London: Macmillan.

Keynes, J. M. (1913) 'Review of Sir David Barbour: *The Standard of Value*', *Economic Journal* 23 (Sept.), 390–3.

Keynes, J. M. (1923) *A Tract on Monetary Reform*, London: Macmillan.

Keynes, J. M. (1925) 'Alfred Marshall' in A. C. Pigou (ed.), *Memorials of Alfred Marshall,* London: Macmillan.

Keynes, J. M. (1930) *A Treatise on Money*, London: Macmillan.

Keynes, J. M. (1936) *The General Theory of Employment, Interest and Money*, London: Macmillan.

Kirtzner, I. (1987) 'L. von Mises' in Eatwell, J., Milgate, M. and Newman, P. (eds) *The New Palgrave – A Dictionary of Economics*, London: Macmillan.

Kohn, M. (1985) 'On the long-run real effects of inside money and outside money: an examination of some propositions stated by Cairnes and Mill', London Ontario: University of Western Ontario (mimeo).

Kompas, T. (1989) *Studies in the History of Long Run Equilibrium Theory*, PhD dissertation, University of Toronto.

Kydland, F. and Prescott, E. (1982) 'Time to Build and Aggregate Fluctuations' *Econometrica* 50 (Sept.), 1345–70.

Laidler, D. (1972) 'On Wicksell's theory of price level dynamics', *Manchester School* 40 (June), 125–44.

Laidler, D. (1973) 'Thomas Tooke on Monetary Reform' in Peston, M. and Corry, B. (eds), *Essays in Honour of Lord Robbins*, London: Weidenfeld and Nicholson.

Laidler, D. (1981) 'Adam Smith as a monetary economist', *Canadian Journal of Economics*, 14 (May), 185–200.

Laidler, D. (1982) 'Jevons on money', *Manchester School* 50 (Dec.), 326–53.

Laidler, D. (1987a) 'The bullionist controversy' in Eatwell, J., Milgate, M. and Newman, P. (eds), *The New Palgrave – A Dictionary of Economics*, London: Macmillan.

Laidler, D. (1987b) 'What was new about liquidity preference theory,' London Ontario: University of Western Ontario (mimeo).

Laidler, D. (1991) 'The Austrians and the Stockholm School – two failures in the development of macroeconomics', in Jonung, L. (ed.).

Laughlin, J. L. (1885) *A History of Bimetallism in the United States*, New York: Appleton.

Laughlin, J. L. (1887) 'Gold and prices since 1873', *Quarterly Journal of Economics* 1 (Apr.), 319–55.

Laughlin, J. L. (1903) *The Principles of Money*, New York: Charles Scribnet's & Sons.

Laughlin, J. L. (1909) 'Gold and prices 1890–1907,' *Journal of Political Economy* 17 (May), 257–71.

Lavington, F. (1921) *The English Capital Market*, London: Methuen.

Leijonhufvud, A. (1968) *On Keynesian Economics and the Economics of Keynes*, London: Oxford University Press.

Leijonhufvud, (1981) 'The Wicksell connection', in *Information and Co-ordination*, London: Oxford University Press.

Lucas, R. E. Jr (1972) 'Expectations and the neutrality of money' *Journal of Economic Theory* 4 (2), 115–38.

Lundberg, E. (1937) *Studies in the Theory of Economic Expansion*, (reprinted 1964, New York: Augustus Kelley).

Malthus, T. R. (1811) 'Depreciation of paper currency' *Edinburgh Review* 17 (Feb.), 340–72.

Marget, A. (1931) 'Leon Walras and the "Cash balance approach to the value of money" ', *Journal of Political Economy* 39 (Oct.), 569–600.

Marget, A. (1938–42) *The Theory of Prices*, 2 vols., New York: Prentice Hall.

Marshall, A. (1871) 'Money' in J. Whittaker (ed.) (1975). *The Early Economic Writings of Alfred Marshall*, 2 vols, London: Macmillan.

Marshall, A. (1887) 'Remedies for fluctuations in general prices', *Contemporary Review*, (reprinted in A. C. Pigou (ed.) (1925), *Memorials of Alfred Marshall*, London: Macmillan).

Marshall, A. (1890) *Principles of Economics*, London: Macmillan.

Marshall, A. (1923) *Money, Credit and Commerce*, London: Macmillan.

Marshall, A. (1926) *Official Papers of Alfred Marshall* edited by J. M. Keynes, London: Macmillan.

Marshall, A. and Marshall, M. P. (1879) *Economics of Industry*, London: Macmillan.

Marx, K. (1867) *Capital* Volume 1 (translated 1883 from 3rd German edn by S. More and E. Aveling and edited by F. Engels, reprinted 1961, Moscow, Foreign Languages Publishing House).

Mason, R. S. (1989) *Robert Giffen and the Giffen Paradox*, Oxford: Philip Allan.

Menger, C. (1893) 'On the origin of money', *Economic Journal* 2 (June), 239–55.

Mill, J. S. (1844) 'On the influence of consumption upon production' in *Essays on Unsettled Questions in Political Economy*, (2nd edn, 1874) London: Longmans, Green, Reader and Dyer, (reprinted 1967 New York: Augustus Kelley).

Mill, J. S. (1871) *The Principles of Political Economy with Some of Their Applications to Social Philosophy* 7th edn, London (reprinted 1965 in 2 vols, edited by J. M. Robson, Toronto: University of Toronto Press.)

Mises, L. von (1912) *The Theory of Money and Credit* 2nd edn (1924) translated by H. E. Batson (1934), London: Jonathan Cape. (reprinted 1953, New Haven: Yale University Press).

Mitchell, W. C. (1896) 'The quantity theory of the value of money' *Journal of Political Economy* 4 (Mar.), 139–65.

Mitchell, W. C. (1914) 'The new banking measure in the United States', *Economic Journal* 24 (Mar.), 130–8.

Myhrman, J. (1991) 'The monetary economics of the Stockholm School: a perspective', in Jonung, L. (ed.) (1991).

Newcomb, S. (1885) *Principles of Political Economy*, New York: Harper & Bros.

Newman, P. (1987) 'F. Y. Edgeworth' in Eatwell, J., Milgate, M. and Newman, P. (eds) *The New Palgrave – A Dictionary of Economics*, London: Macmillan.

Nicholson, J. S. (1893) *A Treatise on Money and Essays on Monetary Problems* 2nd edn, London: A. and C. Black.

Ohlin, B. (1936) 'Introduction' to English translation of Wicksell, K. (1898).

Patinkin, D. (1956) *Money, Interest and Prices*, 1st edn, 2nd edn (1965) New York: Harper & Row.

Patinkin, D. (1965) 'Wicksell's monetary theory', in *Money Interest and Prices*, 2nd edn, New York: Harper & Row.

Patinkin, D. (1973) 'Keynesian monetary theory and the Cambridge School' in Johnson, H. G. and Nobay, A. R. (eds), *Issues in Monetary Economics*, London: Oxford University Press.

Patinkin, D. (1976) *Keynes' Monetary Thought: A Study of its Development*, Durham, NC: Duke University Press.

Peart, S. (1990) 'W. S. Jevons theory of economic fluctuations: the role of expectations', Williamsburgh, Va: College of William and Mary (mimeo).

Pigou, A. C. (1912) *Wealth and Welfare*, London: Macmillan.

Pigou, A. C. (1913a) *Unemployment*, London: Williams and Norgate.

Pigou, A. C. (1913b) 'Review of R. G. Hawtrey: *Good and Bad Trade*', *Economic Journal* 23 (Dec.), 580–3.

Pigou, A. C. (1917) 'The value of money', *Quarterly Journal of Economics*, (reprinted 1954 in Ellis, H. and Haley, W. *Readings in Monetary Economics*, Homewood, IL: Richard Irwin, for the AEA).

Pigou, A. C. (1919) *The Economics of Welfare* London: Macmillan.

Pigou, A. C. (1927) *Industrial Fluctuations*, London: Macmillan.

Presnell, L. R. (1968) 'Gold reserves, banking reserves and the Baring Crisis of 1890' in Whittlesey, C. R. and Wilson, J. S. G. (eds), *Essays in Money and Banking in Honour of R. S. Sayers*, Oxford: The Clarendon Press.

Price, B. (1882) 'Letter to H. R. Grenfell' in Hucks-Gibbs, H. and

Grenfell, H. R. (eds) (1886) *The Bimetallic Controversy*, London: Effingham Wilson, pages 323–4.

Radcliffe Committee (Committee on the Working of the Monetary System) (1959) *Report,* London: HMSO.

Ricardo, D. (1816) *Proposal for an Economical and Secure Currency*, reprinted in Sraffa, P. (ed.) (1956), *Works and Correspondence of David Ricardo*, Volume 3, Cambridge: Cambridge University Press for the RES.

Robertson, D. H. (1915) *A Study of Industrial Fluctuations,* (reprinted 1948 London: London School of Economics).

Robertson, D. H. (1926) *Banking Policy and the Price Level,* London: P. S. King and Son (reprinted 1949, New York: Augustus Kelley).

Rockoff, H. (1990) 'The "Wizard of Oz" as a Monetary Allegory', *Journal of Political Economy* 98 (Aug.), 739–60.

Rolnick, A. and Weber, W. (1986) 'Gresham's Law or Gresham's Fallacy', *Journal of Political Economy* 94 (Feb.), 185–99.

Sargent, T. and Wallace, N. (1983) 'The real bills doctrine and the quantity theory – a reconsideration', *Journal of Political Economy* 90 (Dec.), 1212–36.

Selgin, G. (1988) *The Theory of Free Banking*, Totowa NJ: Rowman and Littlefield.

Senior, N. W. (1840) *Three Lectures on the Value of Money*, reprinted London: London School of Economics and Political Science, *Scarce Tracts in Political Economy*, No. 4, 19.

Sprague, O. (1910) *A History of Crises Under the National Banking System*, Washington DC: Government Printing Office.

Thornton, H. (1802) *An Enquiry into the Nature and Effects of the Paper Credit of Great Britain*, reprinted with an Introduction by F. A. von Hayek, London: George Allen and Unwin (1939).

Tooke, T. (1844) *An Enquiry into the Currency Principle*, 2nd edn, London: Longman, Brown, Green and Longmans.

Uhr, C. (1960) *Economic Doctrines of Knut Wicksell*, Berkeley: University of California Press.

Viner, J. (1937) *Studies in the Theory of International Trade*, New York: Harper & Bros.

Walker, F. A. (1878) *Money*, New York: H. Holt and Co.

Walker, F. A. (1897) *International Bimetallism*, New York: H. Holt and Co.

Walras, L. (1886) *Théorie de la monnaie*, Lausanne: Corbaz.

Walras, L. (1887) 'On the solution of the Anglo-Indian monetary problem', *Report of the British Association for the Advancement of Science*, pages 849–51.

Walras, L. (1889) *Élements d'économie politique pure* 2nd edn (as translated from the 1926 definitive edition by W. Jaffé (1954)), Homewood IL: R. Irwin.

Warburton, C. (1966) *Depression, Inflation and Monetary Policy, Selected Papers 1945–1953*. Baltimore: Johns Hopkins University Press.

White, L. (1984) *Free Banking in Britain: Theory, Experience and Debate*, Cambridge: Cambridge University Press.

Wicksell, K. (1896), *Value, Capital and Rent*, translated by S. W. Frowen, London: Allen and Unwin, (1965).

Wicksell, K. (1898) *Interest and Prices*, translated by Richard Kahn for the Royal Economic Society 1936, (reprinted 1962 New York: Augustus Kelley).

Wicksell, K. (1905) *Lectures in Political Economy*, Volume I (1911 edn, translated by E. Claassen 1935, London: Routledge and Kegan Paul).

Wicksell, K. (1906) *Lectures in Political Economy*, Volume II (1915 edn translated by E. Classen 1935, London: Routledge and Kegan Paul).

Wicksell, K. (1907a) *The Enigma of Business Cycles*, as translated by C. G. Uhr from 'Krisernas Gata' *Statsøkonomisk Tidskrift* 255–84, and included in (1962) Augustus Kelly edition of Wicksell 1898, (223)–(239).

Wicksell, K. (1907b) 'The influence of the rate of interest on prices', *Economic Journal* 17 (June), 213–20.

Williams, A. (1892) 'A "Fixed Value of Bullion" standard: a proposal for preventing general fluctuations of trade', *Economic Journal* 2 (June), 280–9.

Yeager, L. (1966) *International Monetary Relations: Theory, History and Policy* New York: Harper & Row.

Name Index

Aftalion, A., 118n22
Aldenham, Baron *see* Hucks-Gibbs, H.
Arnon, A., 45n14, 47n25

Bagehot, W., 8, 9, 21, 24, 34, 35, 36–40, 42, 100, 116n12, 176, 181, 184, 185, 194
Bailey, R., 150n15
Barbour, D. M. (Sir David), 88n31, 168, 190n10
Barkai, H., 149n2
Baumol, W., 24, 45n18
Becker, G., 24, 45n18
Bickerdike, C., 111
Blomqvist, A., 84n2
Boehm-Bawerk, E. von, 129
Bordo, M., 13, 43n4, 86n13, 152n29, 188n1
Bridel, P., 86n9n10
Bryan, W. J., 165

Cairnes, J., 7, 11, 12–13, 17–18, 30–1, 41–2, 46n22, 156
Cannan, E., 44n10
Cantillon, R., 11, 12, 17
Carver, T. N., 87n21, 118n22
Cassel, G., 151n22, 152n25
Cernuschi, H., 85n6, 157
Chen, C. N., 188n1
Chevalier, M., 30–1, 156
Chipman, J., 118n22
Clark, J. M., 111
Corry, B., 45n15
Cottrell, A., 151n17

Deutscher, P., 44n12, 109, 114
Dornbusch, R., 110
Dowd, K., 192n22

Edgeworth, F. Y., 37, 69, 87n22, 150n9, 171, 172, 176, 184–7, 191n15, 192n22, 193, 194, 196
Engels, F., 20, 145
Eshag, E., 86n9, 88n32

Fetter, F. W., 2, 7, 45n14n18, 47n25, 191n13
Fisher, I., 3, 4, 46n20, 49–88, 90–5, 101, 102, 104, 112–13, 117n21, 124, 129, 136, 139, 141, 142, 143–4, 147, 158–9, 168, 170–1, 174, 176–8, 188, 188n1, 189n7, 190n12, 193, 195
Foxwell, H. S., 153–4, 174, 199n2
Friedman, M., 79, 82, 116n6, 155, 189n8, 190n11, 192n20n21

Giffen, R., 34, 161–3, 164, 176, 188, 189n8, 191n15
Glasner, D., 39, 192n22
Goodhart, C. A. E., 192n19
Goschen, G. J., 28
Gray, M., 192n23
Grenfell, H. R., 160, 161, 189n3
Guillebaud, C., 116n12

Haberler, G., 118n23
Hankey, T., 36
Harrington, R., 86n15
Harrod, R., 152n23
Hawtrey, R., 19, 91, 95, 100–14, 178, 179, 188, 193, 199n2
Hayek, F. A. von, 17, 19, 44n10, 119, 146
Hegeland, H., 43n7
Hicks, J. R., 24, 64, 152n23, 196
Hildreth, C., 192n23

Subject Index